PYTHON IN EXCEL

Hayden Van Der Post

Reactive Publishing

CONTENTS

PREFACE

Welcome to a transformative journey that bridges the powerful worlds of Python and Excel—a journey designed not just to teach you new skills, but to fundamentally change the way you approach data, analysis, and problem solving. In today's fast-paced environment, the ability to transform raw data into actionable insights is more than a competitive advantage; it's a necessity. This book, "Python in Excel: A Comprehensive Guide to Mastering Python for Excel," is your gateway to that future.

Imagine a workplace where complex spreadsheets no longer intimidate you, where repetitive tasks are automated with ease, and where data visualization and financial modeling become intuitive rather than laborious. Whether you're a seasoned professional looking to streamline your workflow, a data enthusiast eager to dive into the world of automation, or a financial analyst aspiring to modernize your models, this book has been crafted to meet your needs—empowering you to harness the full potential of Python integrated with the familiar, yet evolving, landscape of Excel.

In this book, you'll start with the basics, setting up the tools and environments necessary for success. From installing Python and configuring Excel to leveraging Anaconda and Jupyter Notebooks, every step is designed to build a strong foundation. As you progress, you'll learn how to manipulate data, automate routine tasks, and generate stunning reports. We'll guide you through each concept with clear, concise examples, ensuring that the leap into this new integrated approach feels natural and rewarding.

What makes this more than just another technical manual is its focus on real-world applications. You'll discover how to create pivot tables that reveal hidden trends, automate chart generation for instant visual insights, and even convert traditional VBA macros into versatile Python scripts. The book's structure builds from basic operations to advanced applications like financial modeling, statistical analysis, and even machine learning—each chapter designed to challenge you and stimulate both your curiosity and creativity.

The road to mastery involves more than learning techniques; it's about embracing a new way of thinking. Each chapter opens a window into fresh opportunities: from automating web scraping to integrating databases with Excel, from creating interactive dashboards to uncovering insights through data visualization, there's a world of knowledge waiting just for you. As you work through the extensive case studies and explore cutting-edge future trends, you'll not only learn to solve problems but also to innovate and lead in your field.

Throughout this guide, you'll find that every line of code, every automated script, and every visualization is a step toward transforming your daily challenges into moments of triumph. This book is more than instructions on integrating two tools—it's a pathway to dramatically simplify your workflow and amplify your productivity. As you read, experiment, and apply these concepts, remember that the journey ahead is one of continuous growth and discovery.

So take a deep breath, open your mind to new possibilities, and embark on this exciting adventure. We are excited to accompany you as you unlock a future where data works for you in the most efficient and insightful ways imaginable. Here's to your personal and professional evolution— welcome to the world where Python meets Excel, and where you are poised to transform not just your spreadsheets, but your entire approach to problem solving.

Let's begin.

INTRODUCTION

Python and Excel are two heavyweights in the data landscape, each offering unique advantages. Excel, with its intuitive interface, has long been the preferred choice for analysts and decision-makers. It enables quick data manipulation, easy charting, and immediate insights at our fingertips. In contrast, Python provides a level of sophistication and flexibility that can extend our data capabilities well beyond traditional spreadsheets. By integrating these two powerful tools, we unlock an entirely new realm of possibilities.

Imagine you're faced with the challenge of analyzing a large dataset filled with inconsistencies. While Excel efficiently handles basic functions and formulas, it can falter when tackling complex data cleaning tasks or extensive transformations. This is where Python excels. With libraries such as Pandas and NumPy, you can execute intricate data manipulations quickly and seamlessly. This isn't just about speed; it's also about improving accuracy and enabling more thorough analyses.

Now consider a scenario where you need to generate reports that incorporate real-time data from multiple sources. Excel can pull in information through various connectors, but when it comes to automating these processes or conducting advanced statistical analyses, Python truly shines. Take this example, think about automating a report that aggregates sales data from different regions on a weekly basis. By integrating Python scripts with Excel, you can significantly streamline this workflow—saving time and enhancing the consistency of your reports.

This integration not only boosts functionality but also encourages creativity in problem-solving. Picture automating repetitive tasks or visualizing data in innovative ways using Python's extensive libraries for graphics and analytics. You could create interactive dashboards that not only showcase key metrics but also allow stakeholders to dynamically explore the underlying data. Combining libraries like Plotly and Matplotlib with Excel's visualization capabilities enables you to craft experiences that resonate far beyond static charts.

The beauty of this integration is its accessibility; you don't have to be an expert programmer to harness the power of Python within your Excel workflows. In this guide, you'll find that even simple scripts can significantly enhance your productivity and analytical skills. Through practical examples and step-by-step walkthroughs, we will demystify Python, making it approachable for everyone.

As we dive deeper into the world of Python for Excel, you will learn not only how to use these tools independently but also how to effectively leverage their combined power. Each chapter builds on foundational concepts while introducing advanced techniques tailored to your evolving needs as an analyst or developer.

The journey ahead will equip you with a toolkit that enhances your efficiency and empowers you to tackle challenges with renewed confidence. Whether you're automating mundane tasks or engaging in complex analyses, combining Python with Excel will fundamentally transform your interaction with data. Embrace this opportunity to elevate your skill set—your future self will appreciate it!

- ## Overview of Python and Excel Integration

Python and Excel form a dynamic partnership in the world of data analysis, each bringing unique strengths that enhance the overall analytical experience. Excel's popularity is largely due to its intuitive interface, which allows analysts to visualize and manipulate data effortlessly. It excels at quick calculations, basic statistical analyses, and creating visually appealing charts that effectively communicate insights. However, as datasets become larger and more complex, Excel can hit its limits. This is where Python steps in, offering advanced capabilities that significantly improve data manipulation and analysis techniques.

Take, for instance, a marketing analyst who needs to clean a vast dataset containing customer interactions from multiple platforms. While Excel provides basic functions for sorting and filtering, it can quickly become cumbersome when faced with millions of records or complex cleaning tasks. By integrating Python into the workflow, analysts can leverage powerful libraries like Pandas. With just a few lines of code, they can automate the identification of duplicates, fill in missing values, or transform data formats—tasks that might take hours in Excel.

The combination of Python and Excel also unlocks exciting possibilities for generating reports enriched with real-time data. For example, an analyst responsible for tracking sales across various geographic regions would typically face the challenge of manual updates and a multi-step process to gather the necessary information using Excel alone. However, by writing Python scripts that pull data from different APIs or databases directly into an Excel workbook, this process becomes significantly more efficient. A simple script can automate the daily retrieval of updated sales figures and populate them into predefined templates, greatly reducing manual effort while enhancing accuracy.

Visualizations further exemplify how this integration shines. While Excel offers a variety of charting tools, incorporating Python enables analysts to create more sophisticated visualizations. Libraries like Matplotlib and Seaborn allow for the development of intricate visuals that can be seamlessly integrated into Excel reports. Imagine creating an interactive dashboard where stakeholders can not only view metrics but also engage with the data through drill-down capabilities or dynamic filters powered by Python code. This level of interactivity transforms static reporting into a compelling narrative.

Getting started with this integration may seem daunting for those unfamiliar with programming concepts. However, one of the greatest advantages of combining Python with Excel is its accessibility. A basic understanding of Python syntax can empower you to write scripts that enhance your existing workflows without requiring extensive programming expertise. This guide includes practical examples designed to demystify these concepts through hands-on exercises, helping you build your confidence step by step.

As we delve deeper into the fusion of Python and Excel, you'll see how each tool complements the other, creating a robust environment for tackling even the most intricate analytical challenges. Each chapter is structured to build on foundational elements before introducing advanced techniques that enhance both efficiency and creativity in your analyses.

This synergy between Python and Excel not only boosts productivity but also fosters innovation. Whether you're automating repetitive tasks or utilizing advanced statistical models previously out of reach with traditional spreadsheet methods, harnessing the combined power of these tools will transform your approach to data projects in your career. Embrace this opportunity to expand your skill set; mastering this integration will undoubtedly open new doors within your professional landscape and position you as a key contributor capable of driving insightful decision-making processes within your organization.

- **The Need for Python in Excel**

The rapid evolution of data analysis necessitates tools that can adapt to increasing complexities. While Excel remains a staple for many professionals, its limitations become clear when handling large datasets or intricate analytical tasks. This is where Python's integration proves invaluable. The synergy between these two tools arises not only from the quest for efficiency but also from the need to deepen analytical insights and enhance creative problem-solving.

Take, for example, a financial analyst charged with evaluating vast historical datasets to identify trends. Although Excel can manage basic data analysis, it often falters when faced with extensive computations or advanced statistical methods like regression analysis. In contrast, Python thrives in these scenarios, boasting powerful libraries such as NumPy and SciPy that deliver robust mathematical functions and statistical capabilities. With Python, the analyst can effortlessly execute complex algorithms, unlocking insights that would be tedious or even impossible to achieve using Excel alone.

The flexibility of Python further empowers analysts by enabling them to create custom functions tailored to their specific needs. Take this example, a retail manager looking to analyze sales data for seasonal trends can use Python to develop a script that automates the entire process—from gathering sales data across multiple sources and cleaning it to performing time series analyses and generating insightful reports automatically. This not only saves time but also reduces the likelihood of human error, leading to more reliable outcomes.

Incorporating Python into your Excel workflow goes beyond merely enhancing capabilities; it fosters a culture of innovation within your organization. Teams equipped with these skills can tackle problems from fresh perspectives, exploring opportunities that extend beyond traditional reporting methods. For example, a marketing team could leverage machine learning algorithms in Python to predict customer behavior based on historical purchasing patterns —a task that standard spreadsheet formulas would struggle to execute effectively.

And, as organizations increasingly depend on real-time data for decision-making, integrating Python becomes vital for maintaining a competitive edge. Instead of manually updating spreadsheets every time new information arises— an inefficient use of resources—Python scripts can automate these updates seamlessly. Imagine a system where stock levels are continuously monitored through web scraping or API calls; whenever there's a change, the relevant Excel files update instantly without any manual intervention.

It's also important to highlight the accessibility of this integration. Despite the perception that programming may be intimidating for non-technical users, many find that basic Python concepts can be quickly grasped through practice and exploration. Gradually introducing coding within familiar tools like Excel offers a welcoming entry point for analysts who may have previously shied away from programming languages.

As we delve deeper into merging these two worlds effectively, remember that each step forward represents an investment in your professional growth. You're not merely acquiring technical skills; you're transforming your approach to data analysis—turning challenges into opportunities and harnessing technology to amplify your impact within your organization.

Navigating this integration equips you with not only powerful tools but also the mindset necessary for tomorrow's analytical landscape. The convergence of Python and Excel cultivates an environment ripe for experimentation and discovery, perfectly aligning with today's demand for agile and innovative problem-solving strategies across industries. Embrace this dynamic partnership; it promises a journey filled with rich insights and rewarding outcomes that elevate both your work and career trajectory.

- **Benefits of Combining Python with Excel**

Integrating Python with Excel offers a transformative approach that goes beyond mere data manipulation. This powerful combination enhances analytical capabilities, unlocking a range of benefits that boost productivity and encourage innovation. Understanding these advantages can inspire professionals to incorporate this synergy into their daily workflows.

One of the most notable advantages of merging Python with Excel is the ability to manage large datasets with ease. Traditional Excel spreadsheets often struggle with vast amounts of data, leading to sluggish performance. In contrast, Python excels in processing extensive datasets, thanks to its efficient data structures and specialized libraries. Take this example, using Pandas allows analysts to read a CSV file with millions of rows in seconds, turning what can be a tedious task into a streamlined experience. By delegating heavy lifting to Python, users can maintain the familiar interface of Excel for reporting while harnessing Python's capabilities for data manipulation.

Additionally, this integration opens the door to advanced statistical analysis that surpasses Excel's built-in functions.

Take, for example, an analyst tasked with conducting complex multivariate regression analysis. While Excel offers basic regression tools, it lacks the depth required for sophisticated modeling. By utilizing libraries like StatsModels in Python, users can perform intricate analyses and derive more accurate insights. This capability not only enhances the quality of findings but also instills greater confidence among analysts when sharing results with stakeholders.

Automation represents another area where this collaboration shines. Automating repetitive tasks not only saves time but also minimizes errors—crucial advantages in any business setting. Consider a finance team that produces monthly reports by gathering data from various sources and consolidating it in Excel. With Python, they can automate the entire workflow: fetching data from databases or APIs, processing it as needed, and generating comprehensive reports almost instantaneously. This shift enables team members to focus on strategic decision-making instead of mundane data entry.

Collaboration benefits as well from this integration. Many organizations rely on cross-functional teams to analyze and interpret data collectively. When all team members use Excel as their primary tool while integrating Python into their processes, they create a shared foundation that balances technical accessibility with analytical power. A project manager might embed Python scripts within Excel to pull real-time project metrics directly from databases or other platforms, ensuring that everyone has access to consistent and up-to-date information.

Also, embracing this synergy fosters a culture of continuous learning within organizations. Employees proficient in both Excel and Python become adaptable problem solvers who welcome innovation. They are more likely to share insights and techniques across teams, nurturing an environment where experimentation is encouraged—leading not only to improved processes but also to new ideas that drive business growth.

In addition to these practical benefits, the integration of Python and Excel enhances visualization capabilities, allowing for dynamic and insightful representations of data. While Excel provides basic charting functions, incorporating libraries like Matplotlib or Seaborn enables users to create stunning visualizations with just a few lines of code. Imagine generating complex visuals directly from your analysis without switching between applications; this not only streamlines workflows but also makes presentations more engaging.

embracing Python within your Excel workflow transcends merely acquiring new skills—it redefines your approach to data challenges altogether. This blend paves the way for innovative solutions while equipping you with tools tailored to meet modern demands in analytics and reporting. As you explore this powerful combination, you're not just enhancing your technical skillset; you're positioning yourself at the forefront of analytical excellence—ready to tackle complex problems with creativity and insight.

In today's fast-paced environment where timely decisions are crucial, merging Python's flexibility with Excel's familiarity creates an unparalleled toolkit for professionals seeking impactful outcomes in their workspaces. This journey promises not only personal growth but also collective advancement in your organization's capabilities— a commitment worth pursuing as you navigate this exciting frontier in data analysis.

- **Book Structure and Learning Path**

Leveraging Python's strengths within the familiar environment of Excel can lead to a transformative learning experience. This book is structured to guide you through a logical progression, starting with foundational concepts and advancing to more complex applications, ensuring that each chapter builds on the last. As we embark on this journey together, you'll encounter a blend of theory and practical examples that will equip you with the skills needed to effectively harness this powerful integration.

We begin with an overview of Python's capabilities in conjunction with Excel, introducing the essential tools and software required for effective integration. This includes crucial installations such as Python, Anaconda, and Jupyter Notebooks. By establishing these foundational elements early on, you'll be well-prepared to explore more advanced functionalities.

As you progress through the chapters, you'll find detailed walkthroughs of specific libraries designed for Excel automation. You'll delve into OpenPyXL for reading and writing Excel files, Pandas for data manipulation, and other important libraries like XlsxWriter and PyXLL. Each library will be explored through practical examples—such as creating dynamic charts or automating reports—allowing you to understand not just the "how," but also the "why" behind your actions.

The book emphasizes hands-on practice, incorporating real-world scenarios where applicable. This approach ensures that you're actively engaging with the material rather than passively absorbing information. Take this example, while discussing data visualization techniques, you will be guided through creating various types of charts using both Python libraries and Excel's built-in features. This experiential learning fosters a deeper understanding of how Python can enhance Excel's capabilities.

And, each section includes tips and best practices drawn from industry experience. Whether it's optimizing your code for better performance or troubleshooting common errors, these insights will be invaluable as you navigate challenges during implementation. Learning from real-world applications enriches your experience and helps make abstract concepts tangible.

Collaboration is another recurring theme throughout the book; many chapters will highlight how this integration enhances teamwork within organizations. By embedding Python scripts into shared Excel environments, teams can seamlessly access up-to-date information. This not only improves workflow efficiency but also promotes a culture of transparency and knowledge sharing among colleagues.

In the latter sections of the book, we'll tackle advanced topics such as automating financial models and integrating machine learning techniques within Excel. These discussions will push your skills further while showcasing the limitless potential of combining Python with Excel—particularly in fields like finance and data science where precision and adaptability are essential.

To wrap things up, this structured learning path is designed to facilitate incremental mastery of Python within an Excel context. Each chapter invites you to explore specific functionalities while encouraging innovation in your workflows. By embracing these insights and techniques, you'll be well on your way to transforming your engagement with data—turning routine tasks into dynamic processes that drive meaningful results in your professional landscape.

- **Key Tools and Software Required**

To effectively harness the power of Python within Excel, it's essential to start with the right tools and software. The integration of these technologies creates a dynamic platform for data analysis and automation, and understanding the foundational elements is crucial for making the most of this synergy.

The first step is to download and install Python itself, as it serves as the core language you'll be working with. The official Python website provides a straightforward installation process suitable for various operating systems. Alternatively, for those seeking a more user-friendly experience, Anaconda is an excellent option. This open-source distribution not only includes Python but also bundles essential libraries like NumPy and Pandas, which are critical for data manipulation and analysis.

With Python installed, the next logical step is to set up Jupyter Notebooks. This interactive coding environment allows you to experiment with your code seamlessly, running Python scripts line by line. Jupyter Notebooks simplify debugging and testing while enabling you to create visualizations and share your findings in an easily digestible format—ideal for collaboration with colleagues or presenting results to stakeholders.

Now that we have our primary tools in place, we can turn our attention to libraries specifically designed for Excel automation. One of the most widely used libraries is OpenPyXL, which allows you to read from and write to Excel files with ease. Its straightforward syntax makes it easy to manipulate spreadsheets without needing to delve deeply into Excel's native functions. For example, consider this simple code snippet that creates a new Excel workbook:

```python
from openpyxl import Workbook


\#\# Create a new workbook and select the active worksheet

wb = Workbook()

ws = wb.active
```

```
\#\# Add some data
ws['A1'] = "Hello
ws['B1'] = "World!

\#\# Save the workbook
wb.save("hello_world.xlsx")
` ` `
```

This code generates an Excel file named "hello_world.xlsx" with "Hello" in cell A1 and "World!" in cell B1. It's a small yet significant step into the expansive possibilities that OpenPyXL offers.

While OpenPyXL excels at basic tasks, Pandas significantly enhances your data manipulation capabilities. As one of Python's most powerful libraries, Pandas allows you to load data directly from Excel files into DataFrames—a flexible two-dimensional tabular data structure. Here's how you can read an existing Excel file:

```
` ` `python
import pandas as pd

\#\# Load data from an Excel file into a DataFrame
df = pd.read_excel("data.xlsx")

\#\# Display the first few rows of the DataFrame
print(df.head())
` ` `
```

This functionality not only streamlines your workflow but also enables advanced operations such as filtering or aggregating data with minimal code.

Another noteworthy library is XlsxWriter, which specializes in creating complex Excel files from scratch. It supports advanced features like charts, formatting options, and conditional formatting. If you're looking to generate reports with visually appealing presentations directly through Python, XlsxWriter will meet your needs effectively.

For those interested in advanced integration within existing Excel environments, PyXLL offers a unique solution by allowing you to write Python functions that can be called directly from Excel cells as if they were native formulas. This feature bridges traditional spreadsheet calculations with Python's robust capabilities.

Finally, if you need to work with older versions of Excel files (.xls), the xlrd and xlwt libraries become essential tools. While xlrd facilitates reading these legacy files, xlwt enables writing them back into .xls format.

Installing these libraries typically involves using pip—a package management system for Python—with commands like:

```bash
pip install openpyxl pandas xlsxwriter pyxll xlrd xlwt
```

With these tools installed and properly configured, you'll be well-equipped to integrate Python's power into your daily tasks in Excel. This foundational setup will not only streamline your workflow but also empower you to tackle complex data challenges head-on. As we explore specific applications of these libraries in subsequent sections, you'll discover how they can transform mundane tasks into efficient processes—ultimately enhancing your productivity and decision-making capabilities within your organization.

- **Target Audience**

Understanding the target audience for this guide is crucial, as it influences both the depth and breadth of the content. The individuals who will benefit most from mastering Python in Excel come from diverse backgrounds but share a common goal: to enhance their data analysis capabilities and streamline workflows.

A significant portion of our audience consists of data analysts. These professionals are typically well-versed in Excel yet often encounter limitations when handling large datasets or performing complex calculations. By integrating Python into their workflow, they can utilize powerful libraries to automate repetitive tasks, conduct advanced analytics, and visualize data more effectively. Take this example, a financial analyst managing extensive datasets can harness Pandas to quickly aggregate information, facilitating easier report generation without the hassle of manual calculations.

Another important demographic includes business professionals who may lack formal training in data science but understand the importance of data-driven decision-making. These users seek straightforward methods to improve their reporting capabilities and gain insights into their business operations. With the practical examples provided in this guide, they can learn to automate data extraction from various sources directly into Excel, allowing them to focus on interpreting results rather than getting bogged down by tedious data entry.

Students and recent graduates in fields like finance, economics, or data science also represent an eager audience. They often possess foundational knowledge of both Excel and Python but may struggle with effectively merging these skills. This guide not only equips them with technical abilities but also offers real-world applications that can set them apart in the job market. The inclusion of case studies illustrates how these concepts apply in professional scenarios, making learning more relatable.

Educators and trainers looking to incorporate Python into their curriculum or training programs will find this guide invaluable as well. It serves as a resource for teaching advanced data analysis techniques using tools that students are likely to encounter in their careers. By demonstrating how Python enhances Excel's functionality, educators can prepare their students with valuable skills that meet industry demands.

IT professionals and developers tasked with automating business processes will also discover significant value here. As organizations increasingly adopt technology solutions for efficiency, IT teams often seek ways to streamline workflows through automation. The integration of Python with Excel allows these professionals to create customized solutions tailored to specific organizational needs.

Also, entrepreneurs and small business owners who juggle multiple roles within their companies will appreciate the versatility of this guide. With limited resources at their disposal, they require efficient systems for tracking finances, analyzing market trends, and managing inventory. Learning to automate these processes with Python empowers them to make informed decisions without dedicating excessive time to manual tasks.

As we explore specific examples and use cases throughout this book, we will consistently reference these varied perspectives. Each section aims not only to engage seasoned experts but also to welcome newcomers and empower them as they navigate new functionalities within familiar software environments. Our goal is clear: to enable every reader—regardless of their starting point—to harness the combined power of Python and Excel for enhanced productivity and innovative solutions in their respective fields.

- **How to Use This Book**

To use this book effectively, it's essential to grasp both its structure and the practical strategies woven throughout. Each chapter serves as a building block, thoughtfully crafted to enhance your understanding of how Python integrates with Excel, while ensuring that you can apply your newfound knowledge right away.

Begin with the foundational chapters, where you'll uncover the basics of Python and Excel integration, including installation instructions and initial setup. These sections do more than just get you started; they establish a solid foundation for understanding how Python can transform your Excel experience. Pay close attention to the step-by-step walkthroughs provided. Take this example, when writing your first Python script, follow along with the code snippets to gain hands-on experience. Experiment by modifying these examples to see how small changes can lead to different outcomes—this kind of experimentation is vital for reinforcing your learning.

As you continue, take advantage of the practical exercises sprinkled throughout each chapter. These activities serve as checkpoints, allowing you to apply your newly acquired skills in simulated real-world scenarios. Whether you're opening workbooks or reading data from Excel files, actively engaging with these tasks will significantly bolster your retention of the material.

In chapters dedicated to specific libraries like Pandas or OpenPyXL, tap into their unique functionalities by working on concrete projects relevant to your field or interests. For example, if you're handling financial datasets, use the examples on aggregating data with Pandas to streamline your reports. This alignment between what you're learning and your professional tasks creates a more impactful learning experience.

Additionally, delve into the case studies featured within the text. These real-world applications showcase how various professionals have successfully integrated Python into their workflows. By analyzing these examples, you can gain insights into best practices and innovative approaches that may inspire your own projects. Reflect on how these solutions could translate into your context and consider potential obstacles and strategies for overcoming them.

Remember that learning is not just a solitary pursuit; engage with others who are also exploring the integration of Python and Excel. Discussing challenges or sharing discoveries can provide fresh perspectives that enrich your understanding. Consider forming or joining study groups where discussions about chapters can foster deeper insights.

As you approach advanced topics such as automation or data visualization, keep a mindset focused on exploration and curiosity. This journey is not solely about following instructions; it's about leveraging Python's capabilities to tackle complex problems efficiently. As you become more confident in using libraries like Matplotlib or Seaborn for visualizations, challenge yourself by customizing charts beyond basic functionality—experiment with different visual styles and layouts until they align perfectly with your analysis goals.

The final chapters will help you synthesize everything you've learned into cohesive workflows that enhance productivity across various sectors—whether in finance, marketing analytics, or project management. Each technique discussed is designed to save time while increasing accuracy in data handling processes.

view this book as a versatile resource that evolves alongside your journey in mastering Python for Excel. Whether you're revisiting chapters for specific techniques or referencing them during a project, embrace its content as an ongoing toolkit at your disposal.

Engage deeply with this blend of theory and practice; every concept has been curated to empower not just knowledge but actionable skills that can lead to significant improvements in efficiency and decision-making within your role—regardless of whether you're a seasoned analyst or just embarking on this exciting path.

CHAPTER 1: GETTING STARTED WITH PYTHON AND EXCEL

Introduction to Python
and Excel Integration

P ython and Excel have long been essential tools in data analysis, each offering unique strengths and weaknesses. When combined, they create a powerful synergy that significantly enhances the capabilities of both platforms. Python's robust data manipulation libraries and programming flexibility complement Excel's user-friendly interface and extensive functionalities, enabling a level of data handling that neither can achieve on its own.

Consider a scenario where you have a large dataset in Excel containing sales figures from various regions. While Excel provides basic analytical functions, it can become cumbersome for complex analyses or automating repetitive tasks. This is where Python comes into play. By utilizing libraries such as Pandas or OpenPyXL, you can write scripts to efficiently manipulate the data, conduct sophisticated analyses, and create visualizations tailored to your specific needs.

To begin this integration, it's crucial to set up your environment effectively. First, install Python on your machine; distributions like Anaconda can simplify this by bundling essential packages and tools for interacting with Excel. Once Python is installed, configure Excel to accept Python scripts by installing relevant add-ins or using COM objects that facilitate communication between the two applications.

As you explore this integration further, you'll find that Python can automate tedious tasks in Excel. For example, consider the process of data cleaning—a task that can be labor-intensive when performed directly in spreadsheets. With just a few lines of code in Python, you can swiftly clean large datasets by removing duplicates, filling in missing values, or transforming data formats—all while ensuring accuracy and repeatability.

A practical illustration of this might involve reading an Excel file containing customer feedback ratings stored across multiple sheets. Instead of manually reviewing each sheet within Excel to aggregate this information, you can write a simple script using Pandas:

```python
import pandas as pd


\#\# Load multiple sheets from an Excel file

file_path = 'customer_feedback.xlsx'

sheets = pd.read_excel(file_path, sheet_name=None) \# Load all sheets into a dictionary


\#\# Concatenate all sheets into one DataFrame
```

```
feedback_data = pd.concat(sheets.values())
` ` `
```

This code snippet not only streamlines the aggregation process but also ensures consistent handling of data across different sources.

In addition to data manipulation, integrating Python with Excel allows you to leverage visualization libraries like Matplotlib or Seaborn, adding clarity and depth to your analysis. After processing your data with Python scripts, creating graphs becomes straightforward:

```python
import matplotlib.pyplot as plt


\#\# Sample Data
feedback_data['rating'].value_counts().plot(kind='bar')

plt.title('Customer Feedback Ratings')

plt.xlabel('Ratings')

plt.ylabel('Frequency')

plt.show()
` ` `
```

This code generates a bar chart illustrating customer feedback ratings from the previously loaded dataset—something that would require considerable manual effort if done solely within Excel.

Effectively utilizing these tools involves more than just technical proficiency; it requires adopting a mindset focused on efficiency and innovation. As you become adept at navigating both platforms—leveraging Python's scripting capabilities alongside Excel's spreadsheet functionalities—

you'll uncover new opportunities to enhance productivity and improve decision-making processes in your work environment.

mastering the integration of Python and Excel equips you with versatile skills applicable across various industries —from finance to marketing analytics. This combination allows for more efficient handling of large datasets while fostering deeper insights through automation and advanced analysis techniques. Embracing this blend of capabilities will be pivotal in driving your success as a modern analyst navigating the complexities of today's data-driven landscape.

Installing Python

Installing Python is a vital first step in integrating this powerful programming language with Excel. Whether you're an experienced data analyst or just getting started, the right installation will facilitate seamless interactions between these two platforms. Let's explore how to install Python effectively so you can equip yourself with the necessary tools for your upcoming projects.

The process of downloading Python is quite simple. Start by visiting the official Python website at python.org, where you'll find options to download the latest version that suits your operating system. Alternatively, many users opt for Anaconda—a widely-used distribution that includes Python along with a collection of libraries and tools specifically tailored for data science and analytics. Anaconda streamlines package management and deployment, making it an attractive choice for anyone eager to engage in data manipulation and analysis.

Once you've decided on your installation method, follow these steps:

    1. Download the Installer: If you choose Anaconda,

head over to anaconda.com to download the distribution. For a standard Python installation, visit python.org.

2. Run the Installer: Open the installer file. If you selected Anaconda, it's best to stick with the default settings to ensure all essential components are installed.

3. Add Python to PATH: During a standard installation, make sure to select the option to add Python to your system's PATH. This step enables you to execute Python commands directly from your command line or terminal.

4. Verify Installation: Once the installation is complete, open a command prompt (Windows) or terminal (macOS/Linux) and type python --version or conda --version if you used Anaconda. You should see the installed version number, confirming a successful installation.

With Python installed, your next task is setting up an environment that works smoothly with Excel. This typically involves installing additional libraries that enhance communication between Python and Excel files. Key libraries like Pandas, OpenPyXL, and xlrd are essential for reading from and writing to Excel files efficiently.

If you're using pip (Python's package installer), installing these libraries is straightforward:

```bash
pip install pandas openpyxl xlrd
```

For those using Anaconda, consider managing separate environments for different projects; this helps keep dependencies organized and avoids conflicts between packages:

```bash
conda create -n myenv python=3.x

conda activate myenv

conda install pandas openpyxl xlrd
```

Another valuable tool is Jupyter Notebook, an interactive coding environment that allows you to experiment with code snippets and visualizations while working on your data analysis tasks. You can install Jupyter easily using either pip or conda:

```bash
pip install notebook # Using pip

## Or with conda

conda install -c conda-forge notebook
```

After installation, launch Jupyter by typing jupyter notebook in your command line or terminal. This action opens a web interface where you can create new notebooks —perfect for combining code execution with rich text documentation.

It's also important to set up Excel for integration effectively. One efficient way to do this is by utilizing COM objects through the win32com.client library, which allows direct control over Excel using Python scripts:

```bash
pip install pywin32
```

This library lets you open Excel workbooks, manipulate them programmatically, and save changes directly through

Python—making automation tasks much easier.

At this point, you're well-equipped with the tools necessary to leverage Python alongside Excel's user-friendly features. As you embark on this journey of integration, keep in mind that both platforms offer unique strengths that complement each other beautifully. By harnessing their combined power effectively, you'll streamline your workflow and significantly enhance your analytical capabilities.

As you progress into this new phase of your professional development journey, stay curious about how these integrations can boost your productivity and decision-making processes. With every line of code you write alongside Excel's functionalities, you're not just learning; you're transforming how data influences your work and organization as a whole. Embrace this change wholeheartedly—it promises to unlock doors to innovation previously thought unreachable.

Setting Up Excel for Python

First, make sure you have Excel installed on your system. Whether you're using Excel 2016 or a more recent version, the core functionalities remain robust and accessible. Our goal is to configure Python so it can interact directly with Excel files—allowing for easy reading from and writing to them.

The first step in this integration involves installing the necessary libraries. These libraries act as bridges between Python and Excel, facilitating operations such as reading data from spreadsheets and writing results back. One of the most commonly used libraries for this purpose is openpyxl, which allows you to read and write Excel 2010 xlsx/xlsm/xltx/xltm files. To install it, simply run:

```bash
pip install openpyxl
```

` ` `

Another essential library is pandas, renowned for its powerful data manipulation capabilities. It simplifies handling datasets, enabling efficient reading from and writing to Excel files. Install it using the following command:

` ` `bash

pip install pandas

` ` `

Once you have installed these libraries, it's time to explore how they work together in practice. Let's consider an example where you read data from an Excel file using pandas, manipulate it, and then write the results back into a new Excel file.

Imagine you have an Excel file named sales_data.xlsx containing sales figures across different regions, and your objective is to calculate the total sales per region.

Here's how to accomplish this:

1. Reading Data from Excel:

Start by loading the data into a DataFrame using pandas.

` ` `python

import pandas as pd

\#\# Load data from the Excel file

df = pd.read_excel('sales_data.xlsx', sheet_name='Sheet1')

` ` `

1. Data Manipulation:

Next, calculate total sales by region.

` ` `python

\#\# Grouping by 'Region' column and summing 'Sales' column

total_sales = df.groupby('Region')['Sales'].sum().reset_index()

` ` `

1. Writing Data Back to Excel:

Finally, save your results into a new Excel file.

` ` `python

total_sales.to_excel('total_sales_per_region.xlsx', index=False)

` ` `

This example not only demonstrates how to set up your environment but also showcases practical applications in real-world scenarios.

In addition to pandas and openpyxl, you might want to install xlrd if you're working with older .xls files or require specific functionalities related to those formats:

` ` `bash

pip install xlrd

` ` `

Next, let's explore configuring COM objects using the win32com.client library. This library enables Python scripts to automate tasks directly within the Excel application itself —allowing you to create charts or format cells without manual intervention.

To get started with win32com, run:

` ` `bash

pip install pywin32

` ` `

Here's a practical example of how this library can be utilized:

opening an existing workbook and programmatically modifying its content.

```python
import win32com.client

\#\# Start an instance of Excel
excel = win32com.client.Dispatch("Excel.Application")

\#\# Make it visible (optional)
excel.Visible = True

\#\# Open an existing workbook
workbook = excel.Workbooks.Open(r'C:.xlsx')

\#\# Access a specific sheet by name
sheet = workbook.Sheets('Sheet1')

\#\# Read value from cell A1
cell_value = sheet.Range('A1').Value

\#\# Write a value to cell B1
sheet.Range('B1').Value = cell_value * 2

\#\# Save changes and close workbook
workbook.Save()
```

```
workbook.Close()
```

\#\# Quit the application when done (optional)

```
excel.Quit()
```

` ` `

This approach provides extensive control over your spreadsheets through Python scripting, paving the way for complex automation processes tailored specifically to your analytical needs.

While setting up these tools may seem technical at first glance, each installation step adds another layer of capability that empowers you as a data analyst. Think of these configurations as foundational blocks—each one enhancing your ability to derive insights and automate tasks efficiently.

integrating Python with Excel opens up avenues for innovation and efficiency previously unexplored in traditional analytical workflows. By harnessing these tools effectively, you're not just enhancing personal productivity; you're also contributing significantly to your organization's analytical capabilities. As you continue this journey of integration, remain curious—every line of code has the potential to transform how you approach data challenges within your professional landscape.

Introduction to Anaconda and Jupyter Notebooks

The field of data analysis is constantly evolving, and navigating its complexities requires effective tools. Anaconda and Jupyter Notebooks stand out as essential allies in this journey, streamlining the process of managing data and deriving insights. Anaconda serves as a comprehensive platform for managing Python packages, libraries, and environments, while Jupyter Notebooks offers an intuitive interface for writing and executing code.

Together, they not only boost productivity but also facilitate the dynamic sharing of insights in visually engaging formats.

Installing Anaconda is a straightforward process that simplifies package management significantly. After downloading it from the official website and following the setup instructions, you'll find that it automatically installs key libraries like numpy, pandas, and matplotlib. This convenience allows you to dive into your data projects without the need for individual installations, saving you time and reducing potential configuration headaches.

Once Anaconda is up and running, launching Jupyter Notebooks is equally simple. By entering jupyter notebook in your command line, a new tab opens in your default web browser where you can create or access existing notebooks. This interactive environment seamlessly combines code execution with rich text annotations—ideal for documenting your analysis or sharing findings with colleagues.

To illustrate the power of Jupyter Notebooks in action, let's consider analyzing sales data—similar to our previous work with pandas. After launching Jupyter, you can create a new notebook and follow these steps:

1. Importing Libraries: Begin by importing the libraries necessary for your analysis.

``` python
import pandas as pd

import matplotlib.pyplot as plt
```

1. Loading Data: Load your Excel file into a pandas DataFrame.

``` python
```

```python
df = pd.read_excel('sales_data.xlsx')
```

1. Basic Data Exploration: Quickly inspect the dataset using the head function.

```python
print(df.head())
```

1. Visualizing Sales Data: Create a bar chart to visualize total sales by region.

```python
sales_by_region = df.groupby('Region')['Sales'].sum()

sales_by_region.plot(kind='bar', color='skyblue')

plt.title('Total Sales by Region')

plt.xlabel('Region')

plt.ylabel('Total Sales')

plt.xticks(rotation=45)

plt.show()
```

This example not only demonstrates how to load data but also provides immediate visual feedback on sales performance across different regions—an essential component of effective analytical storytelling.

The capabilities of Jupyter extend far beyond mere data manipulation; its support for inline visualizations makes it an invaluable tool for presenting data-driven insights compellingly. Picture working through complex analyses while simultaneously crafting reports within the same environment—this feature revolutionizes collaboration and communication among team members.

Additionally, Jupyter's ability to export notebooks in various formats (such as HTML or PDF) ensures that your analyses can be easily shared with stakeholders who may not have direct access to the notebooks themselves. This functionality streamlines communication between technical teams and decision-makers who rely on clear insights to drive strategic decisions.

As you become more comfortable with these tools, consider how they fit into broader workflows within your organization. Utilizing environments within Anaconda allows you to maintain different projects with specific library requirements, keeping dependencies isolated and minimizing conflicts that could arise from varying project needs.

Exploring these capabilities enables you not only to keep pace with industry standards but also to develop innovative approaches tailored specifically to your tasks at hand. Embracing Anaconda and Jupyter Notebooks cultivates an adaptable mindset—one that embraces continuous learning and exploration as integral parts of your analytical journey.

mastering Anaconda and Jupyter goes beyond merely learning new tools; it transforms your approach to data analysis. Each command executed brings you closer to uncovering deeper insights that can significantly influence decision-making processes within your organization—positioning you as a forward-thinking analyst ready to tackle complex challenges head-on.

Writing Your First Python Script

Writing your first Python script is an exciting milestone in your journey toward mastering Python in Excel. It opens up a world of possibilities, enabling you to harness the power of programming to automate and enhance your data analysis processes. Let's jump right in.

Start by considering what you want your script to accomplish. A practical first step could be automating the opening of an Excel workbook and reading its contents. For this example, we'll use the openpyxl library, which is ideal for working with Excel files. If you haven't installed it yet, run the command pip install openpyxl in your command prompt or terminal.

With the library ready, create a new Python file—let's name it read_excel.py. Open this file in your preferred code editor and start writing the following code:

```python
import openpyxl

\#\# Load the workbook

workbook = openpyxl.load_workbook('your_file.xlsx')

\#\# Select the active sheet

sheet = workbook.active

\#\# Read data from cell A1

data = sheet['A1'].value

print(f'The value in A1 is: data')
```

In this snippet, we begin by importing the openpyxl library. The load_workbook function opens your specified Excel file —be sure to replace 'your_file.xlsx' with the actual path to your file. The next line selects the active worksheet within that workbook. Finally, we retrieve and print the value from cell A1.

After you write this code, save your file and run it from the command line using python read_excel.py. If everything is set up correctly and you have an Excel file named as specified, you should see an output indicating the content of cell A1.

This initial script illustrates a fundamental principle: extracting data from Excel using Python can be both simple and powerful. Consider how much time you usually spend manually opening files and checking specific cells. With just a few lines of code, you've automated part of that tedious process.

Building on this foundation, let's expand our script to read multiple cells from a specific range within your worksheet—an essential skill for any data analyst working with extensive datasets. Modify your script as follows:

```python
import openpyxl


\#\# Load the workbook

workbook = openpyxl.load_workbook('your_file.xlsx')

sheet = workbook.active


\#\# Define the range you want to read

for row in sheet.iter_rows(min_row=1, max_row=5, min_col=1, max_col=3):

for cell in row:

print(cell.value)
```

In this enhancement, we use iter_rows to loop through rows

1 to 5 and columns 1 to 3 of our active sheet. This method allows us to systematically access and print each cell's value within that specified range. Running this updated script will provide values from multiple cells at once—a significant improvement over accessing single cells.

As you experiment with these scripts and gradually increase their complexity—perhaps by adding error handling or data processing functionality—you're cultivating an essential habit: thinking algorithmically about the problems you encounter. Each iteration not only deepens your understanding but also offers immediate utility.

Reflect on how these scripts can integrate into larger workflows within Excel. Consider their potential to pull together multiple datasets or automatically format reports based on predefined criteria.

The excitement of scripting lies not just in seeing results but also in the creative problem-solving process involved. Each new line of code or troubleshooting session enhances your analytical toolkit while building confidence as a programmer —a dual advantage when merging Python with Excel's capabilities.

Now that you've taken these initial steps toward writing effective Python scripts for Excel tasks, envision more complex scenarios where automation can enhance efficiency —like generating monthly reports or dynamically updating dashboards based on real-time data inputs. Every script crafted serves as a stepping stone toward mastering both Python and its integration into Excel's powerful environment.

Running Python Scripts in Excel

Integrating Python scripts into Excel elevates automation, enabling you to perform complex data manipulations and analyses within your familiar spreadsheet environment. This functionality is particularly beneficial for handling large datasets or streamlining repetitive tasks. Let's explore how to effectively run Python scripts in Excel.

First, you'll need a setup that facilitates seamless interaction between Python and Excel. One popular solution is the PyXLL add-in, which allows you to call Python functions as if they were native Excel functions. While installing PyXLL requires some initial configuration, the enhanced functionality it provides makes the effort worthwhile.

Once you've installed PyXLL, open Excel and locate the PyXLL configuration file, typically named pyxll.cfg. In this file, you can specify the Python packages you wish to make available in Excel. For example, if you plan to use Pandas for data manipulation, add the following line under the [PYTHON] section:

```ini
modules = pandas
```

After saving your changes, restart Excel to complete the setup process. You're now ready to run Python scripts directly from within Excel.

Let's consider a practical example: analyzing sales data from a specific worksheet. Start by creating a Python script called sales_analysis.py. Here's a basic outline of what this script might look like:

```python
import pandas as pd

def analyze_sales():
\#\# Load data from an Excel file
df = pd.read_excel('sales_data.xlsx', sheet_name='Sheet1')
```

\#\# Perform analysis: calculate total sales

total_sales = df['Sales'].sum()

return total_sales

` ` `

In this script, we use Pandas to read an Excel file named sales_data.xlsx. The analyze_sales function calculates the total of a column labeled Sales and returns that value. To execute this function directly from Excel, you would simply enter the following formula in a cell:

` ` `excel

=analyze_sales()

` ` `

This integration allows you to trigger your Python script with just a cell formula, displaying the total sales figure right in your spreadsheet.

As your scripts become more complex, you may want to consider error handling and debugging—critical aspects for maintaining robust code. Python offers built-in tools like try and except statements to help manage exceptions gracefully. Here's how you could enhance your previous script with better error management:

` ` `python

def analyze_sales():

try:

df = pd.read_excel('sales_data.xlsx', sheet_name='Sheet1')

total_sales = df['Sales'].sum()

return total_sales

except FileNotFoundError:

return "File not found. Please check the path.

except Exception as e:

return f"An error occurred: e

```
```

With these modifications, if an issue arises—such as the specified file not being found—your function will provide a clear message rather than failing silently or returning an error code.

Beyond simple calculations, imagine the power of automating entire workflows with Python. You could write scripts that pull data from multiple sheets, analyze trends over time, and generate visualizations—all executed with a single command within Excel.

Take this example, consider tracking marketing metrics across various campaigns. You could create a comprehensive script that processes each campaign's data and generates a summary report directly in Excel:

```python
def generate_report():

try:

df = pd.read_excel('marketing_data.xlsx')


\#\# Group by campaign and calculate metrics

report = df.groupby('Campaign').agg('Conversions': 'sum', 'Clicks': 'sum').reset_index()
```

```
return report

except Exception as e:

return f"An error occurred: e

` ` `
```

This function groups your marketing data by campaign and calculates total conversions and clicks—essential metrics for evaluating performance. With such scripts running behind the scenes, you can concentrate on strategy instead of tedious data entry.

As you integrate more sophisticated logic into your scripts, remember to adhere to best practices: keep your code modular for reusability, document each component clearly, and test thoroughly. These practices not only enhance performance but also facilitate future modifications.

Additionally, consider how you might share these tools with colleagues who may not be as comfortable with programming. By encapsulating complex analyses within user-friendly functions callable from Excel itself, you democratize access to insights—empowering others while boosting overall productivity.

Incorporating Python scripts within Excel transforms your workflow into a dynamic and efficient process. As you refine your skills in scripting and automation, you'll discover countless opportunities to leverage these capabilities— ultimately saving time and gaining deeper insights from your data sets.

Understanding Excel COM Objects

Understanding Excel COM objects is essential for effectively utilizing Python in your Excel workflows. COM, or Component Object Model, acts as a bridge between different applications, enabling programs like Python to interact directly with Excel. This powerful integration opens up numerous opportunities for automation and data analysis that would be tedious or impossible to achieve using Excel alone.

To begin working with COM objects in Python, you need the win32com.client library, which grants access to the functionality of COM applications from Python. If you haven't installed this library yet, you can easily do so using pip:

```bash
pip install pywin32
```

Once the library is installed, you can create a simple script that interacts with Excel. The following example demonstrates how to launch an Excel application, create a new workbook, and populate it with data:

```python
import win32com.client

\#\# Start the Excel application
excel = win32com.client.Dispatch("Excel.Application")
excel.Visible = True \# Make Excel visible

\#\# Create a new workbook
workbook = excel.Workbooks.Add()
sheet = workbook.ActiveSheet

\#\# Add data to the sheet
```

```
sheet.Cells(1, 1).Value = "Name

sheet.Cells(1, 2).Value = "Score

\#\# Input sample data
data = [("Alice", 85), ("Bob", 92), ("Charlie", 78)]
for i, (name, score) in enumerate(data):
sheet.Cells(i + 2, 1).Value = name
sheet.Cells(i + 2, 2).Value = score

\#\# Save the workbook
workbook.SaveAs("students_scores.xlsx")
workbook.Close()
excel.Quit()
```
``` `

In this script, we create an instance of Excel and add a new workbook. The sheet.Cells(row, column) method allows you to specify where to place values in the worksheet—an essential feature for dynamically populating data.

After inserting the sample student scores into the worksheet, we save the workbook under the name "students_scores.xlsx". This straightforward example illustrates how easily you can control Excel through Python.

However, working with COM objects requires an understanding of their structure and behavior within Excel. Every aspect of your spreadsheet—from workbooks and sheets to individual cells—is represented as an object that you can manipulate using various properties and methods provided by the win32com interface.
```

If you wish to modify existing data rather than simply entering new information, consider this example:

```python
\#\# Open an existing workbook

workbook = excel.Workbooks.Open("students_scores.xlsx")

sheet = workbook.ActiveSheet


\#\# Modify scores: increase each by 5 points

for i in range(2, sheet.UsedRange.Rows.Count + 1):

current_score = sheet.Cells(i, 2).Value

sheet.Cells(i, 2).Value = current_score + 5


\#\# Save changes

workbook.Save()

workbook.Close()

excel.Quit()
```

This script opens our previously created file and iterates through each student's score to add five points—showcasing how you can programmatically adjust content without manual intervention.

Another important consideration is error handling when working with COM objects. It's essential to ensure that your scripts are resilient against common issues, such as attempting to access files that do not exist or trying to modify locked spreadsheets. Implementing try-except blocks will help you manage potential errors gracefully:

```python
try:

\#\# Open an existing workbook safely.

workbook = excel.Workbooks.Open("students_scores.xlsx")

except Exception as e:

print(f"An error occurred while opening the workbook: e")
```

By catching exceptions this way, your program remains user-friendly and avoids unexpected crashes—a valuable trait when deploying scripts across teams or departments.

As you become more familiar with COM objects in Python for automating tasks in Excel, consider how you might apply these skills to larger projects—such as generating reports or consolidating data from multiple sources seamlessly. With proficiency in manipulating these objects at your disposal, you'll be well-equipped to streamline workflows significantly.

Beyond simple operations on cells and sheets lies a wealth of advanced functionalities, including managing charts and pivot tables directly through Python scripts. The following snippet demonstrates how to create a simple chart based on our student scores:

```python
chart = excel.Charts.Add()

chart.SetSourceData(sheet.Range("A1:B4"))

chart.ChartType                                    =
win32com.client.constants.xlColumnClustered

chart.Name = "Student Scores
```

This addition automatically generates a clustered column chart from our dataset—further highlighting the versatility and power of integrating Python with Excel.

Embracing COM objects not only enhances your capabilities within Excel but also allows for greater customization tailored specifically to your needs. With practice and experimentation using this integration alongside other tools like Pandas or NumPy for deeper analysis tasks, you'll find that managing large datasets becomes more manageable and productive—unlocking possibilities previously unimaginable in standard spreadsheet environments.

CHAPTER 2: PYTHON LIBRARIES FOR EXCEL AUTOMATION

Overview of Python Libraries

Python libraries for Excel automation significantly enhance the capabilities of traditional spreadsheet applications. They provide tools that streamline a range of tasks—from basic data manipulation to intricate analytical processes—while allowing you to leverage Python's extensive functionality. Familiarity with these libraries is essential, as they underpin effective integration between Python and Excel.

At the forefront is Pandas, a vital tool for data analysis in Python. Its strength lies in handling structured data, making it particularly well-suited for working with Excel files. The powerful DataFrame object enables intuitive manipulation of tabular data. For example, consider the following code snippet that loads an Excel file into a DataFrame:

```python
import pandas as pd
```

\#\# Load an Excel file into a DataFrame

df = pd.read_excel("students_scores.xlsx")

\#\# Display the DataFrame

print(df)

` ` `

This straightforward code reads an Excel file and converts it into a DataFrame, facilitating advanced operations like filtering and aggregation with minimal effort.

Another key library is OpenPyXL, specifically designed for reading and writing Excel 2010 xlsx/xlsm/xltx/xltm files. OpenPyXL allows you to create new spreadsheets, modify existing ones, and apply styles or formulas programmatically. Here's how you can create a new workbook and write formatted data using OpenPyXL:

` ` `python

from openpyxl import Workbook

from openpyxl.styles import Font

\#\# Create a new workbook and select the active sheet

workbook = Workbook()

sheet = workbook.active

\#\# Write headers with bold font

headers = ["Name", "Score"]

for col_num, header in enumerate(headers, 1):

```
cell = sheet.cell(row=1, column=col_num)

cell.value = header

cell.font = Font(bold=True)


\#\# Input sample data

data = [("Alice", 85), ("Bob", 92), ("Charlie", 78)]

for row_num, (name, score) in enumerate(data, start=2):

sheet.cell(row=row_num, column=1).value = name

sheet.cell(row=row_num, column=2).value = score


\#\# Save the workbook

workbook.save("formatted_students_scores.xlsx")
```
` ` `

This example demonstrates how easily you can combine styling with data entry using OpenPyXL, as headers are formatted in bold while inputting student scores.

When your work requires creating charts or more complex reports directly from Python scripts, XlsxWriter is an excellent choice. This library enables you to create Excel files that include features such as charts and conditional formatting. Below is an example illustrating how to add a simple bar chart to an Excel file:

` ` `python

```
import xlsxwriter


\#\# Create a new Excel file and add a worksheet

workbook = xlsxwriter.Workbook("chart_example.xlsx")
```

```
worksheet = workbook.add_worksheet()

\#\# Sample data for the chart
data = [10, 20, 30]

\#\# Write data to the worksheet
worksheet.write_column('A1', data)

\#\# Create a chart object
chart = workbook.add_chart('type': 'bar')

\#\# Configure the series of the chart from our worksheet
data
chart.add_series(
'name': 'Data Series',
'categories': '=Sheet1!\(A\)1:\(A\)3',
'values': '=Sheet1!\(B\)1:\(B\)3',
)

\#\# Insert the chart into the worksheet
worksheet.insert_chart('D2', chart)

\#\# Close the workbook (this will save it)
workbook.close()
` ` `
```

With XlsxWriter, you can generate detailed reports complete with visualizations directly from your scripts, transforming raw numbers into meaningful insights.

For users seeking to integrate Python within their Excel environment without leaving Microsoft Office's ecosystem, PyXLL is invaluable. It allows you to write Python functions that can be called directly from Excel formulas, bridging the gap between spreadsheet simplicity and programming power.

Additionally, it's important to mention win32com, which enables communication with COM objects in Windows applications like Excel. This library facilitates operations such as manipulating existing workbooks or interacting with Excel's interface through scripting—especially useful for automating repetitive tasks or generating reports based on live data.

Here's how you might leverage win32com to create an automated report by pulling in data from various sources:

```python
import win32com.client


excel_app = win32com.client.Dispatch("Excel.Application")

excel_app.Visible = True


\#\# Add a new workbook and access its active sheet

workbook = excel_app.Workbooks.Add()

sheet = workbook.ActiveSheet


data_sources = ["source1.xlsx", "source2.xlsx"]
```

```
row_index = 1

for source in data_sources:
source_workbook = excel_app.Workbooks.Open(source)
source_sheet = source_workbook.Sheets(1)

\#\# Assume we want to copy all values from A1:B10 from each source
for i in range(1, 11):
sheet.Cells(row_index + i - 1, 1).Value = source_sheet.Cells(i, 1).Value

sheet.Cells(row_index + i - 1, 2).Value = source_sheet.Cells(i, 2).Value

row_index += 10
source_workbook.Close()

workbook.SaveAs("combined_report.xlsx")
excel_app.Quit()
` ` `
```

This script seamlessly combines multiple sources into one report through automation—a clear testament to Python's capabilities when integrated effectively.

Exploring these libraries not only enhances your ability to work within Excel but also inspires innovative approaches to common business challenges. By integrating various tools based on your specific needs—whether for statistical analysis or report generation—you can develop sophisticated solutions that significantly streamline your processes.

Introduction to OpenPyXL

OpenPyXL is an essential library for anyone interested in Excel automation with Python. It specializes in handling Excel files, particularly in the xlsx format, making it a valuable tool for reading, writing, and modifying spreadsheets programmatically. This capability is especially useful for automating tasks that would otherwise be time-consuming and labor-intensive if done manually.

To begin using OpenPyXL, you'll first need to install the library if you haven't done so already. This can be easily accomplished via pip with the following command:

```bash
pip install openpyxl
```

After installation, you can start creating or manipulating Excel files. One of OpenPyXL's straightforward yet powerful features is its ability to create new workbooks and populate them with data. Take this example, suppose you want to create a new workbook to store sales data. Here's how you can accomplish that:

```python
from openpyxl import Workbook

\#\# Create a new workbook

workbook = Workbook()

sheet = workbook.active

\#\# Define some sample data
```

```
data = [
["Product", "Sales"],
["Widget A", 150],
["Widget B", 200],
["Widget C", 300],
]

\#\# Add data to the sheet
for row in data:
sheet.append(row)

\#\# Save the workbook
workbook.save("sales_data.xlsx")
```

In this example, we start by creating a new workbook and defining a dataset containing product names along with their sales figures. The append method simplifies adding rows of data to the worksheet, eliminating the need to specify each cell individually.

Beyond basic data entry, OpenPyXL also provides functionalities for styling your spreadsheets, enhancing both readability and presentation. Take this example, you can apply styles such as font size and color while inputting data. Consider the following snippet where we format the column headers:

```python
from openpyxl.styles import Font
```

```python
\#\# Set column headers with formatting
headers = ["Product", "Sales"]
for col_num, header in enumerate(headers, 1):
cell = sheet.cell(row=1, column=col_num)
cell.value = header
cell.font = Font(bold=True, color="FF0000") \# Red bold font

\#\# Save changes
workbook.save("styled_sales_data.xlsx")
```

In this case, we make the headers bold and change their color to red for emphasis. Such formatting is crucial when preparing reports or sharing data with stakeholders.

Another common task in data processing is manipulating existing spreadsheets. OpenPyXL allows you to load an existing file and make modifications seamlessly. For example, if you have a file named "sales_data.xlsx" from which you need to read data and possibly update it:

```python
from openpyxl import load_workbook

\#\# Load the existing workbook
workbook = load_workbook("sales_data.xlsx")
sheet = workbook.active

\#\# Read existing data
```

```python
for row in sheet.iter_rows(min_row=2, values_only=True):
    print(f"Product: row[0], Sales: row[1]")


\#\# Update sales for Widget A
sheet["B2"] = 175 \# Updating sales value


\#\# Save the updated workbook
workbook.save("updated_sales_data.xlsx")
```

Here, we load an existing workbook and iterate through its rows while skipping the header. We also demonstrate how easy it is to modify specific cells—updating sales figures for "Widget A"—before saving our changes.

As your needs grow towards more complex operations, such as integrating formulas into your spreadsheets, OpenPyXL accommodates that as well. Take this example, here's how you could add a sum formula that calculates total sales automatically:

```python
\#\# Assuming you have data in cells B2:B4 (sales amounts)
sheet["B5"] = "=SUM(B2:B4)"  \# Adding a formula for total sales


\#\# Save the workbook with formula included
workbook.save("sales_with_formula.xlsx")
```

This formula will dynamically calculate total sales whenever the spreadsheet is opened or refreshed in Excel.

Additionally, OpenPyXL allows users to manage worksheets effectively; adding new sheets or renaming existing ones is straightforward:

``` python
\#\# Add a new worksheet for summary reports

summary_sheet = workbook.create_sheet(title="Summary")


\#\# Rename an existing sheet

sheet.title = "Sales Data


\#\# Save changes again after modifications

workbook.save("final_sales_report.xlsx")
```

By organizing your data into multiple sheets within a single file, you enhance clarity and accessibility.

The flexibility of OpenPyXL extends beyond simple data entry; it enables Python scripts to generate comprehensive reports directly usable within Excel. Whether you're automating routine tasks or creating intricate datasets for analysis, mastering this library equips you with tools that significantly streamline your workflow.

To wrap things up, OpenPyXL serves as a bridge between Python's programming capabilities and Excel's powerful spreadsheet functionalities. As you explore its features— from basic operations like reading and writing files to more advanced functionalities like formula integration—you'll find that it not only enhances efficiency but also elevates your overall productivity in managing Excel-based tasks. This library empowers you to tackle challenges confidently while transforming how you engage with data in Excel.

Exploring Pandas for Excel Operations

Pandas is an essential library for anyone looking to enhance their Excel operations through Python. Its powerful data manipulation capabilities enable users to efficiently handle and analyze large datasets, making it an indispensable tool for data analysts and business professionals alike. The seamless integration between Pandas DataFrames and Excel simplifies the workflow, allowing for a smoother data management experience.

To begin using Pandas, you'll first need to install the library if it's not already on your system. This can be easily accomplished via pip with the following command:

```bash
pip install pandas openpyxl
```

We include openpyxl here because it facilitates reading from and writing to Excel files. Once Pandas is installed, the next step is to load your data into a DataFrame. Take this example, if you have an Excel file named "sales_data.xlsx" containing your sales information, you can read that data into a DataFrame like this:

```python
import pandas as pd

\#\# Load data from an Excel file
df = pd.read_excel("sales_data.xlsx", sheet_name="Sales Data")

\#\# Display the DataFrame
print(df)
```

` ` `

This command reads the contents of the specified sheet and loads it into a DataFrame, allowing you to manipulate your data using Pandas' rich set of functions. If your Excel data includes headers, Pandas will automatically use them as column names.

Once your data is in a DataFrame, you can perform a wide range of operations. For example, if you're interested in filtering the data to show only products with sales greater than 200, you can easily do so:

```python
\#\# Filter products with sales greater than 200

high_sales = df[df['Sales'] > 200]


\#\# Display filtered results

print(high_sales)
```

```python
\#\# Calculate total sales

total_sales = df['Sales'].sum()

print(f"Total Sales: total_sales")
```

In addition to analysis, Pandas excels at transforming and cleaning your data. If your dataset has missing values that need addressing before analysis, you can easily identify and fill or drop those entries:

```python
\#\# Checking for missing values
```

```
missing_values = df.isnull().sum()
```

```
print(missing_values)
```

```
\#\# Filling missing sales with zero
```

```
df['Sales'].fillna(0, inplace=True)
```
` ` `

Merging multiple datasets is another common task that Pandas handles elegantly. For example, if you have another dataset containing promotional information linked by product names, merging them can provide deeper insights:

` ` `python

```
promo_df = pd.read_excel("promotions.xlsx")
```

```
merged_df = pd.merge(df, promo_df, on="Product", how="left")
```

```
\#\# Display the merged DataFrame
```

```
print(merged_df)
```
` ` `

This merge operation enriches your original dataset by appending additional information based on a shared column.

When you're ready to export your manipulated DataFrame back to Excel, Pandas makes this process straightforward as well. You can save your updated DataFrame with a simple command:

` ` `python

```
\#\# Save the modified DataFrame to a new Excel file
```

```
merged_df.to_excel("updated_sales_data.xlsx", index=False)
```

```
` ` `
```

This command not only saves your data but also retains all modifications made during your analysis, ensuring it remains accessible for future use.

Pandas also provides robust support for time series data. If your sales data includes timestamps or dates, you can take advantage of powerful date-based indexing and resampling functionalities for comprehensive time analyses:

```python
\#\# Assuming 'Date' is a column in your DataFrame

df['Date'] = pd.to_datetime(df['Date'])

df.set_index('Date', inplace=True)


\#\# Resample monthly sales totals

monthly_sales = df.resample('M').sum()

print(monthly_sales)
```

This snippet illustrates how easy it is to transition from daily or weekly records to monthly summaries—an essential operation for trend analysis and forecasting.

As you work with Pandas, remember that extensive documentation and community support are available to assist with troubleshooting or exploring advanced features. The flexibility it offers goes beyond mere calculations; it allows for significant customization in how data is managed and presented.

Pandas empowers users to engage deeply with their data while significantly enhancing workflow efficiency within Excel environments. It transforms complex data tasks into manageable operations and provides clarity through its intuitive interface. This integration fosters more informed decision-making processes across various sectors, including finance, marketing, and analytics. By mastering Pandas for Excel operations, you'll not only gain technical skills but also acquire a strategic advantage in effectively managing complex datasets.

XlsxWriter for Excel File Creation

Embarking on the journey of creating Excel files with Python introduces us to XlsxWriter, a powerful library designed specifically for generating Excel spreadsheets. Its ability to produce complex spreadsheets—complete with formatting, charts, and diverse data types—makes XlsxWriter an ideal choice for automating report generation and other tasks that require building Excel files from the ground up.

To begin utilizing XlsxWriter, you'll first need to install the library. If you haven't done this yet, simply run the following command using pip:

```bash
pip install xlsxwriter
```

After installation, you can effortlessly create a new Excel file and input data. The example below shows how to generate a simple Excel file named "report.xlsx" and populate it with some basic information:

```python
import xlsxwriter

\#\# Create a new Excel file and add a worksheet

workbook = xlsxwriter.Workbook('report.xlsx')

worksheet = workbook.add_worksheet()
```

```
\#\# Write headers for the data
worksheet.write('A1', 'Product')
worksheet.write('B1', 'Sales')

\#\# Sample data to include
products = ['Widget A', 'Widget B', 'Widget C']
sales = [100, 150, 200]

for row_num, (product, sale) in enumerate(zip(products, sales), start=1):
    worksheet.write(row_num, 0, product) \# Column A
    worksheet.write(row_num, 1, sale)     \# Column B

\#\# Close the workbook
workbook.close()
```

This snippet creates an Excel file featuring headers for "Product" and "Sales," followed by three rows of sample data. The use of the enumerate function effectively pairs each product with its corresponding sales figure.

Beyond basic data entry, XlsxWriter also supports advanced features such as cell formatting. Take this example, if you wish to highlight sales figures that exceed a specific threshold, applying conditional formatting is straightforward:

```python
```

```
\#\# Define a format for highlighting high sales

high_sales_format = workbook.add_format('bold': True,
'color': 'green')


\#\# Apply conditional formatting to highlight sales greater
than 120

worksheet.conditional_format('B2:B4', 'type': 'cell',

'criteria': '>',

'value': 120,

'format': high_sales_format)
` ` `
```

With this code, any sales figure above 120 will be displayed in bold green text within the specified range. This visual cue is especially helpful when reviewing reports for key performance indicators.

For integrating charts into your Excel reports, XlsxWriter excels once more. The following example demonstrates how to add a simple column chart using the previously entered sales data:

```
` ` `python
\#\# Create a chart object

chart = workbook.add_chart('type': 'column')


\#\# Configure the series for the chart

chart.add_series('name': 'Sales',

'categories': '=Sheet1!\(A\)2:\(A\)4',

'values': '=Sheet1!\(B\)2:\(B\)4')
```

\#\# Insert the chart into the worksheet

worksheet.insert_chart('D2', chart)

` ` `

This code not only generates a chart based on your data but also inserts it directly into the worksheet at cell D2. By visually representing sales data alongside numerical figures, stakeholders can quickly identify trends and insights.

And, XlsxWriter facilitates the management of multiple sheets within a single workbook. If you require separate sheets for various datasets or reports, adding additional worksheets is simple:

` ` `python

\#\# Adding another worksheet for summary statistics

summary_worksheet   = workbook.add_worksheet('Summary')

summary_worksheet.write('A1', 'Total Sales')

summary_worksheet.write('B1', sum(sales)) \# Writing total sales in summary sheet

\#\# Remember to close the workbook after completing all operations!

workbook.close()

` ` `

This example illustrates how easy it is to organize your data across different sheets while maintaining clarity and usability throughout your reports.

Incorporating XlsxWriter into your Python toolkit not only empowers you to automate report generation but also enables you to create visually appealing spreadsheets tailored to your audience's needs. Mastering this library will streamline your workflow considerably while ensuring that your data presentations are both professional and insightful.

By leveraging XlsxWriter's features in conjunction with libraries like Pandas for data manipulation or analysis tasks previously discussed, you can cultivate an efficient approach to managing your Excel documents through Python. This synergy between libraries creates a powerful arsenal that boosts productivity and enhances decision-making capabilities across various business applications.

PyXLL for Advanced Excel Integration

Integrating Python with Excel reveals its true potential through tools like PyXLL, which facilitates a seamless connection between the two platforms. Unlike other libraries, PyXLL enables you to call Python functions directly from Excel as worksheet functions. This integration allows users to leverage Python's robust capabilities within the familiar Excel interface, transforming it into a dynamic tool for complex calculations and data manipulations without ever leaving the spreadsheet.

To begin using PyXLL, you first need to install the tool. This involves downloading the appropriate version for your operating system and following the installation instructions in the documentation. Once installed, you can configure PyXLL by editing its configuration file, typically named pyxll.cfg. Here's a basic example of how this configuration might appear:

```ini
[PYXLL]
modules = mymodule
```

[MYMODULE]

Specify your Python module here

```
```

This setup allows you to define which Python modules are available in your Excel environment. Take this example, if you have a module named mymodule.py containing useful functions, you can configure it in pyxll.cfg and begin using those functions directly within Excel.

Imagine wanting to perform advanced statistical analysis on a dataset stored in an Excel sheet. By writing a function in Python and exposing it through PyXLL, you can enhance your analytical capabilities. Consider this simple function that calculates the mean of a list of numbers:

```python
def calculate_mean(data):

return sum(data) / len(data)
```

To make this function accessible in Excel, simply add the following decorator:

```python
from pyxll import xl_func


@xl_func

def calculate_mean(data):

return sum(data) / len(data)
```

Once defined and configured correctly, this function can be invoked from any cell in Excel as if it were a built-in function. For example, typing =calculate_mean(A1:A10) will compute the average of values in cells A1 through A10.

Additionally, PyXLL supports real-time data updates. If your Python function retrieves live financial data or performs computations based on changing inputs, these updates can be reflected instantly in your spreadsheet without manual refreshes. This feature is especially valuable for applications like financial modeling or inventory management, where timely data is essential.

Another noteworthy aspect of PyXLL is its ability to create custom Excel ribbon menus and user-defined dialog boxes, enhancing user experience by providing an intuitive interface tailored to specific workflows. For example, if you're developing a financial analysis tool that requires user input parameters, you could design a dialog box that prompts users for necessary data before conducting analyses.

Here's how you might create a simple menu item that executes a specific function:

```python
from pyxll import xl_menu


@xl_menu("Run Analysis", "My Tools")

def run_analysis():

\#\# Perform your analysis here

pass
```

With this setup, "Run Analysis" will appear under the "My Tools" tab in the Excel ribbon, making it easy for users to access your functionality without needing to remember complex formulas.

The integration of data visualization tools within PyXLL further enhances its utility. Imagine harnessing powerful Python visualization libraries like Matplotlib or Seaborn while working within Excel. You could generate intricate plots directly from your datasets and present them alongside numerical analyses. Take this example, here's how you might generate a plot using Matplotlib:

```python
import matplotlib.pyplot as plt


@xl_func

def plot_data(x_data, y_data):

plt.figure()

plt.plot(x_data, y_data)

plt.title("Sample Plot")

plt.xlabel("X-axis")

plt.ylabel("Y-axis")

plt.show()
```

After defining this function with PyXLL, calling it from an Excel cell will dynamically display the plot based on the provided input ranges.

Exploring PyXLL's extensive functionalities not only boosts efficiency but also enriches your analytical capabilities by merging the best features of both Python and Excel. As organizations increasingly seek sophisticated data handling and analysis methods, mastering tools like PyXLL positions you as an invaluable asset in any data-driven environment.

embracing PyXLL empowers you to redefine your interaction

with data in Excel—transforming static spreadsheets into dynamic dashboards filled with powerful analytics at your fingertips. The potential for innovation is vast; whether you're building financial models or developing custom analytics tools, leveraging this integration ensures that you're not just keeping pace but leading the way in utilizing technology for enhanced decision-making and reporting processes.

win32com for Excel Automation

The integration of Python with Excel reaches new heights through the win32com library, which facilitates deeper automation and interaction with Excel. Unlike PyXLL, which primarily exposes Python functions as Excel functions, win32com allows for more direct manipulation of Excel objects. This capability opens up a wide array of possibilities, from creating and modifying spreadsheets to automating repetitive tasks.

To begin using win32com, you first need to install the library. If you're working on Windows, you can easily install it via pip:

```bash
pip install pywin32
```

Once the installation is complete, you can import win32com and establish a connection to your Excel application. The following code snippet demonstrates how to create an instance of Excel and make it visible:

```python
import win32com.client


\#\# Start an instance of Excel
```

```python
excel = win32com.client.Dispatch("Excel.Application")

excel.Visible = True
```

This straightforward code opens Excel for the user. Next, you can create a new workbook and access its sheets:

```python
workbook = excel.Workbooks.Add()

sheet = workbook.Sheets(1)
```

With a workbook and sheet set up, let's delve into automating some basic tasks. For example, if you want to enter data into specific cells, you can reference their positions directly:

```python
sheet.Cells(1, 1).Value = "Name

sheet.Cells(1, 2).Value = "Age

sheet.Cells(2, 1).Value = "Alice

sheet.Cells(2, 2).Value = 30
```

Here, the first row is filled with headers while the second row contains data. The power of win32com lies in its ability to programmatically manipulate any aspect of the Excel application. Take this example, if you'd like to format these cells by making the headers bold, you can do so with ease:

```python
header_range = sheet.Range("A1:B1")

header_range.Font.Bold = True
```

```
```

As your tasks become more complex, win32com provides the functionality to loop through data or perform calculations directly within Excel's environment. Suppose you have a list of names in column A alongside their corresponding ages in column B; calculating the average age would be straightforward:

```python
\#\# Assuming ages are in cells B2 through B10

average_age                                                    =
sheet.Application.WorksheetFunction.Average(sheet.Range(
"B2:B10"))

print(f"The average age is: average_age")
```

This snippet utilizes Excel's built-in capabilities to execute calculations seamlessly within your Python script.

Reading data from an existing workbook is just as simple with win32com. If you want to extract values from a specific range and perform operations on them, you can do so with this example:

```python
data_range = sheet.Range("A2:B10")

data = data_range.Value


for row in data:

print(f"Name: row[0], Age: row[1]")
```

This code retrieves values from rows 2 to 10 and prints each name alongside its corresponding age.

Another valuable feature of win32com is its ability to handle charts directly within Excel. If you're interested in creating visual representations of your data without leaving Python, this functionality proves invaluable. For example, consider how to create a simple column chart based on the age data:

```python
chart = workbook.Charts.Add()

chart.SetSourceData(sheet.Range("A2:B10"))

chart.ChartType                                    =
win32com.client.constants.xlColumnClustered
```

This snippet generates a clustered column chart in your workbook using the specified data range.

Win32com also allows for comprehensive control over chart properties. You can customize titles, axis labels, and other attributes programmatically. Here's how you might adjust the chart title:

```python
chart.HasTitle = True

chart.ChartTitle.Text = "Age Distribution"
```

Integrating these features into your workflow not only boosts productivity but also enables you to produce more polished and visually appealing reports.

As with any automation tool, handling exceptions is essential. Take this example, if you're attempting to access a workbook that may not be open or doesn't exist yet, it's wise to wrap your calls in try-except blocks for graceful error management:

```python
```

try:

workbook = excel.Workbooks.Open("C:\\\\.xlsx")

except Exception as e:

print(f"An error occurred: e")

` ` `

mastering win32com empowers you to fully leverage Excel's capabilities through Python programming. As businesses increasingly depend on sophisticated data handling techniques, your expertise in automating workflows with tools like win32com places you at the forefront of innovation. By combining Python's flexibility with Excel's extensive functionalities, you're not merely enhancing efficiency; you're transforming your approach to data analysis and reporting into something far more dynamic and impactful.

xlrd and xlwt for Older Excel Files

The xlrd and xlwt libraries are invaluable tools for working with older Excel file formats, particularly the .xls format. While many users have moved on to the newer .xlsx format, it's important to know how to handle these legacy files, especially in environments that require compatibility with older systems.

Let's begin with xlrd, a library designed for reading data from .xls files. To get started, install xlrd using pip:

` ` `bash

pip install xlrd

` ` `

After installation, you can easily open an Excel workbook and access its contents. Here's a simple code snippet demonstrating how to do this:

` ` `python

```python
import xlrd
```

\#\# Open an existing workbook

workbook = xlrd.open_workbook("path_to_your_file.xls")

\#\# Select the first sheet

sheet = workbook.sheet_by_index(0)
```
` ` `
```

Once you have accessed the workbook and selected a sheet, you can read data from specific cells. Take this example, if you want to extract values from the first column of your worksheet, you can use the following loop:

` ` `python

for row_idx in range(sheet.nrows):

print(sheet.cell_value(row_idx, 0))
` ` `

This loop iterates through all rows in the first column and prints their values. The flexibility of xlrd allows for various operations on data without altering the original Excel file.

While reading old Excel files is straightforward with xlrd, writing or modifying those files necessitates the use of xlwt. To install xlwt, simply run:

` ` `bash

pip install xlwt
` ` `

With xlwt, you can create a new Excel file or update an existing one. Here's a basic example of how to create a new .xls file and write some data into it:

` ` `python

```
import xlwt

\#\# Create a new workbook and add a worksheet
workbook = xlwt.Workbook()
sheet = workbook.add_sheet("Data")

\#\# Write headers
sheet.write(0, 0, "Name")
sheet.write(0, 1, "Age")

\#\# Write some data
data = [("Alice", 30), ("Bob", 25), ("Charlie", 35)]
for row_idx, (name, age) in enumerate(data, start=1):
    sheet.write(row_idx, 0, name)
    sheet.write(row_idx, 1, age)

\#\# Save the workbook
workbook.save("output_file.xls")
```
` ` `

In this example, we create a new workbook called "output_file.xls" and populate it with names and ages while including headers for clarity.

Also, xlrd supports more advanced operations such as formatting cell content during reading. For example, if you want to identify specific types of data within your cells— such as distinguishing between numbers and text—you can use the cell_type method:

```python
for row_idx in range(sheet.nrows):

cell_value = sheet.cell_value(row_idx, 1)

if sheet.cell_type(row_idx, 1) == xlrd.XL_CELL_NUMBER:

print(f"Row row_idx: Number - cell_value")

elif sheet.cell_type(row_idx, 1) == xlrd.XL_CELL_TEXT:

print(f"Row row_idx: Text - cell_value")
```

This technique enhances your ability to manage different data types effectively.

It's worth noting that both libraries have their limitations: xlrd only supports reading older formats (it has dropped support for .xlsx), while xlwt is limited to writing in .xls format without the capability to read back those newly created files directly. To navigate this gap when working with mixed formats or modern applications—where .xlsx is prevalent but legacy datasets are still necessary—requires careful planning.

If you primarily work with newer .xlsx files but occasionally need access to legacy formats due to organizational requirements or historical datasets already present in older systems, utilizing these libraries can streamline your workflow. Understanding when and how to switch between these libraries based on project needs will enhance your efficiency and adaptability as a data professional.

even as technology evolves toward newer formats and Python's capabilities expand—with tools like OpenPyXL gaining popularity—being able to navigate both old and new paradigms ensures you're well-prepared for any challenges that arise in managing Excel-based data tasks. This dual knowledge not only fosters greater versatility but also instills confidence as you tackle projects across diverse domains and client specifications.

Installation and Setup of Libraries

To fully harness the power of Python for Excel, the first crucial step is to install the necessary libraries. Properly setting up these libraries allows for seamless integration of Python into your Excel workflows, enabling you to leverage advanced data manipulation, analysis, and automation capabilities.

Start by ensuring that Python is installed on your system. You can easily check this by running the following command in your terminal or command prompt:

```bash
python --version
```

If Python is not installed, you can download it from the official website and follow the installation instructions tailored to your operating system. After confirming that Python is installed, you should set up a package manager if you haven't done so already. The most common choice is pip, which usually comes pre-installed with Python distributions.

With Python ready, it's time to install essential libraries that enhance your ability to work with Excel files. The most widely used packages include Pandas, OpenPyXL, xlrd, and xlwt. You can install all of these at once using pip:

```bash
pip install pandas openpyxl xlrd xlwt
```

Pandas is a powerful library that simplifies data manipulation and makes working with structured data more intuitive. OpenPyXL allows for direct reading and writing of .xlsx files, while xlrd and xlwt cater to older .xls files, each serving distinct needs depending on the file types you are handling.

After completing the installations, it's a good idea to verify that these libraries are accessible in your Python environment. You can do this by running a simple import test in a Python shell or script:

```python
import pandas as pd

import openpyxl

import xlrd

import xlwt


print("Libraries imported successfully!")
```

If you see no errors upon executing this code snippet, you're ready to start incorporating these libraries into your projects.

To gain a deeper understanding of each library's functionalities, let's examine them more closely. Starting with Pandas, its DataFrame structure resembles an Excel spreadsheet—it's a two-dimensional labeled data structure. Take this example, here's how you can read an Excel file into a Pandas DataFrame:

```python
\#\# Reading an Excel file into a DataFrame

df = pd.read_excel("your_file.xlsx")

print(df.head())
```

` ` `

This snippet reads data from "your_file.xlsx" into a DataFrame and prints the first five rows for a quick overview.

Next, OpenPyXL provides additional flexibility for manipulating .xlsx files directly within Excel workbooks. For example, creating new sheets or modifying existing ones is straightforward. Here's how to create a new workbook and add some data:

` ` `python

from openpyxl import Workbook

\#\# Create a new workbook and select the active worksheet

workbook = Workbook()

sheet = workbook.active

\#\# Add some headers and data

sheet["A1"] = "Name

sheet["B1"] = "Age

data = [("Alice", 30), ("Bob", 25), ("Charlie", 35)]

for row in data:

sheet.append(row)

\#\# Save the workbook

workbook.save("output.xlsx")

` ` `

This example demonstrates how easy it is to generate an .xlsx file with OpenPyXL while organizing data neatly in rows.

For reading older .xls files, xlrd is an effective tool—though keep in mind its limitation to .xls formats. By combining it with other libraries, you can enhance its utility across various projects.

Here's a quick example:

```python
import xlrd

\#\# Read an older format .xls file

workbook = xlrd.open_workbook("legacy_file.xls")

sheet = workbook.sheet_by_index(0)


\#\# Print values from the first column

for row_idx in range(sheet.nrows):

    print(sheet.cell_value(row_idx, 0))
```

In this case, we access legacy data effortlessly while appreciating how different libraries address diverse needs based on file formats.

As you think about future-proofing your projects, it's important to stay informed about evolving technologies and practices. Keeping up with changes within these libraries and any new tools that emerge in the ecosystem will serve you well. Engaging with communities or forums dedicated to Python and Excel will help you discover best practices and innovative approaches.

With all necessary installations complete and initial explorations underway, you're now well-equipped to delve deeper into the specific functionalities offered by each library. This foundation sets you up for developing robust workflows tailored to meet diverse project requirements efficiently. As you embark on your journey of mastering Python for Excel integration, each tool will uniquely contribute to enhancing productivity and facilitating sophisticated analyses like never before.

Comparing Libraries for Different Tasks

When evaluating libraries for integrating Python with Excel, it's crucial to match the features of these tools to your specific tasks. Each library offers unique functionalities that cater to various aspects of data manipulation, file handling, and automation. By understanding these differences, you can significantly improve your efficiency in utilizing Python alongside Excel.

Pandas is particularly noteworthy as a versatile tool for data analysis and manipulation. Its DataFrame structure closely resembles an Excel spreadsheet, making it ideal for handling complex data tasks. Take this example, if you want to analyze sales data across different regions, you can easily load an Excel file into a DataFrame and perform operations such as filtering or aggregating results. Here's a brief example that demonstrates how to filter sales records above a specified threshold:

``` python

import pandas as pd


\#\# Load the sales data

df = pd.read_excel("sales_data.xlsx")


\#\# Filter records where sales exceed 1000
```

```python
high_sales = df[df["Sales"] > 1000]

print(high_sales)
```
```

This snippet showcases the simplicity of using Pandas for filtering while also highlighting how quickly you can extract valuable insights from your dataset.

Complementing this is OpenPyXL, which offers more granular control over .xlsx files. If your task requires creating reports with custom formatting or inserting formulas directly into cells, OpenPyXL excels in those areas. For example, if you need to generate a monthly performance report, this library allows you to embed formulas within your sheets:

```python
from openpyxl import Workbook

workbook = Workbook()
sheet = workbook.active

\#\# Add headers
sheet["A1"] = "Month
sheet["B1"] = "Sales
sheet["C1"] = "Cumulative Sales

\#\# Sample monthly sales data
monthly_sales = [2000, 3000, 2500]
for month, sales in enumerate(monthly_sales, start=2):
```
```

```python
sheet[f"Amonth"] = f"Month month-1

sheet[f"Bmonth"] = sales

\#\# Insert formula for cumulative sales

sheet[f"Cmonth"] = f"=SUM(B2:Bmonth)


workbook.save("monthly_performance.xlsx")
```
` ` `

In this example, you not only create a structured report but also embed dynamic formulas that update automatically as your data changes.

For those working with legacy .xls files—perhaps from older systems—xlrd provides a straightforward solution for reading these formats. Its simplicity is ideal for accessing historical data without requiring extensive modifications:

` ` `python

```python
import xlrd


\#\# Read legacy .xls file

workbook = xlrd.open_workbook("legacy_data.xls")

sheet = workbook.sheet_by_index(0)


\#\# Print all names in the first column

for row_idx in range(sheet.nrows):

print(sheet.cell_value(row_idx, 0))
```
` ` `

This method ensures that older datasets remain accessible and usable within modern workflows.

On another front, if you're looking to automate tasks directly within Excel, the win32com library allows interaction with Excel via COM (Component Object Model). This can be especially powerful when automating repetitive tasks like generating reports based on user input or scheduled triggers. Here's how it looks:

```python
import win32com.client

excel_app = win32com.client.Dispatch("Excel.Application")
excel_app.Visible = True \# Show the Excel application

\#\# Create a new workbook and write some values
workbook = excel_app.Workbooks.Add()
sheet = workbook.ActiveSheet

sheet.Cells(1, 1).Value = "Project
sheet.Cells(1, 2).Value = "Status
sheet.Cells(2, 1).Value = "Project A
sheet.Cells(2, 2).Value = "Completed

workbook.SaveAs("automated_report.xlsx")
excel_app.Quit()
```

With win32com, you can directly manipulate Excel's interface through Python scripts, opening up extensive possibilities for tailored automation.

selecting the right library depends on your specific needs—whether it's data analysis with Pandas, advanced formatting with OpenPyXL, legacy support through xlrd, or automation using win32com. This understanding empowers you to choose the most appropriate tools for each task.

As you integrate these libraries into your projects, consider their distinct strengths and how they align with your objectives. By strategically employing each tool based on task requirements—be it for data manipulation or automation—you can develop efficient workflows that enhance your productivity and effectiveness when working with Python and Excel together. The synergy between these libraries fosters an environment ripe for innovation in managing complex datasets and automating routine processes seamlessly.

Choosing the Right Library for Your Needs

Choosing the right Python library for Excel integration can greatly enhance both the efficiency and effectiveness of your workflow. With a multitude of options available, each designed for specific tasks, it's crucial to understand their unique features and capabilities. This understanding will help you align your needs with the strengths of various libraries, ultimately allowing you to make informed decisions that boost your productivity.

Begin by pinpointing the primary objectives you want to achieve with Excel and Python. Are you aiming to automate repetitive tasks, manipulate data, or generate complex reports? If your goal is to read and write Excel files smoothly, both OpenPyXL and XlsxWriter are strong contenders. OpenPyXL excels in manipulating existing files while also supporting advanced Excel features like charts and styles. Conversely, XlsxWriter is perfect for creating new Excel files from scratch, offering robust formatting options.

If your focus shifts towards data analysis and manipulation,

Pandas emerges as an invaluable resource. Its DataFrame structure facilitates complex operations such as merging, filtering, and aggregating data with ease. The integration of Pandas with Excel is seamless; once you've loaded data into a DataFrame, the opportunities for transformation are nearly endless. Take this example, reading an Excel file into a DataFrame is straightforward with the following command:

```python
import pandas as pd

df = pd.read_excel('your_file.xlsx', sheet_name='Sheet1')
```

This simple line unlocks a range of analytical capabilities, enabling you to perform tasks like calculating summary statistics or visualizing trends in seconds.

For projects requiring extensive automation or interaction with Excel's native functions, libraries such as PyXLL or win32com may be more appropriate. PyXLL allows you to call Python functions directly from Excel cells as if they were built-in Excel functions. This feature creates a seamless bridge between Python scripts and Excel's interface, facilitating real-time calculations without leaving the spreadsheet environment. For example:

```python
from pyxll import xl_func

@xl_func
def add_numbers(a: float, b: float) -> float:
    return a + b
```

By entering =add_numbers(5, 10) in a cell, users can view the result directly within Excel.

Alternatively, win32com provides a traditional automation approach using COM objects, which can be particularly advantageous for those familiar with VBA. It allows for comprehensive programmatic manipulation of Excel. Here's a brief example demonstrating how to open an Excel application and create a new workbook:

```python
import win32com.client


excel = win32com.client.Dispatch("Excel.Application")

workbook = excel.Workbooks.Add()

excel.Visible = True

```

For those working with legacy files or requiring compatibility with older formats like .xls, libraries such as xlrd and xlwt come into play. While xlrd is mainly used for reading data from .xls files, xlwt allows for writing new .xls files. However, keep in mind that both libraries have limitations when it comes to newer file formats (.xlsx), which are commonly used in modern workflows.

When selecting among these libraries, consider factors such as ease of use, community support, documentation quality, and features relevant to your specific tasks. A strong community can significantly aid troubleshooting; libraries like Pandas offer extensive documentation and active forums filled with shared knowledge.

To wrap things up, choosing the right library depends on your specific requirements and familiarity with Python programming. By assessing each library's strengths relative to your tasks—be it automating repetitive actions, conducting in-depth data analyses, or integrating smoothly into existing workflows—you can fully leverage the power of Python within Excel. This thoughtful approach not only improves productivity but also paves the way for deeper insights and innovative solutions in your projects.

CHAPTER 3: BASIC EXCEL OPERATIONS WITH PYTHON

Opening Excel Workbooks

Opening an Excel workbook using Python is a fundamental skill that lays the groundwork for more advanced data manipulation and automation tasks. This straightforward process serves as an entry point to harnessing the power of Python within your data workflows. Whether you're working with existing datasets or preparing to generate new reports, knowing how to initiate an Excel session is essential.

To start, you'll need to choose a library that fits your needs. Take this example, if you're using OpenPyXL, which excels at reading and modifying .xlsx files, the setup is simple. First, ensure you have OpenPyXL installed by running:

```bash
pip install openpyxl
```

Once installed, opening a workbook takes just a few lines of code. Here's how you can do it:

```python
from openpyxl import load_workbook

\#\# Load an existing workbook
workbook = load_workbook('your_file.xlsx')
```

This command opens the specified workbook, making it ready for manipulation. You can access individual sheets within the workbook by calling them directly:

```python
sheet = workbook.active \# Access the active sheet

\#\# Or specify by name
sheet = workbook['Sheet1']
```

Now that you've opened a workbook and accessed its sheets, you can begin reading or writing data. For example, to read a value from cell A1:

```python
value = sheet['A1'].value

print(value)
```

This snippet retrieves the data in cell A1 and prints it to the console. Such simplicity allows users to quickly adapt their Excel workflows.

If your goal includes creating new workbooks instead of merely modifying existing ones, consider using XlsxWriter. This library is specifically designed for creating .xlsx files from scratch and offers extensive formatting options. To get started with XlsxWriter, first install it via pip:

```bash
pip install XlsxWriter
```

Creating a new Excel file with XlsxWriter is straightforward:

```python
import xlsxwriter

\#\# Create a new workbook and add a worksheet
workbook = xlsxwriter.Workbook('new_file.xlsx')
worksheet = workbook.add_worksheet()

\#\# Write some data into the worksheet
worksheet.write('A1', 'Hello')
worksheet.write('A2', 'World')

\#\# Close the workbook to save changes
workbook.close()
```

In this example, we create a new Excel file named new_file.xlsx, add data to cells A1 and A2, and save our work with workbook.close(). This process illustrates how Python can streamline the generation of reports and automate repetitive tasks within Excel.

Another powerful approach is utilizing win32com, which interacts directly with Excel's COM interface. This method is particularly useful if you are already familiar with VBA and want to leverage Python's capabilities.

To get started with win32com, ensure you have it installed:

```bash
pip install pywin32
```

With this library, you can open an instance of Excel and manipulate workbooks much like you would in VBA. Here's how:

```python
import win32com.client

\#\# Start an instance of the Excel application
excel_app = win32com.client.Dispatch("Excel.Application")
excel_app.Visible = True \# Show the application

\#\# Add a new workbook
workbook = excel_app.Workbooks.Add()

\#\# Access the first sheet and write some data into it
sheet = workbook.Worksheets(1)
sheet.Cells(1, 1).Value = "Hello from Python!
```

Executing this code block will launch an Excel window with a new workbook that contains "Hello from Python!" in cell A1. The win32com library effectively bridges Python's capabilities with traditional Excel operations.

Opening workbooks transcends merely accessing data;

it involves forging connections between your code and spreadsheets that house critical information for decision-making processes. Your choice between OpenPyXL's user-friendly interface, XlsxWriter's creation features, or win32com's comprehensive automation will depend on your project's specific requirements.

As you become more adept at opening workbooks and manipulating their contents using these libraries, you'll discover that your ability to automate tedious tasks expands significantly—freeing up valuable time for deeper analysis and strategic planning.

Reading Excel Data

Reading data from Excel is an essential skill that significantly enhances your ability to analyze and manipulate information effectively. Once you have opened a workbook, the next step is to extract the relevant data for your analysis or reporting needs. Whether you're working with large datasets or simple tables, knowing how to read values from an Excel sheet using Python is crucial.

The OpenPyXL library simplifies this process, making it both intuitive and efficient. After loading your workbook, you can easily interact with individual cells or ranges. For example, to read the value of a specific cell, you can access it directly:

```python
\#\# Assuming 'workbook' is already loaded

value = sheet['A1'].value

print(value)
```

This command retrieves the value in cell A1 and prints it out. If your goal is to read an entire row or column, OpenPyXL provides flexible methods to accomplish this. To read all values from a specific column, you can use the following approach:

```python
```

\#\# Read all values from column A

column_values = [cell.value for cell in sheet['A']]

print(column_values)

```
```

This list comprehension gathers each cell's value from column A into a Python list, facilitating further manipulation. You might also consider transforming these lists into pandas DataFrames, which can greatly simplify data analysis, as pandas excels in handling tabular data.

When working with Pandas—a powerful library designed for data analysis—reading Excel files becomes even more streamlined. By utilizing pandas' read_excel() function, you can load entire sheets directly into a DataFrame:

```python
```

import pandas as pd

\#\# Load an Excel file into a DataFrame

df = pd.read_excel('your_file.xlsx', sheet_name='Sheet1')

print(df.head())   \# Display the first few rows of the DataFrame

```
```

This one-liner not only reads the specified sheet but also converts it into a DataFrame format, which is ideal for various analyses. You can perform operations like filtering, grouping, and summarizing on this DataFrame without manually navigating through cells.

Another important consideration when reading data is

handling different data types within your Excel file. Excel does not enforce strict data types; as a result, numeric values may inadvertently be stored as strings if not formatted correctly in the original file. To check and convert these types within Pandas, you can use:

``` python
\#\# Convert a specific column to numeric type, coercing errors

df['NumericColumn'] = pd.to_numeric(df['NumericColumn'], errors='coerce')
```

This method ensures that any non-numeric values are converted to NaN, resulting in cleaner analyses down the line.

If you're using win32com, reading data involves a different approach due to its interaction with Excel's COM interface. After accessing your desired sheet, you can reference ranges similarly to VBA:

``` python
\#\# Read values from A1 to A10

for i in range(1, 11):

value = sheet.Cells(i, 1).Value  \# Column index 1 refers to column A

print(value)
```

In this example, we loop through cells A1 through A10 and print their values. While this method offers flexibility, it may lack some of the convenient features found in libraries like OpenPyXL or Pandas.

When dealing with missing or erroneous data while

reading from Excel files, implementing checks can facilitate smoother processing later on. Both OpenPyXL and Pandas provide functionalities to help identify empty cells or unexpected formats.

Take this example, using OpenPyXL:

```python
if sheet['A1'].value is None:

print("Cell A1 is empty!")
```

With Pandas, you can quickly filter out missing data using methods like dropna():

```python
cleaned_df = df.dropna()  \# Remove rows with any NaN values
```

Each approach has its advantages depending on your workflow needs and preferences. As you deepen your understanding of reading Excel data with Python, you'll find that these skills form the backbone of effective automation and analytics strategies.

With practice comes proficiency; mastering these techniques will empower you to extract valuable insights from your spreadsheets quickly and accurately. The ability to manipulate and analyze data efficiently will undoubtedly distinguish you as a proficient user of both Python and Excel in any analytical setting.

Writing to Excel Cells

Writing data to Excel cells is a crucial skill that enables you to automate report generation, update records, and streamline data entry. With Python's integration, especially through libraries like OpenPyXL and Pandas, this process becomes both manageable and efficient. Transitioning from reading data to writing it enhances the interactivity and dynamism of your Excel workflows.

Using the OpenPyXL library for writing data is straightforward. After loading your workbook and selecting the desired sheet, you can easily write values into specific cells. For example, to insert a value into cell B2, you can use the following code:

```python
from openpyxl import load_workbook

\#\# Load the workbook and select the active sheet
workbook = load_workbook('your_file.xlsx')
sheet = workbook.active

\#\# Write a value to cell B2
sheet['B2'] = 'Hello World!'

\#\# Save the changes
workbook.save('your_file.xlsx')
```

This snippet not only inserts "Hello World!" into cell B2 but also saves the updated workbook. By using load_workbook, you ensure that existing data remains intact while new values are added or modified.

For writing multiple rows or columns of data, OpenPyXL allows for more complex operations through iteration. Take this example, if you want to populate an entire column with numbers from 1 to 10, you can do so efficiently with a loop:

```python
for i in range(1, 11):
sheet[f'Ai'] = i \# Write numbers 1-10 into column A


workbook.save('your_file.xlsx')
```

This example illustrates how easily you can scale your writing operations without resorting to repetitive code.

In addition to inserting static values, OpenPyXL offers dynamic cell formatting capabilities. You can change font styles or cell colors based on specific conditions. For example, if you want to change the font color of cell C3 when its value exceeds 100, you can use:

```python
from openpyxl.styles import Font


if sheet['C3'].value > 100:
sheet['C3'].font = Font(color='FF0000')  \# Change font color to red


workbook.save('your_file.xlsx')
```

This kind of conditional formatting enhances readability and facilitates quick assessments directly within Excel.

Switching gears to Pandas introduces another layer of functionality for writing data back into Excel files. When working with DataFrames, the to_excel() method simplifies exporting an entire DataFrame to a specified worksheet:

```python
import pandas as pd

data =
'Name': ['Alice', 'Bob', 'Charlie'],
'Score': [85, 92, 88]

df = pd.DataFrame(data)

\#\# Write the DataFrame to an Excel file
df.to_excel('output_file.xlsx',          sheet_name='Scores',
index=False)
```

In this example, a new Excel file named output_file.xlsx is created with a worksheet called "Scores," containing names and scores without including DataFrame indices. This functionality is particularly powerful for generating reports based on analytical results.

If your goal is to append data to an existing Excel file rather than overwriting it entirely, Pandas provides flexibility through ExcelWriter. Here's how you can accomplish that:

```python
with pd.ExcelWriter('existing_file.xlsx', mode='a') as writer:

df.to_excel(writer, sheet_name='NewData', index=False)
```

This command opens existing_file.xlsx in append mode and writes your DataFrame into a new worksheet labeled "NewData." This approach is essential for maintaining historical records while adding fresh information without losing previous datasets.

You may also encounter situations where specific formatting or formulas need to be applied when writing data using Pandas. While Pandas primarily focuses on data manipulation rather than formatting, you can effectively bridge this gap by combining it with OpenPyXL. Take this example, after writing a DataFrame using Pandas, you could reload the file with OpenPyXL for any advanced formatting needs.

When working with large datasets or complex structures where performance is crucial, consider strategies like chunking or optimizing memory usage during write operations. Ensuring efficiency will save time and resources in larger projects.

The ability to write effectively back into Excel not only simplifies routine tasks but also boosts your overall productivity by keeping your analyses current and actionable. Mastering these writing techniques allows you to create dynamic reports and dashboards that evolve with your data needs, making them vital skills for any analyst integrating Python into their everyday workflows.

Saving Excel Files

Writing data to Excel files goes beyond simply inserting numbers or text; it's about transforming raw data into meaningful insights that inform decisions and strategies. With Python, you can automate this process, making it both efficient and effective. After learning how to write to Excel cells, it's essential to understand the next crucial step: saving your Excel files. This guarantees that all your hard work is preserved and ready for future use.

When using libraries like OpenPyXL or Pandas to write data to an Excel file, saving your work is vital. If you forget to save, you risk losing all the modifications you've made.

Saving a file isn't merely a straightforward command; it signifies a commitment to preserving your data's structure and integrity for future reference.

With OpenPyXL, the saving process is simple but requires careful attention. After entering your data, you must call the save() method on your workbook object. Here's a quick example:

```python
from openpyxl import Workbook

\#\# Create a new workbook and select a sheet

workbook = Workbook()

sheet = workbook.active


\#\# Write some data

sheet['A1'] = 'Item'

sheet['B1'] = 'Quantity'

sheet['A2'] = 'Apples'

sheet['B2'] = 10


\#\# Save the workbook

workbook.save('inventory.xlsx')
```

In this example, we create an Excel file named inventory.xlsx, add an inventory of apples, and ensure that the file is saved correctly after writing. It's important to remember that if you close the program or navigate away without saving, any unsaved changes will be lost—a critical consideration for any data analyst who relies on accuracy and accountability.

On the other hand, when using Pandas for data manipulation and writing back to Excel, the saving process integrates seamlessly into its functionality. The to_excel() method allows you to save directly while specifying various options like sheet names and whether to include indices. Here's how you can manage saving with Pandas:

```python
import pandas as pd


data =

'Product': ['Bananas', 'Oranges', 'Grapes'],

'Stock': [30, 25, 15]


df = pd.DataFrame(data)


\#\# Save DataFrame to Excel

df.to_excel('fruit_inventory.xlsx', sheet_name='Stock Data', index=False)
```

In this case, fruit_inventory.xlsx will be created with a worksheet named "Stock Data," containing the inventory details without displaying DataFrame indices. This not only streamlines reporting processes but also helps maintain clarity in your datasets.

If you need to modify an existing file instead of creating a new one, Pandas offers methods for appending new data without overwriting existing content. This feature is particularly useful in ongoing projects where historical data must remain intact while allowing for updates:

```python
with pd.ExcelWriter('fruit_inventory.xlsx', mode='a') as writer:

additional_data =

'Product': ['Pineapples', 'Mangoes'],

'Stock': [10, 5]


df_additional = pd.DataFrame(additional_data)

df_additional.to_excel(writer, sheet_name='New Stock', index=False)
```

Using ExcelWriter in append mode enables you to add new sheets while keeping all previous entries safe—an essential strategy for effectively managing evolving datasets.

As we delve deeper into working with Excel files in Python, consider how saving practices can vary based on project needs. Take this example, creating backups of important workbooks before overwriting them or implementing version control strategies can help safeguard against data loss during complex analyses.

Another practical approach involves automating routine saves within long-running scripts. For example, incorporating periodic save commands within loops can ensure that intermediate results are not lost during lengthy calculations:

```python
for i in range(10):

\#\# Perform some calculations

sheet[f'Ai + 2'] = i * 10 \# Write results
```

\#\# Periodically save to avoid losing work

if i % 5 == 0:

workbook.save('periodic_save.xlsx')

` ` `

This snippet not only demonstrates effective writing but also proactive risk management by saving at regular intervals.

mastering the art of saving Excel files enhances workflow efficiency and significantly contributes to maintaining high-quality data integrity. By integrating these practices into your daily tasks with Python, you empower yourself and pave the way for smoother collaboration within teams —ensuring everyone has access to current and accurate datasets at all times.

Managing Worksheets

To begin managing worksheets effectively, it's crucial to learn how to create new sheets within an Excel workbook. With OpenPyXL, you can easily add a new sheet using the create_sheet() method, allowing you to specify the title at the time of creation. Here's a simple example:

` ` `python
from openpyxl import Workbook

\#\# Create a new workbook

workbook = Workbook()

\#\# Create new sheets

workbook.create_sheet(title='Sales Data')

```
workbook.create_sheet(title='Inventory')
```

\#\# Check the names of the sheets

```
print(workbook.sheetnames)
```

` ` `

After executing this code, you'll have two new sheets titled "Sales Data" and "Inventory." You can confirm their creation by printing workbook.sheetnames. Effectively managing multiple sheets is vital for logically separating data while ensuring that all relevant information remains accessible within a single workbook.

Once you've created your worksheets, you may find that some initial names do not adequately reflect the data they contain. Renaming existing worksheets is a straightforward process with OpenPyXL. You can access a sheet by its title or index and assign it a new name:

` ` `python

\#\# Rename 'Sales Data' to 'Q1 Sales'

```
sheet = workbook['Sales Data']

sheet.title = 'Q1 Sales'
```

` ` `

This flexibility enhances your organization of data as projects evolve over time. Maintaining clear naming conventions allows all team members to understand the contents of each sheet at a glance.

Another important aspect of effective data management is deleting unnecessary worksheets. Unused or erroneous sheets can clutter your workbook, making it harder to locate important information. To remove a sheet, simply use the remove() method on your workbook object:

```python
\#\# Remove 'Inventory' sheet

workbook.remove(workbook['Inventory'])

```

This command efficiently deletes the specified worksheet from your workbook. However, exercise caution; once deleted, all data on that sheet is lost unless you have backed it up previously.

Transitioning from OpenPyXL to Pandas opens up additional capabilities for managing worksheets that go beyond basic creation or deletion. Pandas offers a robust way to handle larger datasets through its DataFrame structure and facilitates operations across multiple sheets in an Excel file.

Take this example, if you're loading data from an existing Excel file with multiple sheets into separate DataFrames, you can accomplish this effortlessly with pd.read_excel(). Here's how:

```python
import pandas as pd


\#\# Load all sheets from an Excel file into a dictionary of DataFrames

dfs = pd.read_excel('data.xlsx', sheet_name=None)


\#\# Accessing specific DataFrame for 'Sales Data'

sales_data = dfs['Sales Data']

```

This snippet loads every sheet into a dictionary where the keys are sheet names and the values are their respective

DataFrames. Managing large volumes of data becomes more manageable with this structure since it allows for independent analyses on each dataset.

You can also write multiple DataFrames back to different sheets using ExcelWriter. This method consolidates your workflow as you update or modify individual datasets without affecting others:

```python
with pd.ExcelWriter('updated_data.xlsx') as writer:

sales_data.to_excel(writer, sheet_name='Updated Sales', index=False)

inventory_data.to_excel(writer, sheet_name='Updated Inventory', index=False)
```

This approach preserves existing sheets while creating updated versions alongside them.

Effectively managing worksheets is crucial for maintaining organized datasets that are easily accessible during analysis or reporting phases. Consider implementing version control practices when modifying worksheet structures; retaining previous versions ensures that essential information isn't inadvertently lost during updates.

Automating tasks related to worksheet management can further enhance productivity. For example, setting up scripts that routinely check for redundant sheets and prompt users before deletion can streamline processes and minimize human error.

As we explore these functions throughout this book, reflect on how each method can transform your workflow—turning tedious tasks into streamlined operations and freeing up time for analysis rather than administration. Embracing these techniques will help establish a strong foundation for successful data management in your journey of integrating Python with Excel.

Formatting Cells and Ranges

Formatting cells and ranges in Excel is a crucial aspect of data presentation that significantly improves the readability and professionalism of your reports. By applying proper formatting, you can convey information clearly, enabling stakeholders to interpret data quickly and efficiently. Whether you're highlighting key figures, using conditional formatting to identify trends, or customizing the appearance of charts, the ability to manipulate formatting through Python opens up a world of possibilities.

To start, let's look at how to format individual cells using OpenPyXL. You can easily adjust various attributes, such as font style, size, color, and background fill. Consider this practical example where we format a specific cell:

```python
from openpyxl import Workbook

from openpyxl.styles import Font, PatternFill


\#\# Create a new workbook and access the active sheet

workbook = Workbook()

sheet = workbook.active


\#\# Write data into a cell

sheet['A1'] = 'Sales Amount'


\#\# Apply bold font and red text color

bold_font = Font(bold=True, color='FF0000')
```

sheet['A1'].font = bold_font

\#\# Set a yellow background fill

yellow_fill   =   PatternFill(start_color='FFFF00', end_color='FFFF00', fill_type='solid')

sheet['A1'].fill = yellow_fill

\#\# Save the workbook

workbook.save('formatted_sales.xlsx')

` ` `

In this snippet, we create a new Excel file and apply both font styling and background fill to make the "Sales Amount" label stand out. Such visual cues are essential for ensuring that critical information captures immediate attention.

Next, let's explore how to apply formatting to ranges of cells. Formatting multiple cells at once not only saves time but also ensures consistency throughout your reports. For example, if you wanted to format an entire row with borders and shading:

` ` `python

from openpyxl.styles import Border, Side

\#\# Define border style

thin_border   =   Border(left=Side(style='thin'), right=Side(style='thin'),

top=Side(style='thin'), bottom=Side(style='thin'))

\#\# Apply formatting to an entire range (e.g., A2:C2)

```
for cell in sheet['A2:C2']:

cell.fill = yellow_fill \# Use previously defined yellow fill

cell.border = thin_border \# Apply borders


\#\# Save changes

workbook.save('formatted_range.xlsx')
```
` ` `

This code snippet adds a consistent border around each cell in the specified range while applying the same background fill used earlier. Such bulk formatting methods make it easier to manage larger datasets efficiently.

Another powerful feature to consider is conditional formatting, which can also be automated using Python. With OpenPyXL's conditional_formatting module, you can set rules that dynamically change the appearance of cells based on their values—ideal for highlighting trends or identifying outliers in your data analysis.

Take this example, if you want to highlight any sales figure over (10,000:

` ` `python

```
from openpyxl.formatting.rule import CellIsRule


\#\# Assuming sales data starts from A2 downwards

sheet.add_conditional_formatting('A2:A100',
CellIsRule(operator='greaterThan',        formula=['10000'],
stopIfTrue=True,

fill=PatternFill(start_color='00FF00',    end_color='00FF00',
fill_type='solid')))
```

\#\# Save your workbook with conditional formatting applied

workbook.save('conditional_formatting.xlsx')

` ` `

This script checks each cell in the specified range and applies a green fill if the condition is met. Using such dynamic visual aids transforms how viewers interact with data by drawing immediate attention to critical insights.

Beyond basic styling and conditional formatting lies the realm of Excel charts—integrating visual elements that convey complex datasets at a glance. Although we will delve deeper into charting later on, it's important to note that you can directly apply formats when creating these visuals using libraries like Matplotlib or Seaborn alongside Excel exports.

As you engage with these techniques throughout your projects, think about how different formats can enhance not just aesthetics but also functionality within your reports. Establishing standards for visual consistency will improve readability and strengthen communication across your team or organization.

effective formatting goes beyond aesthetics; it's about making information accessible and actionable. Mastering these skills will significantly elevate your data presentations and empower your analytical efforts as you seamlessly integrate Python into your Excel workflows.

Using Formulas in Excel with Python

Using Excel formulas through Python significantly enhances your analytical capabilities and enables the automation of repetitive tasks, ultimately saving time and minimizing errors. Formulas are at the heart of Excel's functionality, facilitating complex calculations and efficient data manipulation. By leveraging Python's libraries, you can create dynamic spreadsheets that automatically adjust to changes in underlying data.

To get started with using Excel formulas in Python, let's examine how to write formulas directly into cells with OpenPyXL. This method allows you to utilize Excel's built-in functions without the need for manual entry. Take this example, we can calculate total sales from individual sales figures:

```python
from openpyxl import Workbook

\#\# Create a new workbook and access the active sheet

workbook = Workbook()

sheet = workbook.active

\#\# Write sample sales data

sales_data = [1000, 1500, 2000, 2500]

for index, amount in enumerate(sales_data, start=1):

sheet[f'Aindex'] = amount

\#\# Write a formula to calculate total sales in cell B1

sheet['B1'] = '=SUM(A1:A4)'

\#\# Save the workbook

workbook.save('sales_with_formula.xlsx')
```

In this example, we insert sample sales data into column A and write a formula in cell B1 to sum these values. When you open sales_with_formula.xlsx, you'll find that B1 displays the total of all sales amounts.

Next, let's explore more complex scenarios involving conditional calculations or multiple functions within a single formula. For example, if you want to identify which sales figures exceed the average, you can use a combination of the AVERAGE and IF functions in your Python code:

```python
\#\# Write an average formula in cell C1

sheet['C1'] = '=AVERAGE(A1:A4)'


\#\# Write an IF statement in column D to check if each sale is above average

for index in range(1, 5):

sheet[f'Dindex'] = f'=IF(Aindex>C\)1,"Above Average","Below Average")'


\#\# Save changes again

workbook.save('conditional_sales_analysis.xlsx')
```

In this snippet, we first calculate the average of our sales figures in cell C1. Then, we use an IF statement in column D to compare each individual sale against this average. The output will classify each figure as "Above Average" or "Below Average.

Moving beyond basic calculations, you can seamlessly integrate external data or perform lookups using functions like VLOOKUP. For example, if you have a separate list of product IDs with their corresponding prices that you wish to reference:

```python
\#\# Assuming product ID and price are stored in another part of the worksheet

product_data = [('ID001', 10), ('ID002', 15), ('ID003', 20)]

for index, (product_id, price) in enumerate(product_data):

sheet[f'Findex + 2'] = product_id

sheet[f'Gindex + 2'] = price


\#\# Write VLOOKUP formula to find prices based on product IDs (assume input IDs are in E)

sheet['E2'] = 'ID001' \# Example lookup value

sheet['H2'] = '=VLOOKUP(E2,F2:G4,2,FALSE)' \# Looks up price for ID001


\#\# Save final workbook with lookups included

workbook.save('vlookup_example.xlsx')
```

In this case, we create a small dataset with product IDs and prices starting from columns F and G. The VLOOKUP function retrieves prices based on an input ID specified in E2.

As you incorporate formulas into your workflows using Python, it's important to consider how they can adapt dynamically as your datasets change. Formulas should be responsive elements that enhance interactivity within your spreadsheets.

Additionally, remember the importance of error handling when working with formulas—especially when referencing ranges or dependent cells that might change over time. Utilizing Python's error-checking features can help manage these situations effectively.

For example:

``` python

try:

\#\# Attempt to save your workbook after adding complex formulas

workbook.save('error_handling_in_formulas.xlsx')

except Exception as e:

print(f"Error saving workbook: e")

```

Incorporating robust error handling ensures that your scripts run smoothly without unexpected interruptions.

Mastering the use of formulas through Python bridges the gap between programming efficiency and spreadsheet simplicity—enabling advanced data analysis while remaining accessible to those familiar with Excel's interface. By adopting these techniques now, you're not just boosting productivity; you're transforming how data-driven decisions are made within your projects and organization.

Handling Excel Errors

Errors are an inevitable aspect of working with any software, and Excel is no exception. When integrating Python with Excel, effectively managing these errors is essential to maintain the integrity of your data and the reliability of your workflows. By understanding how to handle errors, you can save considerable time and avoid potential data corruption.

Whether facing formula errors, runtime exceptions, or data inconsistencies, a proactive approach enhances overall efficiency.

One of the most frequent types of errors encountered in Excel is the formula error. These errors can arise from various issues, such as incorrect syntax or referencing non-existent cells. For example, if you accidentally type an invalid function name or reference a deleted cell, you will encounter a formula error. Fortunately, when using libraries like OpenPyXL or Pandas in Python, you can automate the detection of these errors.

Let's explore how to encounter a formula error in Excel while executing a basic operation through Python:

```python
from openpyxl import Workbook

\#\# Create workbook and sheet
workbook = Workbook()
sheet = workbook.active

\#\# Intentionally create an incorrect formula
sheet['A1'] = '=SUM(A2:A10)'  \# A2:A10 does not exist

try:
\#\# Save workbook to see if any error is triggered
workbook.save('error_example.xlsx')
except Exception as e:
print(f"Error occurred: e")
```

```
` ` `
```

In this example, attempting to sum a range that doesn't exist won't raise an exception until you open the Excel file and recalculate it. At that point, you might see a #REF! error in Excel indicating an invalid reference.

To manage such scenarios more effectively while developing with Python, it's crucial to implement checks before saving or manipulating Excel files. Take this example, validating that your formulas point to existing ranges can prevent issues:

```python
` ` `python
def validate_formula(sheet):

for cell in sheet['A']:

if isinstance(cell.value, str) and cell.value.startswith('='):

\#\# Perform basic validation on the formula string

if 'A' not in cell.value:  \# Simplistic check just for example

print(f"Warning: cell.coordinate contains an invalid reference.")


validate_formula(sheet)
` ` `
```

In this script, we examine each cell in column A for formulas beginning with '=', offering a preliminary validation step prior to calculations.

Another common challenge arises when dealing with missing or invalid data while reading from spreadsheets using Pandas. When importing data from an Excel file into a DataFrame, NaN values may appear and complicate analysis:

```python
` ` `python
```

```
import pandas as pd

\#\# Load data from an Excel file

df = pd.read_excel('sales_data.xlsx')

\#\# Check for missing values

if df.isnull().values.any():

print("Warning: Missing values detected!")
```
` ` `

This proactive approach enables you to identify issues before they escalate into larger problems during analysis. You can further enhance your workflow by implementing data cleaning functions to fill or drop missing values as necessary.

Building on this foundation of error identification and prevention leads us to effective debugging strategies within our Python scripts. Utilizing Python's built-in debugging tools—such as pdb—can significantly aid in diagnosing more complex issues:

` ` `python

```
import pdb

pdb.set_trace() \# Set a breakpoint here

\#\# Your code logic goes here; execution will pause allowing inspection.
```
` ` `

By pausing execution at strategic points in your code, you can inspect variables and control flow, allowing you to pinpoint precisely where things may be going wrong.

Despite careful planning and coding practices, unexpected errors may still arise during execution—particularly when working with external sources or integrations. To manage these exceptions gracefully within your scripts, it's wise to employ try-except blocks throughout your codebase:

```python
try:

\#\# Execute potentially problematic code here.

result = perform_complex_calculation()

except ValueError as e:

print(f"Value Error encountered: e")

except Exception as general_error:

print(f"An error occurred: general_error")
```

By using specific exception types for targeted responses while maintaining broader exception handling for unforeseen cases, you can navigate errors more effectively.

To wrap things up, mastering the art of error handling not only protects your projects but also equips you with resilience against unexpected challenges. By understanding potential pitfalls within Excel and Python integration and establishing preemptive measures alongside responsive debugging techniques, you're well-prepared to develop robust applications that thrive under pressure. Embracing these strategies will help ensure that your automation processes remain seamless and reliable—a true hallmark of professionalism in today's data-driven landscape.

CHAPTER 4: DATA MANIPULATION WITH PANDAS

Loading Excel Data into DataFrames

Loading Excel data into Pandas DataFrames opens up a powerful avenue for data manipulation and analysis. This integration allows you to combine Excel's user-friendly interface with Python's extensive libraries, enhancing your ability to handle data and amplifying your analytical potential.

To start loading Excel data, you'll typically use the Pandas library, which offers a straightforward method for reading Excel files. For example, imagine you have a workbook named sales_data.xlsx containing sales figures. You can easily import this workbook into a DataFrame using the following code:

```python
import pandas as pd
```

\#\# Load the Excel file into a DataFrame

df = pd.read_excel('sales_data.xlsx')

\#\# Display the first few rows of the DataFrame

print(df.head())
``` `

In this snippet, you begin by importing the pandas module, which grants access to its functionalities. The read_excel function is then used to load your spreadsheet into a DataFrame called df. By using the head() method, you can quickly verify that your data has been loaded correctly by viewing the first five records.

However, it's important to recognize that not all Excel files are structured in the same way. You may encounter situations where your data is located in different sheets or requires specific adjustments for headers. For example, if your relevant data is on a sheet named "2023 Sales," you can specify that directly:

```python

df = pd.read_excel('sales_data.xlsx', sheet_name='2023 Sales')
``` `

In cases where your headers are not formatted as expected —perhaps starting from a different row—you can adjust this with the header parameter:

```python

df = pd.read_excel('sales_data.xlsx', header=1) \# Assuming headers are on the second row

```
` ` `
```

Once your data is in a DataFrame, it may contain various types of values that require cleaning and formatting before any analytical processing can occur. Common tasks include checking for NaN values and ensuring that data types are suitable for calculations.

Take this example, after loading sales data, you might want to confirm that numeric columns are recognized as numbers:

``` `python
\#\# Convert 'Sales Amount' column to numeric type if needed

df['Sales Amount'] = pd.to_numeric(df['Sales Amount'], errors='coerce')

\#\# Check for missing values after conversion

print(df['Sales Amount'].isnull().sum(), "missing values found in 'Sales Amount'")
` ` `
```

Here, we use pd.to_numeric() with the parameter errors='coerce', which gracefully converts any non-numeric entries into NaN values. Following this step with a check ensures you're fully aware of your dataset's state.

DataFrames also allow for easy subsetting operations. If you want to analyze only those sales exceeding (5000, you can do so with conditional filtering:

``` `python
high_sales_df = df[df['Sales Amount'] > 5000]

\#\# Display high sales records
```

```
print(high_sales_df)
```

This method enables you to extract relevant segments without needing complex loops or manual checks.

Additionally, efficiently loading large datasets is crucial for performance-sensitive applications. When working with extensive spreadsheets, Pandas provides options such as specifying particular columns to load or utilizing chunking to handle large datasets in manageable portions:

```python
chunk_iter = pd.read_excel('large_dataset.xlsx', chunksize=1000)


for chunk in chunk_iter:

\#\# Process each chunk independently

print(chunk.describe()) \# Example operation on each chunk
```

Chunking is particularly effective when performance considerations arise since it allows for processing smaller portions of your dataset one at a time.

On another note, combining multiple sheets from an Excel workbook can be done easily if they are structured correctly. Take this example, if you have several sheets representing different months of sales data and wish to consolidate them into one DataFrame, Python simplifies this process:

```python
sheets = ['January', 'February', 'March']

all_data = []
```

```
for sheet in sheets:

monthly_data      =      pd.read_excel('monthly_sales.xlsx',
sheet_name=sheet)

all_data.append(monthly_data)


\#\# Concatenate all monthly data into one DataFrame

consolidated_df = pd.concat(all_data)

print(consolidated_df)
` ` `
```

This loop iterates through each specified sheet name, loading the respective data into individual DataFrames before appending them collectively using pd.concat(). The resulting consolidated_df provides an aggregated view of your multi-sheet sales information.

The transition from raw Excel files to actionable insights involves more than just loading data; it's about creating an adaptable framework that enhances efficiency and effectiveness in analysis. As you navigate these processes—loading diverse datasets while managing their complexities—you'll find yourself equipped not only with tools but also with insights that drive impactful decision-making across projects.

Data Cleaning Techniques

Data cleaning techniques are fundamental to the success of any data analysis project. Once you load your Excel data into a Pandas DataFrame, the next crucial step is to ensure that the data is clean and prepared for insightful analysis. Raw data often contains errors, missing values, or inconsistencies that can significantly skew your results. Addressing these issues is essential—not merely for tidying up but to ensure that your analyses are built on a reliable foundation.

A common challenge in data cleaning is dealing with missing values. These gaps can arise from various sources, such as data entry errors, incomplete surveys, or unrecorded information. Identifying missing values early on enables you to address them effectively. With Pandas, you can quickly check for NaN (Not a Number) entries using the isnull() method:

```python
\#\# Checking for missing values in each column

print(df.isnull().sum())
```

This command provides a count of missing entries across all columns, allowing you to decide whether to fill these gaps or remove affected rows. The fillna() function can replace NaN values with a specified value or interpolate based on surrounding data:

```python
\#\# Filling missing values with the average of the column

df['Sales    Amount'].fillna(df['Sales    Amount'].mean(), inplace=True)
```

In this example, we use the mean to fill gaps in the 'Sales Amount' column. However, depending on the context, you might choose other strategies such as forward filling, backward filling, or setting specific defaults.

In addition to handling missing values, it's common to encounter duplicates within datasets. These redundancies can distort your results and mislead interpretations. Fortunately, removing duplicates is straightforward in

Pandas:

```python
\#\# Dropping duplicate rows

df.drop_duplicates(inplace=True)
```

This command eliminates any exact duplicate rows from your DataFrame.

Another important consideration is formatting issues with categorical data. Take this example, a 'Region' column may contain variations like "East", "east", and "EAST". Inconsistent casing can complicate accurate grouping and analysis. Normalizing these entries facilitates easier comparisons and aggregations:

```python
\#\# Standardizing categorical variable casing

df['Region'] = df['Region'].str.lower()
```

With this simple line of code, all entries in the 'Region' column are converted to lowercase, ensuring consistency across your dataset.

Data types also play a critical role in effective analysis. If numeric data is mistakenly stored as strings due to formatting errors, it can lead to computation failures. Therefore, it's wise to check and convert data types as needed:

```python
\#\# Converting 'Sales Amount' to numeric if it was read incorrectly

df['Sales Amount'] = pd.to_numeric(df['Sales Amount'], errors='coerce')
```

` ` `

This line ensures that any string representations of numbers are converted into actual numeric types; invalid characters (like currency symbols) result in NaN for further handling.

Another often-overlooked aspect of cleaning involves trimming whitespace from string entries. This detail can lead to mismatches during analyses:

` ` `python

\#\# Stripping whitespace from string columns

df['Product Name'] = df['Product Name'].str.strip()

` ` `

By eliminating leading and trailing spaces from product names or other textual entries, you enhance matching accuracy when conducting joins or filters.

Additionally, filtering out outliers is sometimes necessary to avoid distorting statistical analyses. A practical approach involves using Z-scores or IQR (Interquartile Range) methods for identifying such anomalies:

` ` `python

\#\# Filtering out outliers based on Z-score method

from scipy import stats

z_scores = stats.zscore(df['Sales Amount'])

filtered_entries = (abs(z_scores) < 3)

clean_df = df[filtered_entries]

` ` `

In this example, any row with a Z-score exceeding three standard deviations from the mean is flagged as an outlier and excluded from clean_df.

When working with dates imported from Excel via Pandas, ensuring correct date formats is essential for analyses like time series forecasting or trend detection:

``` python
\#\# Converting string dates into datetime objects

df['Order Date'] = pd.to_datetime(df['Order Date'], errors='coerce')
```

With this conversion, date-related operations become more efficient and reliable.

As you implement these cleaning techniques—addressing missing values, removing duplicates, normalizing text entries—you will find that your analytical tasks progress more smoothly and accurately. Each step not only enhances data quality but also bolsters confidence in the insights derived from this information-rich environment. Properly cleaned data paves the way for deeper exploration and more meaningful conclusions about trends and patterns within your datasets.

Merging and Joining DataFrames

Once your data is clean and well-prepared, the next step often involves integrating information from multiple sources. Merging and joining DataFrames in Pandas enables you to consolidate disparate datasets into a single, coherent view, which is essential for thorough analysis—especially when your data is spread across different tables or files but connected by common fields.

At the heart of this process is the merge function, which allows you to combine DataFrames based on key columns. For example, imagine you have one DataFrame containing sales data and another with customer information. Merging these datasets can help you analyze sales performance in relation to customer demographics.

Here's a simple illustration of how to perform a basic merge:

```python
\#\# Sample DataFrames
sales_data = pd.DataFrame(
'CustomerID': [1, 2, 3],
'SalesAmount': [150, 200, 300]
)


customer_data = pd.DataFrame(
'CustomerID': [1, 2],
'Region': ['East', 'West']
)


\#\# Merging DataFrames on CustomerID
merged_data = pd.merge(sales_data, customer_data, on='CustomerID', how='inner')
print(merged_data)
```

In this code snippet, we merge sales_data and customer_data on the 'CustomerID' column using an inner join. This operation retains only those customers present in both DataFrames. The output will appear as follows:

```

CustomerID SalesAmount Region
```

0 1 150 East

1 2 200 West

` ` `

Depending on your analytical needs, you can also utilize different types of joins. Take this example, if you want to include all customers regardless of whether they have corresponding sales records, an outer join would be more suitable:

` ` `python

\#\# Performing an outer join

merged_outer = pd.merge(sales_data, customer_data, on='CustomerID', how='outer')

print(merged_outer)

` ` `

This approach preserves all records from both DataFrames and fills any missing values with NaN as needed.

Another powerful feature of merging in Pandas is the ability to concatenate multiple DataFrames along a specific axis using the concat() function. If you have several months of sales data stored in separate DataFrames that require consolidation for analysis, you can do it like this:

` ` `python

\#\# Sample monthly DataFrames

january_sales = pd.DataFrame('SalesAmount': [100, 200])

february_sales = pd.DataFrame('SalesAmount': [150, 250])

\#\# Concatenating monthly sales data

all_sales = pd.concat([january_sales, february_sales], axis=0)

```
print(all_sales)
```
` ` `

This concatenation stacks the January and February sales records vertically into one comprehensive DataFrame.

Sometimes merging tasks may involve more complex relationships. In such cases, the join() method becomes particularly useful when working with indices rather than columns. Consider two DataFrames where one contains time series data indexed by dates while another holds related metrics indexed similarly:

` ` `python

\#\# Sample time series DataFrame

time_series = pd.DataFrame('Metric1': [1.5, 2.5], index=pd.to_datetime(['2023-01-01', '2023-01-02']))

metrics = pd.DataFrame('Metric2': [10, 20], index=pd.to_datetime(['2023-01-01', '2023-01-03']))

\#\# Joining using indices

joined_metrics = time_series.join(metrics)

print(joined_metrics)

` ` `

The output will display NaN for dates without corresponding entries in either DataFrame:

` ` `

Metric1 Metric2

2023-01-01 1.5 10.0

2023-01-02 2.5 NaN

2023-01-03 NaN 20.0

` ` `

When merging or joining DataFrames, it's important to monitor potential duplicates that may arise from overlapping keys. Addressing these duplicates before or after merging can help maintain data integrity.

To ensure the accuracy of your merges, consider utilizing the validate parameter in the merge() function to enforce constraints on the relationships between your datasets:

` ` `python

\#\# Validating merge integrity (one-to-one)

merged_validated = pd.merge(sales_data, customer_data, on='CustomerID', how='inner', validate='one_to_one')

` ` `

In this scenario, if any duplicate keys are detected in either source DataFrame that violate the specified relationship type (like one-to-one), Pandas will raise an error.

Once your datasets are successfully merged, exploring and analyzing them becomes much easier. You can apply all the cleaning techniques previously discussed alongside these merged datasets to uncover deeper insights and enhance decision-making capabilities.

By mastering merging and joining techniques within Pandas, you'll significantly improve your ability to analyze interconnected datasets effectively—transforming raw information into actionable insights that can drive better business decisions and strategies across various domains.

Calculating Aggregates in Excel

Calculating aggregates in Excel using Python can significantly enhance your data analysis capabilities. Whether you are working with sales data, customer information, or financial reports, the ability to compute sums, averages, counts, and other statistical measures directly within your Excel workflows not only saves time but also improves accuracy.

To begin, it's essential to understand the fundamental aggregates you might require. The most common functions include:

1. SUM: Adds up all values.

2. AVERAGE: Calculates the mean of the values.

3. COUNT: Counts the number of entries.

4. MAX: Finds the largest value.

5. MIN: Identifies the smallest value.

These functions can be executed through Python libraries such as Pandas and OpenPyXL, enabling scalable data manipulation within your Excel files.

Using Pandas for Aggregate Calculations

Pandas excels at managing large datasets and performing complex computations efficiently. Take this example, let's consider an Excel file named sales_data.xlsx that contains sales records across multiple regions. We can load this file into a Pandas DataFrame and calculate some aggregates.

```python
import pandas as pd


\#\# Load the Excel file

file_path = 'sales_data.xlsx'

df = pd.read_excel(file_path)


\#\# Display the first few rows of the DataFrame
```

```
print(df.head())
```

Assuming this dataset includes columns like Region, Sales, and Date, you can calculate total sales per region with the following code:

```python
total_sales_per_region = df.groupby('Region')['Sales'].sum()

print(total_sales_per_region)
```

This command outputs the total sales for each region, offering insights into which areas are performing best.

Averages and Other Aggregates

To derive averages or other statistics, you can expand upon this method:

```python
average_sales_per_region = df.groupby('Region')['Sales'].mean()

count_of_sales_entries = df.groupby('Region')['Sales'].count()

print("Average Sales:", average_sales_per_region)

print("Count of Sales Entries:", count_of_sales_entries)
```

These commands provide a comprehensive view of performance metrics and data entry volume by region.

Exporting Results Back to Excel

After computing your aggregates, exporting the results back into Excel for reporting or further analysis is straightforward with Pandas:

```python
\#\# Create a new DataFrame to hold aggregates

aggregates_df = pd.DataFrame(

'Total Sales': total_sales_per_region,

'Average Sales': average_sales_per_region,

'Count of Entries': count_of_sales_entries

)


\#\# Save it to a new sheet in the existing workbook or a new workbook

aggregates_df.to_excel('sales_data_aggregates.xlsx', sheet_name='Aggregates', index=True)
```

This snippet generates a new workbook containing your aggregated results in an organized format.

Using OpenPyXL for Simple Aggregates

If you prefer a more direct approach without utilizing DataFrames, OpenPyXL allows you to manipulate cells directly in an existing workbook. Here's how you can compute totals without creating additional DataFrames:

```python
from openpyxl import load_workbook


\#\# Load your workbook and select a sheet

wb = load_workbook('sales_data.xlsx')

ws = wb.active
```

```
\#\# Assuming sales are in column B from row 2 onwards

total = 0

for row in ws.iter_rows(min_row=2, max_col=2, values_only=True):

total += row[0] if row[0] is not None else 0


ws['D1'] = 'Total Sales'

ws['D2'] = total


wb.save('sales_data_updated.xlsx')
```
` ` `

In this example, we loop through each row starting from row 2 (skipping headers) and sum up values from column B before writing the result into cell D2.

Using Python to calculate aggregates not only streamlines your workflow but also enhances accuracy—eliminating manual errors in calculations. By leveraging libraries like Pandas and OpenPyXL, you can efficiently handle large datasets. This proficiency allows you to concentrate on interpreting results rather than being bogged down by tedious calculations. Each technique presented here serves as a stepping stone toward more complex analyses that Python can facilitate within Excel's environment. Embrace these tools; they will profoundly change how you interact with your data!

Filtering and Sorting Data

Filtering and sorting data are essential skills for anyone working with Excel, and Python can greatly enhance your efficiency in these tasks. Whether you're analyzing customer records, sales figures, or inventory lists, the ability to manipulate data effectively can significantly improve your analysis and decision-making processes.

To start, it's important to identify the specific criteria you'll use for filtering or sorting your data. Filtering helps you isolate certain rows based on defined conditions, while sorting organizes your data in a specified order, either ascending or descending. This functionality is crucial for identifying trends and making informed decisions.

Filtering Data with Pandas

Pandas provides powerful filtering options that allow you to apply multiple conditions seamlessly. Take this example, consider a dataset named customer_data.xlsx, which includes columns like CustomerID, Country, and PurchaseAmount. To load this dataset and filter for customers from a specific country, you can use the following code:

```python
import pandas as pd

\#\# Load the Excel file
file_path = 'customer_data.xlsx'
df = pd.read_excel(file_path)

\#\# Filter customers from 'USA'
us_customers = df[df['Country'] == 'USA']

print(us_customers)
```

This code creates a DataFrame containing only customers from the USA. You can also combine conditions using logical operators. For example, if you want to find customers from the USA who have made purchases over)500:

```python
us_high_value_customers = df[(df['Country'] == 'USA') & (df['PurchaseAmount'] > 500)]


print(us_high_value_customers)
```

Sorting Data with Pandas

After filtering your data, sorting it can help you quickly identify patterns. Continuing with the example of us_high_value_customers, you might want to sort these entries by PurchaseAmount in descending order:

```python
sorted_us_customers = us_high_value_customers.sort_values(by='PurchaseAmount', ascending=False)


print(sorted_us_customers)
```

This rearrangement allows you to see the highest purchases first, making it easier to identify key customers.

Exporting Filtered Results Back to Excel

Once you've filtered and sorted your data, saving these results back into an Excel file can facilitate further analysis or reporting. The following snippet demonstrates how to export your sorted DataFrame into a new sheet within an existing workbook:

```python
```

\#\# Save the filtered and sorted results back to Excel

sorted_us_customers.to_excel('filtered_sorted_customers.xlsx', sheet_name='HighValueCustomers', index=False)

```
```

This action creates a new workbook that retains only the relevant customer information in a structured format for easy review.

Filtering and Sorting with OpenPyXL

If you prefer a more hands-on approach without relying on Pandas, OpenPyXL allows for direct manipulation of Excel files. For example, suppose you want to filter out high-value transactions directly from an existing workbook. Here's how you might do that for purchase amounts greater than (500:

```python
```

from openpyxl import load_workbook

\#\# Load workbook and select active worksheet

wb = load_workbook('customer_data.xlsx')

ws = wb.active

\#\# Create a new worksheet for filtered results

filtered_ws = wb.create_sheet('FilteredCustomers')

\#\# Set headers in new sheet

filtered_ws.append(['CustomerID', 'Country', 'PurchaseAmount'])

```
for row in ws.iter_rows(min_row=2, values_only=True):

if row[1] == 'USA' and row[2] > 500: \# Assuming Country is at index 1 and PurchaseAmount at index 2

filtered_ws.append(row)


wb.save('filtered_customer_data.xlsx')
` ` `
```

In this code block, we loop through each row of the original worksheet starting from row 2 (to skip headers) and check if each customer meets our filtering criteria before appending them to a new worksheet.

Mastering filtering and sorting techniques using Python transforms how you work with large datasets in Excel. Libraries like Pandas simplify complex operations through intuitive syntax, while OpenPyXL allows for direct workbook manipulation. These skills not only save time but also enhance the accuracy of your analyses. By embracing these methods, you can effortlessly distill critical insights from vast amounts of data—turning raw numbers into actionable intelligence for decision-making.

Handling Missing Data

Handling missing data is a crucial part of data analysis, particularly when working with Excel datasets. Missing values can distort your results, lead to incorrect conclusions, and complicate further analyses. Therefore, it is vital to recognize and manage these gaps to maintain the integrity of your data-driven decisions.

To start, it's important to clarify what a missing value entails. In datasets, missing values may manifest as blank cells, NaN (Not a Number), or other placeholders depending on the context. Identifying these gaps is essential, as it enables you to implement appropriate strategies for addressing them. Take this example, consider a dataset named sales_data.xlsx, which includes columns such as Date, Product, Quantity, and Revenue. Missing entries in this dataset may stem from various sources like incomplete records, data entry errors, or even system malfunctions.

Identifying Missing Data with Pandas

Pandas offers convenient functions for detecting missing values. To illustrate this, you can load the sales data and check for missing entries with the following code:

```python
import pandas as pd


\#\# Load the Excel file
file_path = 'sales_data.xlsx'
df = pd.read_excel(file_path)


\#\# Check for missing values
missing_data = df.isnull().sum()
print(missing_data)
```

This code provides a clear overview of the number of missing values in each column. For example, if the Quantity column shows five missing entries while Revenue has none, you can prioritize your cleaning efforts accordingly.

Dropping Missing Values

One straightforward strategy for managing missing data is to remove entire rows that contain any gaps. This method can be effective if the proportion of missing data is small relative to the overall dataset and does not significantly impact your analysis. You can drop rows with missing values using the following command:

```python
\#\# Drop rows with any missing values
df_cleaned = df.dropna()

print(df_cleaned)
```

While this approach is simple and effective in many situations, it's important to use it judiciously; dropping too many rows can result in valuable information being lost.

Filling Missing Values

When removing data isn't practical, filling in gaps— commonly referred to as imputation—becomes a preferred method. The strategy you choose should align with the nature of your dataset and your analytical goals. Take this example, if dealing with numerical data like Revenue, you might fill in missing values with the mean or median:

```python
\#\# Fill missing Revenue with mean value
mean_revenue = df['Revenue'].mean()
df['Revenue'].fillna(mean_revenue, inplace=True)

print(df)
```

For categorical data such as Product, you might opt to fill in missing values with the most frequently occurring item (the mode):

```python
\#\# Fill missing Product values with mode

mode_product = df['Product'].mode()[0]

df['Product'].fillna(mode_product, inplace=True)


print(df)
```

This approach helps preserve more of your dataset while making informed estimates about what the missing entries should be.

Advanced Techniques: Interpolation

For time series or ordered datasets, interpolation presents a more advanced solution for handling missing values. This technique estimates gaps based on surrounding available data points. Here's how to apply it:

```python
\#\# Assume Date is datetime type and set as index

df['Date'] = pd.to_datetime(df['Date'])

df.set_index('Date', inplace=True)


\#\# Interpolate missing Quantity values

df['Quantity'] = df['Quantity'].interpolate()


print(df)
```

Interpolation can offer a more nuanced approach than

simply filling in static numbers since it leverages existing trends within your dataset.

Exporting Cleaned Data Back to Excel

After effectively addressing missing data issues, saving your cleaned dataset for future use is essential. Exporting it back to Excel ensures that all modifications are retained:

```python
\#\# Save the cleaned DataFrame back to Excel

df.to_excel('cleaned_sales_data.xlsx', index=False)
```

This keeps your workspace organized and provides an updated version of your data for further analysis or reporting.

Effectively managing missing data transforms potential challenges into opportunities for improving data quality. By utilizing tools available in Pandas—from detection to imputation—you create a robust framework that ensures your analyses remain accurate and insightful. Mastering these techniques not only helps maintain data integrity but also enhances your decision-making capabilities across various analytical contexts.

Exporting DataFrames to Excel

Exporting data from Pandas DataFrames back into Excel is a crucial skill for anyone aiming to integrate Python into their Excel workflows. After manipulating and analyzing your data, the next step is to save your results in a format that can be easily shared and utilized by others. This not only enhances collaboration but also allows for further analysis in Excel's familiar environment.

Preparing Your Data for Export

Before you export, it's essential to ensure that your

DataFrame is in the desired format. Take a moment to clean up any unnecessary columns or rename them for clarity if needed. Take this example, if you have a DataFrame containing sales data with columns such as Date, Product, Quantity, and Revenue, you might want to filter out or reorder these columns before exporting, especially after performing operations like handling missing values.

Here's how you can prepare your DataFrame:

```python
import pandas as pd

\#\# Load your cleaned DataFrame

df_cleaned = pd.read_excel('cleaned_sales_data.xlsx')

\#\# Rename columns for clarity if necessary

df_cleaned.rename(columns='Product':   'Item',   'Revenue':
'Sales Revenue', inplace=True)

\#\# Optionally select only relevant columns for export

df_export   =   df_cleaned[['Date',   'Item',   'Quantity',   'Sales
Revenue']]
```

This preparation ensures that the exported file is user-friendly and contains only the necessary information.

Exporting to Excel Using Pandas

Pandas simplifies the process of exporting your DataFrame to an Excel file through the to_excel() function. Here's how you can do it:

```python
```

\#\# Specify the path where you want to save the file

output_file_path = 'final_sales_report.xlsx'

\#\# Export the DataFrame to Excel

df_export.to_excel(output_file_path, index=False)

` ` `

By setting index=False, you prevent Pandas from including row indices in the Excel file, resulting in a cleaner presentation of your data.

Customizing Your Export

Sometimes, you may need more than just a basic export. Pandas offers customization options, such as defining specific sheet names or exporting multiple DataFrames to different sheets within the same workbook. For example:

` ` `python

with pd.ExcelWriter('multi_sheet_report.xlsx') as writer:

df_export.to_excel(writer, sheet_name='Sales Report', index=False)

df_other_data.to_excel(writer, sheet_name='Other Metrics', index=False)

` ` `

This flexibility makes it easy to organize related datasets within one file, enhancing both accessibility and usability.

Ensuring Compatibility with Excel Features

When exporting data intended for further analysis in Excel, it's important to consider compatibility with features like formulas and formatting. While Pandas does not directly support advanced formatting during export, you can apply basic styles using libraries such as OpenPyXL or XlsxWriter after creating your initial export.

Take this example, if you want to highlight certain cells based on their values or add conditional formatting, you can do so as follows:

```python
import xlsxwriter


\#\# Create an Excel writer object using XlsxWriter

with                    pd.ExcelWriter('styled_report.xlsx',
engine='xlsxwriter') as writer:

df_export.to_excel(writer,    sheet_name='Sales    Report',
index=False)


\#\# Access the XlsxWriter workbook and worksheet objects

workbook = writer.book

worksheet = writer.sheets['Sales Report']


\#\# Define a format for highlighting high sales revenue

highlight_format    =    workbook.add_format('bg_color':
'\#FFEBCC')


\#\# Apply conditional formatting: highlight if Sales Revenue > 1000

worksheet.conditional_format('D2:D100', 'type': 'cell',

'criteria': '>',

'value': 1000,

'format': highlight_format)
```

` ` `

Incorporating these techniques into your workflow ensures that your exported data not only conveys accurate information but also promotes actionable insights.

Final Touches: Testing Your Exports

Once you've exported your data, it's important to verify its integrity by opening the generated Excel file. Check that all values are correctly represented and confirm that there are no unexpected changes due to formatting issues or data loss during export. This step helps prevent miscommunication or confusion when others utilize your reports.

By effectively preparing and customizing your exports, you're equipped to deliver polished datasets ready for collaboration and strategic decision-making in any environment where Excel thrives. The integration of Python's analytical capabilities with the accessibility of Excel creates a powerful synergy that enhances productivity across various domains—whether it's financial reporting, marketing analytics, or inventory management—wherever data-driven decisions are critical.

Best Practices for Data Manipulation

Data manipulation transcends mere technical skill; it is an art form that demands finesse and a solid grasp of best practices. When using Pandas, particularly in conjunction with Excel, following certain principles can transform a chaotic dataset into one that effectively communicates its narrative.

Structuring Your DataFrame Wisely

Efficient data manipulation begins with the thoughtful structuring of your DataFrame. Meaningful column names and consistent data types are essential for clarity. Take this example, in a dataset of employee records, using column names like Employee ID, Name, Department, and Salary provides immediate understanding.

Here's how to create a well-structured DataFrame:

``` `python

import pandas as pd

\#\# Creating a sample DataFrame for employee records

data =

'Employee ID': [101, 102, 103],

'Name': ['Alice', 'Bob', 'Charlie'],

'Department': ['HR', 'Finance', 'IT'],

'Salary': [70000, 80000, 90000]

df_employees = pd.DataFrame(data)
` ` `

This initial structuring lays the groundwork for further operations. It's important to anticipate the types of manipulations you'll perform—such as grouping by department or calculating average salaries—and design your DataFrame accordingly.

Emphasizing Data Cleaning

Data cleaning is often the most tedious yet crucial aspect of data manipulation. Before diving into analysis or exporting data, it's vital to ensure that your dataset is free from errors and inconsistencies. This may involve addressing missing values or correcting incorrect entries.

For example, if some salary entries are recorded as strings
```

instead of numbers, you can fix it like this:

```python
\#\# Simulating a dataset with incorrect types

df_employees['Salary'] = df_employees['Salary'].astype(str) \# Incorrectly set as string


\#\# Correcting the data type

df_employees['Salary'] = pd.to_numeric(df_employees['Salary'], errors='coerce')
```

This snippet demonstrates how to convert values while managing potential conversion errors gracefully. By cleaning your data upfront, you can avoid complications later during analysis and reporting.

Leveraging Group Operations

Group operations offer an efficient way to summarize your data. If you wish to analyze average salaries by department, Pandas simplifies this task:

```python
\#\# Calculating average salary by department

average_salary_by_department = df_employees.groupby('Department')['Salary'].mean().reset_index()
```

This operation not only computes averages but also resets the index for improved readability. Mastering grouping and aggregation techniques enables deeper insights into your datasets.

Employing Functions for Repetitive Tasks

In many scenarios, you may find yourself performing similar manipulations across various datasets or different parts of your workflow. This is where defining functions becomes invaluable.

Take this example, if you frequently need to standardize names (ensuring consistent capitalization), you could create a function like this:

```python
def standardize_names(name):

    return name.title()


df_employees['Name'] = df_employees['Name'].apply(standardize_names)
```

This approach streamlines your workflow and guarantees uniformity across all entries in that column.

Keeping Performance in Mind

As datasets expand in size, performance considerations become increasingly significant. It's best to avoid operations that unnecessarily copy data; instead, aim to work in place whenever possible. For example:

```python
\#\# Instead of creating copies, modify directly when possible

df_employees.dropna(inplace=True)   \# Drop rows with missing values in place
```

Using inplace=True helps maintain efficient memory usage without generating additional copies of your DataFrame.

Documenting Your Process

While often overlooked, documentation is crucial for maintaining clarity regarding the transformations applied to your data. Adding comments on complex lines of code or keeping a change log can be immensely helpful when revisiting projects or collaborating with others.

Take this example:

```python
\#\# Dropping rows where Salary is NaN to ensure accurate calculations later on

df_employees.dropna(subset=['Salary'], inplace=True)
```

Such comments elucidate the intentions behind each line of code and enhance maintainability.

Final Checks Before Export

After manipulating your data and before exporting it back into Excel or another format, it's important to conduct a final review. Look for anomalies such as unexpected null values or outliers that could distort results in reports.

By adhering to these best practices—thoughtful structuring, prioritizing data cleaning, utilizing functions for repetitive tasks, focusing on performance efficiency, and thorough documentation—you not only improve the quality of your datasets but also foster a more productive environment for yourself and your collaborators. Mastery in these areas leads to reliable insights and ultimately empowers informed decision-making in any analytical endeavor using Python alongside Excel.

CHAPTER 5: ADVANCED EXCEL REPORTING

Creating Pivot Tables with Python

C reating pivot tables using Python is a valuable skill for anyone who wants to harness the analytical capabilities of Excel. Pivot tables simplify the process of summarizing and analyzing complex datasets, and by incorporating Python into this workflow, you can enhance flexibility and automate tasks, fundamentally changing how you engage with your data.

To begin, it's essential to understand the structure of your dataset. For example, if you're dealing with sales figures categorized by product and region, organizing your data correctly is vital for effective pivot table creation. Consider this sample sales dataset:

```python
import pandas as pd


\#\# Sample sales data
```

```
data =

'Product': ['A', 'B', 'A', 'B', 'A'],

'Region': ['North', 'North', 'South', 'South', 'East'],

'Sales': [100, 150, 200, 300, 250]


df_sales = pd.DataFrame(data)
```
` ` `

With this DataFrame in place, you are poised to generate valuable insights. Next, you can create a pivot table using the built-in functionality of the Pandas library.

Creating the Pivot Table

Pandas provides an intuitive method for generating pivot tables through the pivot_table() function. To summarize sales by product and region, you can use the following code:

` ` `python

```
pivot_table        =        df_sales.pivot_table(values='Sales',
index='Product',      columns='Region',       aggfunc='sum',
fill_value=0)
```
` ` `

This line of code performs several key actions:

- values='Sales' specifies the data to summarize.
- index='Product' designates products as rows.
- columns='Region' sets regions as column headers.
- aggfunc='sum' instructs Pandas to sum sales values.
- fill_value=0 fills any missing values with zero.

So, you'll obtain a pivot table that summarizes total sales for each product across different regions.

Reviewing Your Pivot Table

After creating your pivot table, reviewing it for accuracy is essential. The output might appear as follows:

```
` ` `

Region East North South
Product
A 250 100 200
B 0 150 300
` ` `
```

This table clearly illustrates where sales are strong and where there may be opportunities for growth. However, generating the table is just one part of the process; manipulating it for deeper analysis is equally crucial.

Advanced Manipulations

You may want to delve deeper into your analysis by making additional modifications to your pivot table. Take this example, if you wish to focus on total sales per region rather than by product, you can adjust your approach:

```python
pivot_table_region = df_sales.pivot_table(values='Sales', index='Region', aggfunc='sum')
` ` `
```

This will produce a new pivot table that summarizes total sales by region.

Exporting Your Pivot Table

Once you've created your desired pivot table, exporting it back to Excel is straightforward using Pandas. The to_excel()

function enables you to save your pivot table directly into an Excel file:

``` python

pivot_table.to_excel('sales_summary.xlsx')
```

This command generates an Excel file named sales_summary.xlsx, maintaining all formatting and structure from your pivot table.

Enhancing Your Workflow

Using Python to create pivot tables not only automates repetitive tasks but also facilitates advanced analyses that would be cumbersome in Excel alone. If you're frequently generating similar reports, consider creating reusable functions to streamline your workflow.

For example, you could define a function that accepts parameters like the DataFrame and aggregation method:

``` python

def create_pivot(dataframe, value_col, index_col, column_col):

return dataframe.pivot_table(values=value_col, index=index_col, columns=column_col, aggfunc='sum', fill_value=0)


\#\# Usage

my_pivot = create_pivot(df_sales, 'Sales', 'Product', 'Region')
```

Leveraging Python for creating and manipulating pivot tables in Excel not only boosts efficiency but also unlocks advanced analytical capabilities. By mastering this integration, you position yourself at the forefront of data analysis innovation within your organization. Embrace these techniques as tools for not just reporting but also driving strategic decisions based on solid insights drawn from your data.

Automating Chart Generation

Automating chart generation in Excel using Python not only boosts efficiency but also revolutionizes data visualization. Manually creating charts can be tedious, especially when dealing with large datasets or repetitive tasks. However, Python simplifies this process significantly. By utilizing libraries like Matplotlib and Pandas, you can produce insightful visualizations with minimal effort.

To begin, it's important to have your data structured properly. Take this example, consider a scenario where you have monthly sales data for various products. Here's how such a dataset might look:

```python
import pandas as pd


\#\# Sample sales data

data =

'Month': ['January', 'February', 'March', 'April'],

'Product A': [1500, 2000, 2500, 3000],

'Product B': [1800, 2200, 2700, 3200]


df_sales = pd.DataFrame(data)
```

With this DataFrame prepared, the next step is to create

visualizations that effectively represent the data. You can use Matplotlib to generate a simple line chart that illustrates sales trends over the months.

Generating a Line Chart

The first step in generating a chart involves importing the necessary library and configuring it to work seamlessly with your DataFrame:

```python
``` python
import matplotlib.pyplot as plt


\#\# Set the figure size for better visibility

plt.figure(figsize=(10, 5))


\#\# Plotting the sales data

plt.plot(df_sales['Month'], df_sales['Product A'], marker='o',
label='Product A')

plt.plot(df_sales['Month'], df_sales['Product B'], marker='o',
label='Product B')


\#\# Adding titles and labels

plt.title('Monthly Sales Data')

plt.xlabel('Months')

plt.ylabel('Sales (\))')

plt.legend()
```

This code snippet performs several key tasks:

- It initializes a figure with specified dimensions.
```

- It plots each product's sales as a line graph, using markers for clarity.

- Titles and labels are included to enhance readability.

Customizing Your Chart

Customization plays a crucial role in making your charts both informative and visually appealing. You might want to adjust colors or add grid lines for improved clarity. Here's how you can enhance your existing chart:

```python
\#\# Customize colors and grid lines

plt.plot(df_sales['Month'], df_sales['Product A'], marker='o', color='blue', linestyle='-', linewidth=2)

plt.plot(df_sales['Month'], df_sales['Product B'], marker='o', color='orange', linestyle='--', linewidth=2)


\#\# Add grid lines

plt.grid(True)


\#\# Show the updated chart

plt.show()
```

By modifying colors and line styles, your visualization becomes more distinct and easier to interpret at a glance.

Saving Your Chart

Once you've created your chart and are satisfied with its appearance, saving it for future use or sharing is simple. You can use Matplotlib's savefig() function:

```python
\#\# Save the figure as a PNG file
plt.savefig('monthly_sales_chart.png')
```

This command saves your chart in PNG format in your current working directory.

Automating Multiple Charts

For those who regularly need to generate similar charts from varying datasets, automation becomes essential. Consider encapsulating your plotting logic within a function that accepts parameters like the DataFrame and column names:

```python
def plot_sales_chart(dataframe, product_columns):

plt.figure(figsize=(10, 5))

for product in product_columns:

plt.plot(dataframe['Month'], dataframe[product], marker='o', label=product)


plt.title('Monthly Sales Data')

plt.xlabel('Months')

plt.ylabel('Sales (\()')

plt.legend()

plt.grid(True)

plt.show()


\#\# Usage of function
```

plot_sales_chart(df_sales, ['Product A', 'Product B'])

` ` `

This approach allows you to easily adapt to different datasets by simply calling plot_sales_chart() with new parameters.

Final Thoughts on Automation

Automating chart generation with Python not only saves time but also enhances consistency across visual reports. The combination of libraries like Matplotlib and Pandas opens new avenues for presenting complex data in an understandable format. This method transforms raw numbers into compelling narratives that drive insights and decisions within any organization. Embracing these tools as integral components of your data analysis toolkit will significantly improve your efficiency as you continue to master the integration of Python with Excel.

Building Dashboards in Excel

Creating effective dashboards in Excel is an essential skill for anyone aiming to improve data visualization and enhance decision-making processes. A well-designed dashboard can distill complex datasets into easily digestible insights, allowing stakeholders to quickly understand critical information. By integrating Python with Excel, you gain powerful tools that automate and enrich the dashboard-building process.

To begin crafting your dashboard, identify the key performance indicators (KPIs) you wish to highlight. For example, if you're analyzing sales data across various regions, it's crucial to pinpoint metrics—such as total sales, growth percentages, and comparisons against targets—that will provide the most value. With these metrics defined, you can utilize Python libraries to dynamically pull in data, ensuring your dashboard remains up-to-date.

Setting Up Your Dashboard Framework

First, prepare your Excel workbook by creating a dedicated sheet for the dashboard. Aim for a clean layout that promotes readability and clarity. Consider organizing sections to focus on different facets of the data, such as sales trends or customer demographics. This thoughtful organization streamlines the presentation of information.

Importing Data with Python

Leveraging Python scripts to import data into your Excel dashboard simplifies updates and enhances accuracy. Take this example, if your sales data is stored in a CSV file, you can effortlessly read it into a Pandas DataFrame. Here's how:

```python
import pandas as pd


\#\# Load sales data from a CSV file

df_sales = pd.read_csv('sales_data.csv')


\#\# Display the first few rows of the DataFrame

print(df_sales.head())
```

This code snippet enables you to load the latest sales information dynamically without manual effort. Once your data is in Python, you can further manipulate or analyze it before sending it back to Excel for visualization.

Creating Visual Elements

Excel offers a variety of visual elements, including charts and tables, but enhancing these with Python can lead to even more impactful results. For example, after processing your sales data, you may want to create a bar chart illustrating sales by region. This can be accomplished using Matplotlib:

```python
import matplotlib.pyplot as plt

\#\# Grouping sales data by region

region_sales        =        df_sales.groupby('Region')
['Sales'].sum().reset_index()

\#\# Creating a bar chart

plt.figure(figsize=(10, 6))

plt.bar(region_sales['Region'],          region_sales['Sales'],
color='skyblue')

plt.title('Sales by Region')

plt.xlabel('Region')

plt.ylabel('Total Sales (\))')

plt.xticks(rotation=45)

plt.tight_layout()
```

In this example, you aggregate sales by region and generate a bar chart, providing a clear visual representation of performance differences among regions.

Integrating Visuals into Excel

To effectively incorporate your visualizations back into Excel, save them as image files and use Python's openpyxl library to insert them directly into your dashboard sheet:

```python
\#\# Save the figure as an image
```

```
plt.savefig('sales_by_region.png')


\#\# Using openpyxl to insert the image

from openpyxl import Workbook

from openpyxl.drawing.image import Image


\#\# Create a new workbook or load an existing one

wb = Workbook()

ws = wb.active


\#\# Load and add the image to the worksheet

img = Image('sales_by_region.png')

ws.add_image(img, 'A1')


\#\# Save the workbook with the new image

wb.save('dashboard.xlsx')
` ` `
```

This code snippet illustrates how to programmatically insert your generated chart back into an Excel workbook, allowing for seamless automation from data analysis to visualization.

Final Touches on Dashboard Design

Once all visual elements are integrated, it's time to refine your dashboard's overall appearance. Consider adding interactive features like slicers or timelines that enable users to filter views based on specific criteria such as date ranges or product categories.

By combining Excel's built-in features with Python's

automation capabilities, you can create dynamic dashboards that not only inform but also engage users. Take this example, using slicers linked to Pivot Tables allows viewers to interactively explore various aspects of your data without requiring extensive technical knowledge.

on Building Dashboards

Building dashboards in Excel using Python unlocks countless opportunities for dynamic reporting and insightful presentations. By merging structured data management with advanced visualization techniques, you develop a powerful tool that enhances decision-making across any organization. As you refine your skills in this area, remember that the key is understanding what information is most relevant and presenting it in a manner that resonates with your audience. this approach empowers you to convey complex narratives through concise and visually appealing formats.

Conditional Formatting through Python

Integrating conditional formatting with Python elevates your Excel reporting, allowing for dynamic adjustments that respond to changes in data. This feature highlights key trends and anomalies, directing users' attention to vital insights without the need for manual updates. The true advantage of using Python lies in its ability to automate what can often be a tedious process in Excel.

Understanding Conditional Formatting

Before we delve into the coding aspect, let's define what conditional formatting is. In Excel, this feature enables cells to be formatted based on specific criteria; for instance, a cell's color might change according to its value. Imagine wanting cells containing sales figures below a certain threshold to appear red, while those exceeding it turn green. Such visual cues provide immediate insight into performance status at a glance.

Setting Up Your Environment

To implement conditional formatting through Python, you'll need the openpyxl library, which offers tools for programmatically manipulating Excel files. If you haven't installed it yet, you can easily do so via pip:

```bash
pip install openpyxl
```

With openpyxl, you can create or modify Excel workbooks and worksheets. The next step is to prepare your data in Excel so that you can apply your conditional formatting rules effectively.

Preparing Your Data

Suppose you have an Excel file named sales_data.xlsx that contains sales figures in one column. Here's a simple snippet that demonstrates how to read this data into a Python script using openpyxl:

```python
from openpyxl import load_workbook

\#\# Load the workbook and select the active worksheet
wb = load_workbook('sales_data.xlsx')
ws = wb.active

\#\# Read sales data from column B (assuming it starts from row 2)
sales_data = [cell.value for cell in ws['B'][1:]]
```

This code loads your existing sales data into a list called sales_data. With this information ready, you're well-prepared to apply conditional formatting based on defined rules.

Applying Conditional Formatting

Now let's create two rules: one that formats cells red if sales are less than (1,000 and another that formats them green if they exceed)5,000. Here's how you can implement these conditions programmatically:

``` python

from openpyxl.styles import PatternFill


\#\# Define fill colors for conditional formatting

red_fill          =          PatternFill(start_color="FF9999", end_color="FF9999", fill_type="solid")

green_fill          =          PatternFill(start_color="99FF99", end_color="99FF99", fill_type="solid")


\#\# Apply conditional formatting

for i, cell in enumerate(ws['B'][1:], start=2): \# Start from row 2

if cell.value < 1000:

cell.fill = red_fill

elif cell.value > 5000:

cell.fill = green_fill

```

In this snippet, we loop through each cell in column B starting from row 2 (where our data begins). Based on each cell's value, we apply either a red or green fill. This automation ensures visual clarity as your dataset changes over time.

Saving Your Changes

Once you've applied the desired formatting, it's important to save your workbook:

```python
\#\# Save changes back to the same file or as a new file

wb.save('sales_data_conditional_formatting.xlsx')
```

This command saves all modifications—including your newly applied conditional formats—into an Excel file.

Testing and Validation

After running your script and saving the changes, open sales_data_conditional_formatting.xlsx in Excel to assess the effectiveness of your conditional formatting. Experiment with different scenarios by adjusting sales figures and rerunning your Python script; this automated approach ensures that visual cues adapt accordingly.

Benefits of Automation with Conditional Formatting

Utilizing Python alongside Excel not only speeds up workflows but also enhances accuracy and consistency. Automating conditional formatting reduces manual oversight and minimizes opportunities for human error when adapting visual cues based on evolving datasets.

This integration fosters improved decision-making by ensuring that stakeholders can quickly identify critical issues or opportunities within their data. As organizations increasingly handle complex datasets, mastering these techniques positions you as an invaluable asset capable of transforming raw numbers into actionable insights.

on Conditional Formatting with Python

Implementing conditional formatting through Python streamlines both data visualization and decision-making processes. It transforms static spreadsheets into responsive tools that signal urgency where it matters most. Whether analyzing financial trends or operational metrics, automating these processes enhances productivity and clarity within any reporting framework.

Using Python for Excel Financial Analysis

Using Python for financial analysis in Excel unlocks a range of possibilities that enhance data-driven decision-making. The synergy between Python's computational strength and Excel's intuitive interface can significantly transform how financial professionals analyze data, build models, and generate reports. With Python, you can automate tedious tasks, execute complex calculations, and handle large datasets with ease, ultimately leading to more accurate and timely insights.

Understanding Financial Analysis

At its essence, financial analysis involves scrutinizing historical and current financial data to make predictions and informed decisions about the future. Traditional methods in Excel often require extensive manual data entry and formula application. However, incorporating Python introduces a more dynamic approach that streamlines data retrieval, processing, and reporting through automation.

Take this example, when creating a cash flow forecast in Excel, you might need to set up multiple sheets for manual calculations of inflows and outflows. This method can be labor-intensive and error-prone. In contrast, using Python allows you to automate data collection from various sources, apply calculations programmatically, and generate comprehensive reports with minimal manual effort.

Setting Up Your Environment for Financial Analysis

To effectively integrate Python with Excel for financial analysis, you'll need libraries that simplify data manipulation. The two most popular choices are Pandas and openpyxl. You can install these libraries by running:

```bash
pip install pandas openpyxl
```

With these libraries in place, you can easily load data from your Excel files into Pandas DataFrames—an essential step for conducting effective analysis.

Loading Financial Data into Python

Suppose you have an Excel file named financial_data.xlsx, containing multiple sheets with various financial metrics such as revenue, expenses, and profits. Here's how you can load this data into Python:

```python
import pandas as pd

\#\# Load the financial data from an Excel file
file_path = 'financial_data.xlsx'
data = pd.read_excel(file_path, sheet_name=None)

\#\# Display the names of the sheets loaded
print(data.keys())
```

This code snippet loads all sheets into a dictionary where the keys represent the sheet names. You can then access individual sheets easily by name. For example:

```python
revenue_df = data['Revenue']

expenses_df = data['Expenses']
```

Analyzing Financial Metrics

Once your financial data is loaded into Pandas DataFrames, performing calculations is straightforward. Take this example, to calculate net income from revenue and expenses:

```python
\#\# Assuming both DataFrames have columns 'Amount' with numeric values

revenue_total = revenue_df['Amount'].sum()

expenses_total = expenses_df['Amount'].sum()


net_income = revenue_total - expenses_total

print(f"Net Income: \(net_income:.2f")
```

This simple yet effective calculation illustrates how quickly you can analyze key metrics with just a few lines of code compared to traditional Excel formulas.

Automating Report Generation

To further streamline your workflow, consider automatically generating a summary report using Python. You can compile essential financial figures into a new DataFrame and export it back to an Excel file:

```python
```

```
summary_data =

'Metric': ['Total Revenue', 'Total Expenses', 'Net Income'],

'Value': [revenue_total, expenses_total, net_income]


summary_df = pd.DataFrame(summary_data)

\#\# Save the summary report to a new Excel file

summary_df.to_excel('financial_summary_report.xlsx',
index=False)
```
` ` `

This efficient report generation not only saves time but also minimizes the risk of errors associated with manual reporting processes.

Visualizing Financial Data with Python

To elevate your analysis even further, consider visualizing your financial data using libraries like Matplotlib or Seaborn. Visual representations can reveal trends that may not be immediately obvious through raw numbers alone. For example:

` ` `python

```
import matplotlib.pyplot as plt


\#\# Plotting total revenue vs expenses

plt.bar(['Revenue', 'Expenses'], [revenue_total,
expenses_total], color=['green', 'red'])

plt.title('Total Revenue vs Expenses')

plt.ylabel('Amount (\))')
```

plt.show()

```
` ` `
```

This bar chart provides immediate visual insight into how revenues compare to expenses—an invaluable tool for stakeholders assessing financial health at a glance.

on Using Python for Financial Analysis

Integrating Python into your financial analysis workflows not only enhances efficiency but also significantly boosts your analytical capabilities. By automating tasks such as data loading, calculations, and reporting, you free up valuable time for deeper analysis and strategic thinking. Additionally, visualizations created with Python offer critical insights that support decision-making processes within organizations.

As you continue to explore this powerful integration of tools, you'll uncover countless ways to refine your analytical methods—transforming raw data into meaningful narratives that drive organizational success. Your journey toward mastering this integration will position you as a leader in financial analysis within your field.

Automation of Report Generation

In today's fast-paced business landscape, the ability to generate reports quickly and accurately is essential. Automating report generation in Excel with Python simplifies this process, allowing professionals to shift their focus from manual data manipulation to meaningful analysis. By harnessing Python's powerful capabilities alongside Excel's user-friendly interface, you can create intricate reports that save time and enhance accuracy.

Consider the task of compiling a weekly sales report, which involves gathering data from various sources, performing calculations, and formatting the final output. Traditionally, this process requires tedious manual entry and carries the risk of human error. However, by employing Python, you can automate each step, ensuring consistency and reliability in your reporting.

Setting Up for Automation

Before you begin automating your reports, it's important to prepare your environment. You will need the openpyxl library for manipulating Excel files and the pandas library for efficient data handling. If you haven't installed these libraries yet, you can do so by running:

```bash
pip install openpyxl pandas
```

These tools will form the foundation of your automated reporting tasks.

Automating Data Retrieval

Let's take a scenario where you need to collect sales data from an Excel workbook named sales_data.xlsx, which contains sheets dedicated to different regions. Here's how you can load this data programmatically:

```python
import pandas as pd

\#\# Load sales data from multiple sheets
file_path = 'sales_data.xlsx'
sales_data = pd.read_excel(file_path, sheet_name=None)

\#\# Accessing specific region data
north_sales = sales_data['North']
```

```
south_sales = sales_data['South']
```
` ` `

By utilizing the sheet_name=None parameter, you can load all sheets at once into a dictionary format. This approach allows easy access to each region's data without repetitive code.

Data Processing with Python

After retrieving the necessary data, the next step is processing it to extract insights or compute totals. For example, if each sheet contains monthly sales figures that need summation:

` ` `python

\#\# Calculate total sales for each region

north_total = north_sales['Sales'].sum()

south_total = south_sales['Sales'].sum()

print(f"Total Sales - North: \(north_total:.2f, South: \)south_total:.2f")

` ` `

This simple calculation illustrates how Python can streamline operations that might otherwise take significantly longer using manual formulas in Excel.

Creating Automated Reports

To generate a comprehensive report from the processed data automatically, consider compiling your findings into a summary DataFrame before exporting it back to Excel:

` ` `python

\#\# Compiling results into a summary DataFrame

```
summary_data =

'Region': ['North', 'South'],

'Total Sales': [north_total, south_total]


summary_df = pd.DataFrame(summary_data)

\#\# Saving summary report to a new Excel file

summary_df.to_excel('weekly_sales_report.xlsx',
index=False)
```
` ` `

This script organizes total sales by region into a summary and exports it as an Excel file named weekly_sales_report.xlsx, ready for distribution.

Enhancing Reports with Visuals

Visualizing your report can significantly enhance its effectiveness. By using libraries like Matplotlib, you can create charts that complement your textual findings:

` ` `python
```
import matplotlib.pyplot as plt


\#\# Create a pie chart of sales distribution by region

labels = ['North', 'South']

sizes = [north_total, south_total]

colors = ['gold', 'lightskyblue']


plt.pie(sizes, labels=labels, colors=colors, autopct='%1.1f%
```

%', startangle=140)

plt.axis('equal') \# Equal aspect ratio ensures that pie chart is circular.

plt.title('Sales Distribution by Region')

plt.show()

` ` `

This pie chart visually represents the contribution of each region to overall sales, providing stakeholders with immediate insights into performance.

Final Thoughts on Automating Report Generation

Automating report generation with Python not only boosts efficiency but also transforms how reports are created and shared within organizations. The capability to seamlessly pull data from multiple sources, perform calculations without manual input errors, and visualize results fosters improved decision-making processes.

As you explore further into automating workflows with Python and Excel integration, consider delving into more complex scenarios that involve conditional logic or dynamic datasets. The potential for automation is limitless when combined with creativity and analytical thinking—setting the stage for impactful insights derived from your financial analyses.

Tips for Effective Report Design

Effective report design is essential for conveying insights clearly and engagingly. A well-structured report not only emphasizes key findings but also enhances understanding and encourages action among stakeholders. To achieve this, prioritize clarity, consistency, and visual appeal throughout your reports.

Begin by defining the purpose of your report. Understanding

your audience and their specific needs is a crucial first step that influences every design choice you make. Take this example, a financial report aimed at senior management may emphasize high-level summaries and forecasts, whereas a detailed operational report might delve into granular data analysis. Tailoring your content to meet these diverse expectations ensures that your reports resonate with readers.

Structuring Your Report

The layout of your report significantly affects how information is absorbed. Start with an executive summary that encapsulates the main points—consider it the "elevator pitch" of your document. Following this, organize your findings into well-defined sections that guide readers logically through the content. Use consistent headings and subheadings to create a clear hierarchy of information.

For example, in a sales report, structure it into sections such as Introduction, Methodology, Results, Analysis, and Conclusion. This format not only organizes your thoughts but also helps readers navigate complex datasets without feeling overwhelmed.

Leveraging Visuals for Impact

Visual elements play a crucial role in effective communication within reports. Charts, graphs, and tables can present large volumes of data succinctly while highlighting trends or patterns at a glance. When designing visuals:

1. Choose the Right Type: Select chart types based on the data you want to convey. For example, line charts are ideal for showing trends over time, while bar charts excel at comparing categories.

2. Keep It Simple: Avoid cluttering visuals with excessive information or decorative elements that

detract from the message.

3. Label Clearly: Ensure axes are properly labeled and legends are included where necessary to aid interpretation.

Instead of presenting raw sales figures in a table, consider using a bar graph to visually contrast monthly performance across different regions. This approach makes trends immediately recognizable.

Consistency Is Key

Maintaining a cohesive visual style throughout your report enhances professionalism and readability. Stick to a uniform color palette and font style across all pages; this includes text size for headings versus body content as well as colors used in graphs or tables.

Consider establishing a reusable template for different reports within your organization—this promotes brand consistency and saves time when creating new documents.

Utilizing White Space Effectively

White space is often overlooked but plays an essential role in report design by improving readability and reducing cognitive overload. Ensure there are adequate margins around text blocks and visuals to allow each element to breathe. Avoid cramming too much information onto one page; instead, break complex sections into digestible chunks spread across multiple pages if needed.

This strategy helps keep the reader's attention focused on critical insights rather than becoming overwhelmed by dense content.

Incorporating Feedback Loops

After drafting your report, seek feedback from peers or stakeholders before finalizing it. Fresh eyes can identify areas needing clarification or improvement that you might overlook after working on it for extended periods.

Encourage colleagues to critique both content accuracy and design aspects; their insights could reveal opportunities for enhancing clarity or engagement in ways you hadn't considered.

Finalizing Your Report Design

Once you've made revisions based on feedback received, thoroughly proofread the document to eliminate typos or errors that could undermine its credibility with readers. A polished presentation signifies professionalism and attention to detail—qualities that stakeholders value when evaluating data-driven decisions.

To wrap things up, effective report design combines structured layouts with thoughtful visuals while maintaining consistency throughout the narrative flow of each document. The effort invested in crafting clear reports empowers decision-makers to act confidently based on accurate insights derived from complex data analyses— setting the stage for informed business strategies moving forward.

CHAPTER 6: PYTHON SCRIPTING FOR EXCEL MACROS

Understanding Excel
Macros and VBA

Excel macros are a powerful resource for automating repetitive tasks, significantly boosting productivity. At the heart of this automation is Visual Basic for Applications (VBA), a programming language integrated into Excel. VBA empowers users to write scripts that manipulate Excel in various ways, making it essential for anyone seeking to streamline their workflows and maximize efficiency.

The true advantage of macros is their ability to record sequences of actions that can be executed repeatedly with just a click. Take this example, if you regularly format monthly sales reports—applying specific font styles, cell colors, and border settings—this process can take up valuable time. By recording a macro to handle these tasks, you can run it whenever necessary, allowing you to focus on more analytical or strategic responsibilities.

Creating a macro is quite simple. Start by enabling the

Developer tab in Excel, which grants access to the tools needed for macro creation. Once activated, you can begin recording your actions—everything from opening files and entering data to formatting cells. After you finish recording, Excel automatically generates the corresponding VBA code, which you can modify or expand as needed.

Consider a scenario where you frequently generate a report that consolidates data from various sheets into one summary sheet. Writing a macro can automate this entire process. The VBA code would utilize loops to navigate through each sheet, apply conditions to check for specific data criteria, and execute commands to copy and paste information into your summary sheet. Here's a basic example:

```vba
Sub CompileReports()

Dim ws As Worksheet

Dim summarySheet As Worksheet

Dim lastRow As Long

Set summarySheet = ThisWorkbook.Sheets("Summary")


For Each ws In ThisWorkbook.Worksheets

If ws.Name <> "Summary" Then

lastRow = summarySheet.Cells(summarySheet.Rows.Count, 1).End(xlUp).Row + 1

ws.Range("A1:B10").Copy summarySheet.Cells(lastRow, 1)

End If

Next ws
```

End Sub

` ` `

In this snippet, we loop through all worksheets except the "Summary" one, copying data into the next available row of the "Summary" sheet. Such automation not only saves time but also minimizes the risk of human error during manual processes.

However, while macros offer significant benefits, they also come with important considerations—particularly regarding security and complexity. If not managed properly, macros can introduce vulnerabilities; malicious code may be hidden within seemingly harmless scripts. Thus, understanding how to enable macro security settings is crucial. Always ensure you trust the source of any macros before activating them.

Also, mastering VBA allows users to create more than simple automation scripts; it enables the development of comprehensive applications within Excel itself. With structured programming concepts such as loops, conditionals, and user-defined functions at your disposal, your potential for achieving complex tasks in Excel expands dramatically.

Learning how to debug VBA code is another essential skill for anyone working with macros. Common errors often arise from minor mistakes like misspelled variable names or incorrect object references. The VBA editor provides debugging tools like breakpoints and watches that help monitor variables during runtime and efficiently identify issues.

In summary, mastering macros and VBA equips you with an invaluable toolkit that enhances productivity in Excel while allowing extensive customization of your workflows. As we delve into more advanced topics—such as integrating Python with these macros—you'll find that this foundational knowledge serves as a crucial building block for greater capabilities in your data analysis journey. Embrace this learning path; it's where true efficiency begins in your professional toolkit.

Python vs. VBA: Pros and Cons

VBA has long been a cornerstone for Excel users looking to automate tasks, but Python is emerging as a compelling alternative that many find advantageous. Each language has its strengths and weaknesses, making it crucial to evaluate them carefully when deciding which to adopt for your automation needs.

Let's start with VBA. Its seamless integration within Excel makes it incredibly convenient. Users can write and execute scripts directly in the application without needing any external tools. The simplicity of recording macros—where actions are captured as code—allows even non-programmers to achieve significant automation with minimal effort. Take this example, if you regularly send out reports or format data in a specific way, recording a macro can drastically cut down the time spent on these repetitive tasks.

However, while VBA excels in ease of use for straightforward tasks, its limitations become evident when more complex functionality is required. It lacks the versatility and extensive libraries that Python offers. For example, if you're engaged in advanced data manipulation or need to connect to external APIs, Python provides powerful libraries like Pandas and Requests that streamline these processes.

Consider a situation where you want to analyze large datasets from various sources or apply machine learning algorithms. In such cases, VBA may struggle due to performance constraints and limited capabilities. Conversely, Python thrives in this environment, allowing you to leverage packages like NumPy for numerical calculations and Matplotlib for data visualization. These tools open up new avenues for data analysis that VBA simply cannot match.

Security is another important factor to consider. VBA scripts can pose risks if not managed correctly; malicious macros can compromise systems if users inadvertently enable them without understanding their origin. While Python also faces security challenges—especially when using third-party libraries—it benefits from better isolation through virtual environments. This feature allows you to manage dependencies more effectively and reduces the risk of introducing vulnerabilities into your workflows.

Debugging is another area where Python tends to outperform VBA. Modern integrated development environments (IDEs) like PyCharm or Jupyter Notebook offer extensive debugging capabilities, providing clearer error messages that offer insights into what went wrong during execution. This makes troubleshooting much easier compared to the often cumbersome debugging process in VBA.

For community support and learning resources, Python has gained considerable traction in recent years. The availability of online tutorials, forums like Stack Overflow, and a wealth of documentation contribute to a rapidly expanding knowledge base. While there are resources available for VBA —often found within Microsoft's own documentation—the community is not as vibrant or active as that surrounding Python.

Integration is another area where both languages excel but serve different purposes. If you work primarily within the Microsoft ecosystem and require tight integration with other Office applications like Word or Outlook, VBA offers seamless interaction due to its native support within those applications. On the other hand, if your workflow involves pulling data from web services or databases beyond what Excel natively supports, Python stands out for its ability to handle various file formats and connections with ease.

To wrap things up, the choice between Python and VBA largely depends on your specific requirements and workflows. If your tasks are centered around Excel-centric operations with moderate complexity and an emphasis on user-friendliness, VBA remains a valuable tool. However, as your projects become more sophisticated—requiring advanced analytics or integration across multiple platforms —Python emerges as a formidable alternative that promises greater efficiency and flexibility.

understanding both languages will enhance your capabilities. Mastering them not only allows you to automate mundane tasks but also empowers you to innovate within Excel's framework like never before. Embracing this duality unlocks true potential in optimizing your workflows while helping you stand out in a competitive landscape.

Writing Python Scripts for Macro Automation

Automation in Excel can significantly boost productivity, especially when combined with Python. By writing Python scripts for macro automation, you can transform tedious, repetitive tasks into streamlined workflows that execute with a simple click. The journey begins by learning how to effectively translate your needs into functional scripts that automate various Excel operations.

Consider a common task: regularly updating a financial report. If you need to gather the latest sales figures from multiple sheets and compile them into a single summary sheet, it may seem straightforward at first. However, doing this manually every week can quickly become tedious and error-prone. This is where Python proves invaluable.

To get started, ensure your environment is set up correctly with the necessary libraries. The openpyxl library is particularly useful for managing Excel files. You can install it using pip:

```bash
pip install openpyxl
```

Now, let's create a script that automates the process of compiling data from various sheets into one summary sheet:

```python
import openpyxl

\#\# Load the workbook and select sheets
workbook = openpyxl.load_workbook('sales_data.xlsx')
summary_sheet = workbook.create_sheet('Summary')

\#\# Initialize variables
total_sales = 0

\#\# Loop through all sheets except 'Summary'
for sheet_name in workbook.sheetnames:
if sheet_name != 'Summary':
sheet = workbook[sheet_name]
\#\# Assuming sales data is in column B
for row in range(2, sheet.max_row + 1):  \# Skip header row
total_sales += sheet.cell(row=row, column=2).value

\#\# Write total to the summary sheet
```

```python
summary_sheet['A1'] = 'Total Sales'

summary_sheet['B1'] = total_sales


\#\# Save the workbook

workbook.save('sales_data_updated.xlsx')
```
```

This script performs several important functions: it loads an existing Excel file containing sales data, iterates through each relevant worksheet while skipping the summary, aggregates sales figures from column B, and writes the calculated total into a newly created summary worksheet.

You might also consider error handling—what if there are non-numeric values or missing cells? Adding basic error checks will enhance your script's robustness:

```python
for row in range(2, sheet.max_row + 1):

try:

value = sheet.cell(row=row, column=2).value

if isinstance(value, (int, float)):  \# Check for numeric type

total_sales += value

except Exception as e:

print(f"Error processing row row in sheet_name: e")
```
```

With this addition, your script can continue executing even when it encounters problematic data—an essential feature when dealing with large datasets.

Once you've written your script and tested it on sample data, integrating this automation into your regular workflow is crucial. The goal is to ensure ease of execution; consider setting up a shortcut or an Excel button to trigger the script whenever needed.

Debugging is also an integral part of coding. Python offers several effective methods for troubleshooting issues:

1. Print Statements: Use print statements to display variable values at critical points in your code.

2. Logging: Take advantage of Python's logging module to track events during script execution.

3. Debugging Tools: IDEs like PyCharm or Visual Studio Code provide interactive debugging tools that allow you to step through your code line-by-line.

Take this example:

```python
import logging

logging.basicConfig(level=logging.DEBUG)

for row in range(2, sheet.max_row + 1):

try:

value = sheet.cell(row=row, column=2).value

logging.debug(f'Row row, Value: value')

if isinstance(value, (int, float)):

total_sales += value

except Exception as e:
```

```
logging.error(f"Error processing row row in sheet_name: e")
```
` ` `

Using logging instead of print statements in production code enhances traceability and maintainability.

By writing Python scripts for macro automation, you not only streamline workflows but also gain greater flexibility and control over processes that would be cumbersome with VBA alone. As you become more adept at scripting these automations, you'll discover opportunities to incorporate more complex operations—such as data visualization within Excel using libraries like Matplotlib or Seaborn—and integrate APIs that provide real-time data relevant to your reports.

Embracing Python within Excel fosters a culture of innovation and efficiency—a transformative approach for any data analyst eager to leverage powerful tools. Whether you're automating reports or constructing intricate models requiring real-time updates from various sources, mastering these skills positions you as a vital asset in any organization striving to maximize its analytical capabilities.

Integrating Python with VBA

Integrating Python with VBA unlocks a world of possibilities for automating and enhancing workflows within Excel. While VBA has traditionally been the go-to language for creating macros, Python serves as a modern, powerful alternative that can simplify complex tasks and introduce a level of flexibility that VBA often lacks. By harnessing Python's extensive libraries and its clear syntax, you can streamline processes that previously required significant manual effort.

To begin integrating Python scripts into your Excel workflow, you can utilize libraries such as pywin32 or xlwings, which facilitate communication between Python and Excel. These tools enable you to execute Python scripts directly from within Excel, allowing you to take advantage of the strengths of both languages.

For example, imagine you need to automate the updating of data in an existing workbook. You might have a worksheet dedicated to monthly sales figures, and each month, you receive a CSV file containing updated data. Rather than manually importing this data into Excel, you could write a Python script to automate the entire process seamlessly.

Here's how to get started:

1. Install Required Libraries: Begin by ensuring that xlwings is installed. You can do this easily via pip:

```bash
pip install xlwings
```

1. Create Your Script: Next, write a script that opens your existing workbook, reads the CSV file, and updates the relevant worksheet.

```python
import xlwings as xw

import pandas as pd


\#\# Load the existing workbook

wb = xw.Book('monthly_sales.xlsx')

sheet = wb.sheets['Sales']


\#\# Read new data from CSV

new_data = pd.read_csv('new_sales_data.csv')
```

\#\# Update worksheet with new data

sheet.range('A2').options(index=False, header=False).value = new_data

\#\# Save and close the workbook

wb.save()

wb.close()

` ` `

In this example, the xlwings library allows for seamless interaction with Excel while leveraging Pandas for efficient data manipulation. The script opens the specified workbook and reads new sales figures from the CSV file before placing those values directly into the designated sheet.

When working with files and user input, it's essential to incorporate error handling. Take this example, checking whether the specified CSV file exists before attempting to read it can prevent runtime errors. Here's how to enhance your script with this check:

```python
import os

csv_file_path = 'new_sales_data.csv'

if os.path.exists(csv_file_path):

new_data = pd.read_csv(csv_file_path)

sheet.range('A2').options(index=False, header=False).value = new_data
```

else:

print(f"Error: The file csv_file_path does not exist.")

` ` `

This simple verification ensures that your script remains robust by avoiding errors related to non-existent files.

Once you execute this script directly from Excel—using a button or shortcut key set through VBA or xlwings—you'll notice a significant increase in your workflow efficiency. Integrating Python not only saves time but also enhances your capacity to process and analyze data dynamically.

Debugging is another area where Python excels compared to traditional VBA methods. With tools like pdb (Python Debugger), you can execute code step-by-step, making it easier to pinpoint issues in complex scripts. Additionally, incorporating logging capabilities offers insights into your script's performance without disrupting its flow.

Consider adding logging features as shown below:

` ` `python

import logging

logging.basicConfig(level=logging.INFO)

try:

if os.path.exists(csv_file_path):

new_data = pd.read_csv(csv_file_path)

sheet.range('A2').options(index=False, header=False).value = new_data

logging.info("Data updated successfully.")

```
else:

logging.warning(f"File csv_file_path not found.")

except Exception as e:

logging.error(f"An error occurred: e")
```

` ` `

This integration not only helps monitor script performance but also provides critical feedback for troubleshooting during execution.

Transitioning from VBA-centric automation to integrating Python scripts within Excel workflows opens avenues for greater efficiency and adaptability in your data processes. As you become more comfortable with these advanced operations—such as building predictive models or generating reports linked to live datasets—you will find yourself equipped with tools that meet today's fast-paced analytical demands.

As automation continues to evolve in the data analytics landscape, mastering the integration between Python and Excel positions you at the forefront of innovation in your workplace. Embracing these tools not only enhances your personal productivity but also significantly contributes to organizational success by enabling smarter decision-making based on real-time insights.

Converting VBA Macros to Python

Converting VBA macros to Python scripts marks a significant advancement in automating Excel tasks, allowing users to tap into Python's extensive libraries and clearer syntax for enhanced functionality. While VBA has served its purpose over the years, transitioning to Python unlocks new possibilities that can streamline processes and alleviate the complexities often associated with traditional macro coding.

To embark on this conversion journey, it's essential to analyze the existing VBA code and grasp its underlying logic. For example, consider a straightforward VBA macro that updates a sales report by pulling data from another sheet. The corresponding Python code can accomplish this task with improved readability and superior error handling capabilities.

Here's a simple example of a VBA macro:

```vba
Sub UpdateSalesReport()

Dim wsSource As Worksheet

Dim wsTarget As Worksheet

Set wsSource = ThisWorkbook.Sheets("Source")

Set wsTarget = ThisWorkbook.Sheets("SalesReport")


wsTarget.Range("A1").Value = wsSource.Range("A1").Value

End Sub
```

In this snippet, the macro retrieves a value from the "Source" sheet and places it in cell A1 of the "SalesReport" sheet. The same functionality can be achieved in Python using the xlwings library, which facilitates seamless integration between Python scripts and Excel workbooks.

First, ensure you have xlwings installed:

```bash
pip install xlwings
```

Now, let's write a Python script to perform the same

operation:

```python
import xlwings as xw

def update_sales_report():
    wb = xw.Book('YourWorkbook.xlsx')
    ws_source = wb.sheets['Source']
    ws_target = wb.sheets['SalesReport']

    ws_target.range('A1').value = ws_source.range('A1').value
    wb.save()
    wb.close()

update_sales_report()
```

This code clearly demonstrates how Python simplifies macro creation while maintaining clarity. The use of descriptive variable names enhances readability, making it easier for others—or even yourself at a later date—to understand each part of the script.

When converting more complex VBA macros that involve loops or conditions, you'll find Python's syntax to be more straightforward. Take this example, take a macro that loops through a range of cells to update values based on specific criteria:

Here's an example of such a VBA code snippet:

```vba
Sub UpdateValues()
```

```
Dim cell As Range

For          Each          cell          In
ThisWorkbook.Sheets("Data").Range("A1:A10")

If cell.Value > 100 Then

cell.Offset(0, 1).Value = "High

Else

cell.Offset(0, 1).Value = "Low

End If

Next cell

End Sub
```
` ` `

The equivalent Python script utilizing pandas for advanced data manipulation would look like this:

` ` `python

```python
import pandas as pd


def update_values():
    df = pd.read_excel('YourWorkbook.xlsx', sheet_name='Data')


    df['B'] = df['A'].apply(lambda x: 'High' if x > 100 else 'Low')


    with          pd.ExcelWriter('YourWorkbook.xlsx',
    engine='openpyxl', mode='a') as writer:

        df.to_excel(writer, sheet_name='Data', index=False)
```

update_values()

``` ` ` ` ```

This transition not only preserves the original functionality but also leverages powerful data manipulation capabilities offered by pandas. The use of DataFrames simplifies handling larger datasets efficiently and reduces reliance on cumbersome loops.

Error handling is another area where Python excels compared to VBA. Instead of depending on sometimes unclear error messages, you can implement try-except blocks in Python for graceful exception management. Take this example:

```python
try:

df = pd.read_excel('YourWorkbook.xlsx', sheet_name='Data')

except FileNotFoundError:

print("Error: The specified workbook does not exist.")
```

This clear feedback during script execution enhances usability and minimizes frustration when errors occur.

As you continue transitioning from VBA to Python, consider creating a library of common functions that replicate frequently used macros. This modular approach allows you to easily adjust and reuse your code across different projects without starting from scratch each time.

Additionally, with tools like pywin32, you can call your converted Python scripts directly from Excel via macros or buttons, effectively blending both worlds. This capability ensures that you retain your existing workflows while
```

gaining the benefits of modern programming practices.

To wrap things up, converting your existing VBA macros into Python scripts not only enriches your coding experience but also paves the way for more efficient automation processes within Excel. By embracing this transition, you'll equip yourself with a flexible toolkit capable of managing complex data tasks while maintaining clarity and performance. The time invested in mastering this shift will undoubtedly enhance both your productivity and versatility in analytical work.

Scheduling Python Scripts in Excel

Integrating the scheduling of Python scripts into your Excel workflows greatly enhances automation, enabling more sophisticated data management with minimal manual intervention. By scheduling these scripts, you can execute them at specific times or in response to particular events, which streamlines your processes significantly. This capability is especially beneficial for tasks that require timely data updates, such as daily reports or real-time data analysis.

To get started, you'll need to use a task scheduler. On Windows, this is typically the Task Scheduler application, while macOS utilizes its own Launchd system. Both tools allow you to set up tasks that run Python scripts at predefined intervals or under specific conditions. Let's walk through the setup process step-by-step.

Scheduling a Python Script on Windows

1. Prepare Your Python Script: Before scheduling, ensure your script is working correctly. For example, consider a script that retrieves updated sales data from a database and writes it to an Excel file. Here's a simplified version:

``` python

import pandas as pd
```

import datetime

def update_sales_data():

\#\# Simulate fetching data

data = 'Date': [datetime.datetime.now().strftime('%Y-%m-%d')],

'Sales': [100] \# Placeholder for actual data fetching logic

df = pd.DataFrame(data)

\#\# Save to Excel

with pd.ExcelWriter('SalesData.xlsx', engine='openpyxl', mode='a') as writer:

df.to_excel(writer, index=False)

update_sales_data()
```

1. Create a Batch File: To run the Python script through Task Scheduler, create a batch file (.bat). Open Notepad and enter the following:

```bat
@echo off
cd C:\
python your_script.py
```

Save this file with a .bat extension.

1. Open Task Scheduler: Search for "Task Scheduler"
```

in the Windows start menu and open it.

2. Create a New Task: Select "Create Basic Task" from the right panel and follow the wizard:

3. Name your task (e.g., "Update Sales Data").

4. Choose how often you want it to run (daily, weekly, etc.).

5. Set the start time and any recurrence options.

6. Configure the Action: When prompted for an action, select "Start a program" and browse to choose your .bat file.

7. Complete the Setup: Finalize the wizard and verify that everything is configured correctly. Your script will now run according to the schedule you defined.

Scheduling on macOS

On macOS, you will use launchd, which may seem more complex but offers powerful options:

1. Prepare Your Script: Just like on Windows, ensure your Python script is ready for execution.

2. Create a Property List File (plist): Open TextEdit and create a .plist file that specifies when and how your script runs:

```xml
```

Label

com.yourusername.updatesalesdata

ProgramArguments

/usr/local/bin/python3

/path/to/your/script.py

StartInterval

86400

```
` ` `
```

Save this file in ~/Library/LaunchAgents/ with an appropriate name like com.yourusername.updatesalesdata.plist.

1. Load Your Job: Open Terminal and load this job into launchd using the following command:

```bash
launchctl load ~/Library/LaunchAgents/com.yourusername.updatesalesdata.plist
```

Verifying Script Execution

Once you've scheduled your script on either platform, it's important to verify its successful execution:

- On Windows, check if the output Excel file updates as expected after the scheduled time.

- On macOS, look for any log files generated by launchd, which can provide insights into whether your script ran successfully or encountered errors.

Enhancing Your Scheduled Scripts

To improve monitoring and maintenance of your scripts over time, consider adding error handling and logging features:

```python
import logging

logging.basicConfig(filename='script.log', level=logging.INFO)

def update_sales_data():
```

try:

\#\# Data fetching logic...

logging.info("Sales data updated successfully.")

except Exception as e:

logging.error(f"Error occurred: str(e)")

` ` `

Implementing logging gives you visibility into failures or unexpected behavior without needing constant manual oversight.

Incorporating scheduled Python scripts into your Excel workflows not only boosts productivity but also ensures consistency in managing repetitive tasks efficiently— freeing up more time for analytical insights rather than administrative upkeep of data processes. While setting up tools like Task Scheduler or launchd may require an initial investment of time and learning, these skills are invaluable for enhancing both efficiency and precision in data handling tasks over time.

Debugging Python-Excel Macros

Debugging Python-Excel macros is an essential skill that enables you to efficiently resolve issues and optimize your automation processes. As you integrate Python with Excel, you will likely encounter a variety of errors, ranging from syntax mistakes in your code to misconfigurations within the Excel environment. Developing the ability to diagnose and fix these issues not only enhances your technical expertise but also builds your confidence in managing complex workflows.

To begin, it's important to familiarize yourself with common sources of error in Python scripts that run within Excel. These might include incorrect cell references, incompatible data types, or unhandled exceptions. Take this example, trying to write a string value into a numeric cell can trigger a type error, disrupting your execution flow.

Debugging Techniques

1. Use Print Statements: One of the simplest yet most effective debugging techniques is inserting print statements at various points in your script. This approach allows you to track variable values and the flow of execution. Here's an example:

```python
import pandas as pd

def update_sales_data():
try:
sales_data = 'Q1': [100], 'Q2': [150]
print(f"Retrieved data: sales_data") \# Debug statement

df = pd.DataFrame(sales_data)
print("DataFrame created successfully.") \# Debug statement

df.to_excel('SalesData.xlsx', index=False)
print("Data saved to Excel.")
except Exception as e:
print(f"An error occurred: e")

update_sales_data()
```

The output from these print statements can help pinpoint where issues arise.

1. Use the Logging Module: For more robust error tracking, consider utilizing Python's built-in logging module. This allows you to save messages to a file for later review:

```python
import logging

logging.basicConfig(filename='debug.log',
level=logging.DEBUG)

def update_sales_data():
try:
sales_data = 'Q1': [100], 'Q2': [150]
logging.debug(f"Retrieved data: sales_data")

df = pd.DataFrame(sales_data)
logging.debug("DataFrame created successfully.")

df.to_excel('SalesData.xlsx', index=False)
logging.info("Data saved to Excel.")
except Exception as e:
logging.error(f"An error occurred: e")

update_sales_data()
```

` ` `

With this setup, you'll generate a debug.log file that records all debug messages and errors, simplifying the process of tracing your code's execution.

1. Utilize Breakpoints: If you're using an Integrated Development Environment (IDE) like PyCharm or VSCode, take advantage of their debugging features such as breakpoints and step-through execution. Setting breakpoints lets you pause the script at specific lines and interactively inspect variable states:

2. Place breakpoints where you suspect issues may occur.

3. Run the debugger to execute your script.

4. Use the interactive console for examining variables or executing additional commands.

5. Reviewing Error Messages: Pay close attention to error messages generated while running scripts in Excel. These messages often provide crucial information about what went wrong and where it happened. For example, receiving an AttributeError indicates that you're trying to access an attribute that doesn't exist for a particular object—typically due to typos or outdated method calls.

Handling Common Issues

While debugging can sometimes feel overwhelming, certain strategies can help simplify common problems:

- Cell Reference Errors: Always double-check that cell references in your scripts are accurate when working with ranges or specific cells.

- File Path Issues: Ensure paths are formatted

correctly; consider using raw strings (r'path') if working in Windows environments.

- Compatibility Checks: Verify that libraries such as Pandas or OpenPyXL are compatible with your version of Python and are properly installed.

Testing Your Scripts

Testing is another critical aspect of effective debugging. Before running scripts on important datasets, try them on smaller sample files or controlled datasets where potential errors won't have significant consequences:

- Develop test cases for various scenarios that your script will encounter.

- Assess edge cases where unexpected data formats may arise.

For example, if you're processing sales data from multiple regions, test how the script behaves with missing data points or outliers.

Mastering debugging within Python-Excel integration not only enhances the reliability of your automated processes but also equips you with problem-solving skills applicable across many programming contexts. By employing tools like print statements for tracking flow and logging for persistent records, along with strategic testing practices, you'll navigate complexities with greater confidence.

This journey through debugging not only improves individual projects but also fosters a culture of resilience against errors—an invaluable trait for anyone engaged in automation within data management tasks. Each issue resolved strengthens your skill set further, propelling you toward increased efficiency and effectiveness in your workflows.

Security Considerations for Macros

Understanding security considerations when working with Python macros in Excel is essential for protecting your data and ensuring the integrity of your workflows. As automation increasingly becomes a staple in business processes, the risk of security vulnerabilities also rises. While Python provides powerful tools that can significantly enhance Excel's functionality, these same tools can expose your system to potential threats if not handled with care.

Enabling macros in Excel means allowing external code—potentially harmful—to run within your environment. The risks associated with Python scripts are heightened by the language's flexibility and the numerous libraries that may access external resources. That's why, adopting security best practices is not just advisable; it is imperative.

Secure Coding Practices

1. Input Validation: Always validate any input received from users or external files before processing it in your Python scripts. This practice helps prevent common attacks, such as injection attacks, where malicious code could be introduced:

```python
def validate_input(data):

if isinstance(data, str) and len(data) < 100:

return True

else:

raise ValueError("Invalid input")


user_input = "Sample Data

if validate_input(user_input):

\#\# Proceed with data processing
```

```python
print("Input is valid.")
```

By enforcing strict validation rules, you significantly reduce the likelihood of executing unintended commands.

1. Limit File Access: When saving or opening files within your scripts, restrict access to only the necessary directories. Utilizing relative paths instead of absolute ones can further protect your file structure:

```python
import os

file_path = os.path.join('data', 'sales_data.xlsx')

\#\# Open the file only if it exists
if os.path.exists(file_path):
df = pd.read_excel(file_path)
else:
print("File not found.")
```

This approach minimizes exposure to unwanted file manipulations.

1. Environment Isolation: For added security, consider using virtual environments for your Python projects. This practice isolates dependencies and reduces potential conflicts or vulnerabilities from globally installed packages:

```bash
```

```
python -m venv myenv
source myenv/bin/activate # On Windows use myenv
```

By keeping project dependencies contained, you lower the risk of unintentionally relying on older or vulnerable library versions.

User Permissions

Establishing appropriate user permissions within Excel is crucial when deploying Python macros. Ensure that only authorized personnel can access sensitive data and executable scripts:

- Implement password protection for critical Excel files.

- Set different access levels based on user roles; for example, only grant edit permissions to those who genuinely need them.

- Regularly review user permissions and revoke access for individuals who no longer require it.

Robust access controls significantly mitigate the risks associated with unauthorized script execution.

Handling Sensitive Data

If your Python scripts deal with sensitive information—such as personal identification details or financial data—encryption must be an integral part of your workflow:

1. Data Encryption: Use libraries like cryptography to encrypt sensitive information both during transmission and while stored:

```python
from cryptography.fernet import Fernet
```

```
\#\# Generate a key for encryption/decryption
key = Fernet.generate_key()
cipher_suite = Fernet(key)

sensitive_data = b"Super Secret Information
encrypted_data = cipher_suite.encrypt(sensitive_data)
decrypted_data = cipher_suite.decrypt(encrypted_data)

print(f"Encrypted:        encrypted_data,        Decrypted:
decrypted_data")
` ` `
```

1. Secure Storage: Store sensitive credentials (like API keys) in environment variables rather than hardcoding them into your scripts:

```
` ` `python
import os

api_key = os.getenv('API_KEY') \# Ensure API_KEY is set in
the environment variables
` ` `
```

These strategies help ensure that sensitive data remains confidential and protected from unauthorized access.

Continuous Monitoring and Updating

Security is not a one-time setup; it demands ongoing attention. Establish regular audits of your codebase and automated processes:

- Review logs for suspicious activities or failed attempts to access files.

- Keep all dependencies updated to address known vulnerabilities.

- Implement a process for regular code reviews where peers evaluate security implications.

By maintaining a vigilant approach toward security issues, you build resilience into your automation efforts and create a safer environment for yourself and others.

As you integrate Python with Excel, prioritize these security considerations at every step of your development process. By cultivating secure coding practices, enforcing strict user permissions, managing sensitive data thoughtfully, and ensuring continuous monitoring, you not only protect your work but also uphold trust in the systems that underpin modern businesses.

CHAPTER 7: DATA VISUALIZATION WITH PYTHON AND EXCEL

Introduction to Data Visualization in Excel

Data visualization serves as a powerful tool for converting raw data into clear, actionable insights. In the context of Excel, it enables users to visually represent trends, patterns, and relationships within their datasets. While Excel offers a robust set of built-in tools for creating charts and graphs, integrating Python can elevate these capabilities, providing the means for more sophisticated visualizations and increased flexibility.

Consider the impact of data visualization on decision-making. A simple chart can convey insights that pages of text cannot. Take this example, when analyzing sales data for a retail store, a well-crafted bar chart can instantly highlight underperforming products, driving action more effectively than raw numbers alone.

The Power of Python in Visualization

Incorporating Python with Excel enhances your ability to create complex visualizations that may be difficult or impossible to achieve using Excel's native tools. Libraries such as Matplotlib and Seaborn allow you to design aesthetically pleasing graphics that are highly customizable. While Excel might limit your options in terms of chart types and styles, Python opens up a world of possibilities, enabling you to create everything from interactive dashboards to intricate scatter plots.

To illustrate this, let's explore how to generate a simple line graph using Python's Matplotlib library based on data stored in an Excel file named sales_data.xlsx, which contains monthly sales figures. Here's how you can read that data into Python and visualize it:

```python
import pandas as pd

import matplotlib.pyplot as plt


\#\# Load the data from Excel

df = pd.read_excel('sales_data.xlsx')


\#\# Assuming the dataframe has columns 'Month' and 'Sales'

plt.figure(figsize=(10, 5))

plt.plot(df['Month'], df['Sales'], marker='o')

plt.title('Monthly Sales Data')

plt.xlabel('Month')

plt.ylabel('Sales')
```

```python
plt.grid(True)

plt.xticks(rotation=45)

plt.tight_layout()

plt.show()
```
` ` `

In this example, we first load the sales data into a Pandas DataFrame. Using Matplotlib, we then plot the sales figures against the months. The extensive customization options available through Matplotlib allow you to enhance both the readability and aesthetic appeal of your charts.

Customizing Visualizations

Customization is crucial in data visualization. Tailoring your charts to meet specific needs or branding guidelines can significantly influence how information is perceived. You might want to adjust colors or add labels for clarity.

Seaborn—a higher-level interface built on top of Matplotlib —makes this process more intuitive. Here's how you might create a similar line graph with added features using Seaborn:

` ` `python
```python
import seaborn as sns


\#\# Set the aesthetics for the plots

sns.set(style='whitegrid')


\#\# Create a line plot

plt.figure(figsize=(10, 5))

sns.lineplot(data=df,    x='Month',    y='Sales',    marker='o',
```

```
color='blue', linewidth=2.5)
```

plt.title('Monthly Sales Data')

plt.xlabel('Month')

plt.ylabel('Sales')

plt.xticks(rotation=45)

plt.tight_layout()

plt.show()

` ` `

This code snippet not only produces a visually appealing chart but also enhances interpretability at a glance thanks to Seaborn's refined default styles.

Interactive Visualizations

While static charts are valuable, interactive visualizations engage users on a deeper level. Libraries like Plotly allow users to create dynamic dashboards where stakeholders can explore data interactively. This interactivity fosters deeper insights as users manipulate visual elements directly.

Here's an example of setting up an interactive scatter plot using Plotly:

` ` `python

import plotly.express as px

\#\# Create an interactive scatter plot

fig = px.scatter(df, x='Month', y='Sales', title='Interactive Monthly Sales Data',

labels='Sales': 'Sales Amount',

hover_data=['Sales'])

```
fig.show()
```
` ` `

This snippet generates an interactive scatter plot that lets users hover over points to view specific sales figures for each month. Such features not only make presentations more engaging but also empower users to draw their conclusions from the presented data.

Best Practices in Data Visualization

As you delve into creating visual representations of your data with Python and Excel, keep these best practices in mind:

1. Know Your Audience: Tailor your visualizations according to who will view them. Technical stakeholders may appreciate more detail than those without a technical background.

2. Choose Appropriate Chart Types: Different types of data require different kinds of visual representations. Use line charts for trends over time, bar charts for category comparisons, and pie charts sparingly for part-to-whole relationships.

3. Simplify: Avoid cluttering visuals with unnecessary information; every element should have a purpose.

4. Highlight Key Insights: Use color or annotations strategically to draw attention to critical insights within your visuals.

By mastering these techniques through Python's powerful libraries alongside Excel's capabilities, you'll be well-equipped to transform complex datasets into compelling narratives that facilitate informed decision-making across your organization. effective visual storytelling is about clarity and impact—essential components of communication in any data-driven environment.

Creating Charts with Matplotlib

Creating compelling charts with Matplotlib can significantly enhance your data visualization toolkit. Clear and informative visuals not only aid in interpreting data but also effectively communicate insights to stakeholders. As you explore the integration of Python and Excel, mastering Matplotlib will elevate your reporting and presentation capabilities.

To start crafting your first chart, ensure you have the necessary libraries installed. If you haven't done so yet, you can install Matplotlib and Pandas using the following command:

```bash
pip install matplotlib pandas openpyxl
```

With your environment set up, let's jump into an example. Imagine you have a dataset stored in an Excel file named sales_data.xlsx, which contains monthly sales figures. To visualize these sales trends with a line chart, follow these steps:

1. Load the Data: Use Pandas to read the Excel file into a DataFrame.

2. Plot the Data: Utilize Matplotlib to create the line chart.

3. Customize Your Visualization: Adjust aesthetics for improved clarity and engagement.

Here's how the code would look:

```python
import pandas as pd
```

```
import matplotlib.pyplot as plt

\#\# Load the data from Excel
df = pd.read_excel('sales_data.xlsx')

\#\# Assuming the dataframe has columns 'Month' and 'Sales'
plt.figure(figsize=(10, 5)) \# Set the figure size
plt.plot(df['Month'], df['Sales'], marker='o') \# Create line plot with markers
plt.title('Monthly Sales Data') \# Add title
plt.xlabel('Month') \# X-axis label
plt.ylabel('Sales') \# Y-axis label
plt.grid(True) \# Add grid for better readability
plt.xticks(rotation=45) \# Rotate x labels for clarity
plt.tight_layout() \# Adjust layout for better fit
plt.show() \# Display the plot
```
` ` `

This code snippet generates a straightforward yet informative line chart that displays monthly sales data. The marker='o' parameter adds points at each data value, providing a clearer visual reference.

Customization Options

Customizing your charts is essential for maximizing their impact. From colors to line styles, every detail contributes to how effectively your message is conveyed. Consider enhancing your charts with features like annotations or color changes based on specific criteria to emphasize key data points.

For example, if you want to highlight months where sales spiked or dropped, you can annotate those points directly on the chart:

```python
\#\# Plotting with annotations for peak sales months

plt.figure(figsize=(10, 5))

plt.plot(df['Month'], df['Sales'], marker='o', color='blue')

plt.title('Monthly Sales Data with Highlights')

plt.xlabel('Month')

plt.ylabel('Sales')

plt.grid(True)

plt.xticks(rotation=45)


\#\# Annotate peak sales months (for example)

for i in range(len(df)):

if df['Sales'][i] > threshold_value:    \# Define your threshold_value

plt.annotate(f"df['Sales'][i]", (df['Month'][i], df['Sales'][i]),

textcoords="offset points",

xytext=(0,10),

ha='center', fontsize=9)


plt.tight_layout()

plt.show()
```

` ` `

In this example, each month exceeding a predefined threshold is annotated with its sales figure directly above the point on the graph. Such visual cues guide viewers' attention toward significant fluctuations in data.

Advanced Visualizations with Seaborn

While Matplotlib serves well for basic visualizations, Seaborn enhances functionality by simplifying complex representations and offering aesthetically pleasing defaults. Transitioning from Matplotlib to Seaborn can streamline your workflow significantly.

Here's how to create a similar line graph using Seaborn:

` ` `python

import seaborn as sns

\#\# Set aesthetic style using Seaborn

sns.set(style='whitegrid')

\#\# Create a line plot using Seaborn

plt.figure(figsize=(10, 5))

sns.lineplot(data=df, x='Month', y='Sales', marker='o', color='blue', linewidth=2.5)

plt.title('Monthly Sales Data Using Seaborn')

plt.xlabel('Month')

plt.ylabel('Sales')

plt.xticks(rotation=45)

plt.tight_layout()

plt.show()

``` `

This code snippet produces a cleaner output with enhanced aesthetics due to Seaborn's styling features. The process becomes intuitive while allowing for intricate customization where needed.

Interactive Visualizations

Static visualizations have their place, but incorporating interactivity can make your reports more engaging. Libraries such as Plotly enable users to explore datasets interactively by allowing them to hover over points or zoom in on specific areas of interest.

Here's how to create an interactive scatter plot with Plotly:

``` `python

import plotly.express as px

\#\# Create an interactive scatter plot using Plotly

fig = px.scatter(df, x='Month', y='Sales',

title='Interactive Monthly Sales Data',

labels='Sales': 'Sales Amount',

hover_data=['Sales'])

fig.show()

``` `

This snippet generates an interactive visualization where viewers can hover over each point to see exact figures for monthly sales. Such features enhance user engagement and allow deeper exploration of the data.
```

Best Practices

As you embrace these tools for data visualization in Python alongside Excel, keep these best practices in mind:

- Audience Awareness: Tailor visuals according to your audience's expertise level—simpler charts for general stakeholders and detailed graphs for technical teams.

- Appropriate Chart Types: Choose chart types that best fit your data—line graphs for trends over time and bar graphs for comparisons.

- Simplicity is Key: Avoid cluttering visuals with unnecessary information; prioritize clarity.

- Highlight Insights: Use color strategically to emphasize important trends or findings within your data.

By employing these techniques, you'll not only present your data effectively but also foster meaningful discussions within your team or organization. Integrating Python's visualization capabilities with Excel transforms how insights are shared—shaping decisions and strategies based on clear visual narratives rather than raw numbers alone.

Visualizing Data with Seaborn

Visualizing data with Seaborn opens up a world of possibilities for analysts and decision-makers alike. Renowned for its ability to create stunning and informative graphics, Seaborn enhances the foundational capabilities of Matplotlib, making complex visualizations more accessible and aesthetically pleasing. As you explore the intersection of Python and Excel, mastering Seaborn will significantly elevate your data storytelling skills.

To get started with Seaborn, ensure you have it installed alongside Pandas. If you haven't added it to your environment yet, you can do so by running:

```bash
pip install seaborn
```

With the library ready, you're poised to create visualizations that not only convey information but also capture attention through their design. Take this example, if you have a dataset in sales_data.xlsx that contains monthly sales data, here's how to visualize this information using Seaborn.

1. Load Your Data: Utilize Pandas to read your Excel file into a DataFrame.

2. Create Your Visualization: Take advantage of Seaborn functions to produce charts with minimal code while maintaining advanced features.

3. Customize for Impact: Adjust elements such as color palettes or themes to align with your desired aesthetic.

Here's an example illustrating these steps:

```python
import pandas as pd

import seaborn as sns

import matplotlib.pyplot as plt


\#\# Load the data from Excel

df = pd.read_excel('sales_data.xlsx')


\#\# Set the aesthetic style

sns.set(style='darkgrid')
```

```python
\#\# Create a line plot with Seaborn

plt.figure(figsize=(10, 5))

sns.lineplot(data=df, x='Month', y='Sales', marker='o')

plt.title('Monthly Sales Trends')

plt.xlabel('Month')

plt.ylabel('Sales Amount')

plt.xticks(rotation=45)

plt.tight_layout()

plt.show()
```
` ` `

This simple yet effective snippet generates a visually appealing line chart that encapsulates sales trends over time. The marker='o' parameter ensures each point is clearly marked, enhancing clarity in presentation.

Customizing with Color Palettes

One of Seaborn's standout features is its ability to easily manage color palettes. A thoughtful color scheme can significantly improve the readability and appeal of your charts. If you wish to apply a specific palette that aligns with your company's branding or simply enhances visual appeal, consider using:

` ` `python

sns.set_palette("husl") \# Setting a vibrant color palette

\#\# Create the same line plot with new aesthetics

plt.figure(figsize=(10, 5))

```
sns.lineplot(data=df, x='Month', y='Sales', marker='o')

plt.title('Monthly Sales Trends Enhanced')

plt.xlabel('Month')

plt.ylabel('Sales Amount')

plt.xticks(rotation=45)

plt.tight_layout()

plt.show()
```
` ` `

Switching palettes is effortless yet can transform how viewers interpret your charts.

Highlighting Specific Data Points

Seaborn also provides built-in functionality for highlighting certain data points based on conditions—an essential feature for drawing attention to key insights within larger datasets. For example, if you want to spotlight sales months where figures exceeded an established threshold:

` ` `python

```
threshold_value = df['Sales'].mean()  \# Define threshold as
average sales


\#\# Plotting with highlighted points above the threshold

plt.figure(figsize=(10, 5))

sns.lineplot(data=df,    x='Month',    y='Sales',    marker='o',
color='blue')


\#\# Highlighting points above the threshold value

highlights = df[df['Sales'] > threshold_value]
```

```python
sns.scatterplot(data=highlights,    x='Month',    y='Sales',
color='red', s=100)
```

\#\# Title and labels remain unchanged

```python
plt.title('Monthly Sales Trends with Highlights')

plt.xlabel('Month')

plt.ylabel('Sales Amount')

plt.xticks(rotation=45)

plt.tight_layout()

plt.show()
```
` ` `

The addition of red markers emphasizes significant months directly on the line chart without cluttering it.

Advanced Visualizations: Pair Plots and Heatmaps

Beyond basic line plots, Seaborn excels at producing advanced visualizations such as pair plots and heatmaps that provide deeper insights from multidimensional datasets.

A pair plot allows you to visualize relationships between multiple variables simultaneously:

` ` `python

\#\# Assuming df has additional columns like 'Profit' or 'Expenses'

```python
pair_plot = sns.pairplot(df[['Month', 'Sales', 'Profit']])

pair_plot.fig.suptitle("Relationships    Between    Sales    and
Profit", y=1.02)

plt.show()
```
` ` `

This snippet creates a matrix of scatterplots showing how different metrics relate—a valuable tool for exploratory analysis.

Heatmaps are another powerful visualization tool particularly useful for displaying correlation matrices or frequency distributions:

```python
\#\# Generate correlation matrix first if applicable

correlation_matrix = df.corr()


\#\# Create heatmap

sns.heatmap(correlation_matrix, annot=True)

plt.title("Correlation Matrix Heatmap")

plt.show()

```

Using heatmaps helps identify potential relationships between numerical variables quickly—saving time during analysis while revealing hidden patterns.

Best Practices for Using Seaborn

As you integrate Seaborn into your workflow alongside Excel data analyses, keep these best practices in mind:

- Consistency in Style: Maintain uniform styling across all visualizations; use similar fonts and colors for cohesiveness in reports.

- Appropriate Use of Annotations: Use annotations sparingly but effectively; they should clarify insights without overwhelming viewers.

- Understanding Your Audience: Tailor complexity based on who will be viewing the visuals

—executives might prefer simpler visuals while analysts may benefit from detailed representations.

By implementing these techniques and principles within your Python visualizations using Seaborn alongside Excel data sources, you'll be well-equipped to craft meaningful narratives from complex datasets. Elevating how insights are presented fosters better decision-making across teams —transforming raw numbers into compelling stories that drive action forward.

Advanced Excel Charts with Python

Advanced Excel Charting with Python

Harnessing the capabilities of Python for advanced Excel charting opens the door to creating visually compelling narratives that surpass the limitations of built-in Excel features. By integrating powerful libraries like Matplotlib and Seaborn, you can produce graphics that are both aesthetically pleasing and rich in insights. These advanced visualizations enable you to effectively communicate trends, patterns, and critical insights derived from your data— an essential component of any data-driven decision-making process.

To start, we'll lay a solid foundation by utilizing Matplotlib for sophisticated visualizations. Imagine you're analyzing a dataset containing monthly sales figures for various products. With just a few lines of code, you can create an insightful bar chart to compare product performance:

```python
import pandas as pd

import matplotlib.pyplot as plt


\#\# Load data from an Excel file
```

```python
df = pd.read_excel('sales_data.xlsx')


\#\# Set up the bar chart
plt.figure(figsize=(10, 6))

plt.bar(df['Product'], df['Sales'], color='skyblue')

plt.title('Sales Comparison by Product')

plt.xlabel('Product')

plt.ylabel('Sales Amount')

plt.xticks(rotation=45)

plt.tight_layout()

plt.show()
```
` ` `

This straightforward visualization immediately reveals which products are thriving compared to others, but there is ample room for customization to enhance its effectiveness.

Enhancing Charts with Custom Features

Incorporating custom features into your charts can significantly elevate their impact. Take this example, adding data labels directly on the bars enhances clarity:

` ` `python

```python
bars = plt.bar(df['Product'], df['Sales'], color='skyblue')

plt.title('Sales Comparison by Product')


\#\# Adding data labels

for bar in bars:

yval = bar.get_height()
```

```python
plt.text(bar.get_x() + bar.get_width()/2 - 0.1, yval + 5,
round(yval), va='bottom')
```

```
plt.xlabel('Product')

plt.ylabel('Sales Amount')

plt.xticks(rotation=45)

plt.tight_layout()

plt.show()
```
` ` `

This modification allows viewers to easily interpret the exact values represented by each bar, making it particularly effective for presentations or reports.

Advanced Chart Types: Stacked Bar Charts

When comparisons require additional layers of information, stacked bar charts can provide deeper insights by depicting subcategories within your main categories. Here's how to implement this using the same dataset:

` ` `python

\#\# Suppose we have additional columns like 'Region' indicating sales distribution.

\#\# Restructure DataFrame accordingly.

```
stacked_df                =               df.groupby(['Product',
'Region']).sum().unstack()
```

\#\# Creating a stacked bar chart

```
stacked_df.plot(kind='bar', stacked=True, figsize=(10, 6),
colormap='viridis')
```

```python
plt.title('Sales Distribution by Region and Product')

plt.xlabel('Product')

plt.ylabel('Sales Amount')

plt.xticks(rotation=45)

plt.tight_layout()

plt.show()
```
` ` `

This visualization offers immediate insight into how different regions contribute to overall product sales—an invaluable tool for strategic decision-making.

Leveraging Seaborn for Enhanced Aesthetics

To further elevate your visualizations, Seaborn provides pre-styled themes and enhanced functionalities. When visualizing categorical data such as sales performance across multiple months or products, Seaborn's catplot offers rich options while keeping your code concise.

For example, here's how to visualize average sales per month using a point plot:

` ` `python

```python
import seaborn as sns


\#\# Prepare DataFrame if necessary (pivoting might be needed)
sns.set_theme(style="whitegrid")


\#\# Creating a point plot
sns.catplot(data=df, x='Month', y='Sales', kind='point',
```

hue='Product', markers=["o", "D"], height=6)

plt.title('Average Monthly Sales by Product')

plt.xlabel('Month')

plt.ylabel('Average Sales Amount')

plt.xticks(rotation=45)

plt.show()

` ` `

The use of color-coded markers helps viewers easily distinguish between products while clearly illustrating trends over time.

Heatmaps: Visualizing Correlation

Heatmaps are particularly effective for examining relationships among variables in a dataset. If you want to analyze how features like pricing or marketing spend correlate with monthly sales figures, here's how to proceed:

` ` `python

\#\# Assuming df contains features relevant for correlation analysis.

correlation_matrix = df.corr()

\#\# Create heatmap using Seaborn

sns.heatmap(correlation_matrix,   annot=True, cmap="coolwarm", fmt=".2f")

plt.title("Correlation Heatmap of Sales Factors")

plt.show()

` ` `

The annotations within the heatmap provide essential

context at a glance—especially useful in presentations where time is limited and insights need to be conveyed quickly.

Best Practices for Chart Design

While developing these advanced visualizations is crucial, adhering to best practices enhances their clarity and usability:

- Limit Clutter: Avoid overwhelming visuals with excessive information; focus on key insights.

- Consistent Color Schemes: Utilize coherent color palettes throughout different charts; this consistency aids visual storytelling across multiple slides or reports.

- Test Audience Understanding: Before finalizing charts for stakeholders or presentations, gather feedback to ensure the messages are clear.

By merging advanced visualization techniques through Matplotlib and Seaborn with practical design principles, you empower yourself not only to present numbers but also to craft compelling stories through data. This powerful combination enhances your analytical capabilities and improves overall communication effectiveness within your organization.

Interactive Dashboards with Plotly

Creating interactive dashboards in Excel with Plotly is a powerful way to visualize data and engage users. Unlike static charts, these dashboards allow for dynamic exploration of data, enabling users to filter, zoom, and gain insights on demand. This level of flexibility not only enhances how data is presented but also deepens understanding.

To begin building an interactive dashboard using Plotly, you'll first need to ensure that you have the necessary libraries installed. If you haven't done so already, you can easily install Plotly via pip:

```bash
pip install plotly
```

Once the library is set up, kick off your project by importing the essential modules in Python. A typical setup might look like this:

```python
import plotly.express as px
import pandas as pd
```

Next, let's prepare some sample data for our dashboard. Imagine we have a dataset capturing sales across various regions and product categories. You can create a DataFrame to simulate this data as follows:

```python
data =
'Region': ['North', 'South', 'East', 'West'] * 25,
'Category': ['A', 'B', 'C'] * 33 + ['A'],
'Sales': [200 + x*10 for x in range(100)]

df = pd.DataFrame(data)
```

With our DataFrame ready, we can create a simple bar chart illustrating sales by region. Using Plotly Express makes this process straightforward:

```python
```

```
fig = px.bar(df, x='Region', y='Sales', color='Category',
barmode='group')
```

fig.show()

` ` `

This code produces an interactive bar chart where users can hover over the bars to view detailed sales figures by category and region.

To enhance this foundation, let's introduce interactivity through filters. Dash by Plotly allows for the creation of web applications featuring interactive dashboards with ease. If you haven't installed Dash yet, do so using pip:

` ` `bash

pip install dash

` ` `

Now, let's expand our previous example into a Dash application. Here's how to set it up:

` ` `python

from dash import Dash, dcc, html

app = Dash(__name__)

app.layout = html.Div([

dcc.Dropdown(

id='region-dropdown',

options=['label': region, 'value': region for region in df['Region'].unique()],

value='North',

multi=True

```
),
dcc.Graph(id='sales-graph')
])


@app.callback(
Output('sales-graph', 'figure'),
Input('region-dropdown', 'value')
)
def update_graph(selected_regions):
filtered_df = df[df['Region'].isin(selected_regions)]
fig = px.bar(filtered_df, x='Region', y='Sales', color='Category',
barmode='group')
return fig


if __name__ == '__main__':
app.run_server(debug=True)
```

This code constructs a basic web application featuring a dropdown menu that allows users to dynamically select different regions. The callback function updates the bar graph based on the selected values from the dropdown.

When you run this application, it will open a local server on your machine where you can interact with your dashboard in real time. As you select different regions from the dropdown, you'll see how sales vary across categories.

Interactive dashboards go beyond merely displaying data; they empower users to engage with information meaningfully. To enhance user experience further, consider incorporating additional elements such as sliders for date ranges or checkboxes for product categories.

Take this example, adding a date slider could dramatically improve usability if your dataset includes time-series data. You can seamlessly implement this feature using dcc.Slider from Dash.

Creating interactive dashboards with Plotly paves the way for engaging presentations of your data analysis work—be it in financial reporting or tracking key performance indicators (KPIs). As users delve deeper into their datasets with these tools at their disposal, they uncover insights that static reports simply cannot offer.

The true beauty of integrating Python's capabilities with Excel lies not only in automating mundane tasks but also in empowering users with sophisticated visualization options that enhance decision-making processes. The adaptability provided by interactive dashboards positions them as essential tools in modern data analysis workflows—enabling analysts like you to transform raw numbers into compelling narratives that resonate with stakeholders' needs and interests.

Customizing Visual Elements

Customizing the visual elements of your dashboards is essential for making data resonate with your audience. While Plotly provides a wide range of default styles and options, personalizing these elements can greatly enhance both clarity and engagement. By concentrating on colors, fonts, layout, and interactivity, you can create visuals that are not only visually appealing but also effectively convey your intended message.

Let's start with color schemes. The strategic use of color can significantly improve how information is understood and retained. Take this example, a color palette that aligns with your brand or emphasizes key data points can effectively guide users' attention to where it's needed most. Plotly supports various color scales and custom colors for your plots. You might consider modifying the color palette in your existing bar chart like this:

```python
fig = px.bar(df, x='Region', y='Sales', color='Category',

color_discrete_sequence=px.colors.sequential.Plasma)
```

This code replaces the default colors with a gradient from the Plasma color scale, resulting in a visually striking representation that clearly distinguishes between categories.

Next, let's turn our attention to titles and labels, which are crucial for articulating your data's narrative. Clear titles and axis labels provide important context for viewers. For example:

```python
fig.update_layout(

title='Sales Data by Region and Category',

xaxis_title='Region',

yaxis_title='Sales',

legend_title='Product Category'

)
```

This snippet updates the chart's layout with informative titles, allowing viewers to quickly understand what they are observing.

You can further enrich your visuals by adding annotations or shapes to highlight specific insights directly on the chart.

Take this example, if you want to emphasize a peak sales figure in one region, you could add an annotation like this:

```python
fig.add_annotation(

x='North', y=250,

text="Peak Sales!",

showarrow=True,

arrowhead=2,

ax=20,

ay=-30

)
```

This annotation draws attention to significant data points, enhancing the storytelling aspect of your dashboard.

To increase user engagement, consider incorporating hover information that provides additional context about each data point. While Plotly offers default tooltips, you can customize them to display specific details:

```python
fig.update_traces(hoverinfo='x+y+name')
```

This customization ensures that users receive comprehensive information when they hover over different segments of the chart.

The layout of your dashboard also plays a crucial role in its effectiveness. A cluttered dashboard can overwhelm users and obscure insights. Organizing your visuals logically enhances readability. Using Plotly's make_subplots function allows you to create multi-panel layouts where each subplot represents different dimensions of your analysis:

```python
from plotly.subplots import make_subplots

fig = make_subplots(rows=1, cols=2,
subplot_titles=("Sales by Region", "Sales by Category"))

\#\# Add first plot
fig.add_trace(px.bar(df, x='Region', y='Sales').data[0], row=1, col=1)

\#\# Add second plot
fig.add_trace(px.bar(df.groupby('Category').sum().reset_index(),
x='Category', y='Sales').data[0], row=1, col=2)

fig.update_layout(title_text="Sales Overview")
```

In this example, two distinct visualizations are displayed side by side—one focusing on region-specific sales and the other emphasizing product categories—allowing viewers to compare these metrics effortlessly.

Lastly, it's important to incorporate accessibility considerations into your design choices. Choosing high-contrast colors can help individuals with visual impairments access information more easily. Additionally, maintaining consistent font sizes and styles across your dashboard fosters familiarity for all users.

By strategically customizing visual elements—such as colors, titles, and annotations—you not only enhance aesthetics but also improve comprehension and usability for stakeholders who rely on these insights for decision-making. Striking a balance between design flair and functional clarity leads to impactful presentations that elevate the narrative quality of your data analysis endeavors.

With these techniques at your disposal, you're now ready to create dashboards that showcase data while engaging users meaningfully. The art of customization transforms standard charts into dynamic storytelling tools that resonate across various sectors—from finance to marketing—ensuring every visual serves its purpose effectively while inviting exploration and discovery.

Combining Excel and Python Plots

Integrating Python plots with Excel significantly enhances both the analytical capabilities of your spreadsheets and the storytelling aspect of data presentation. By leveraging Python's robust plotting features within the familiar Excel environment, you can create a seamless workflow that maximizes the strengths of both platforms. This combination leads to deeper insights, clearer visualizations, and ultimately more impactful communication of your findings.

To begin this integration, consider using Plotly, a versatile library known for its ability to create interactive plots. Imagine you have a dataset tracking sales across various regions and product categories. Rather than relying solely on Excel's built-in charts, which can be somewhat limiting, Python allows you to generate dynamic visualizations that enable users to explore data interactively.

For example, if you want to create an interactive line chart displaying sales trends over time, you can start by importing the necessary libraries and loading your data:

```python
import pandas as pd

import plotly.express as px

\#\# Load your data

df = pd.read_excel('sales_data.xlsx')
```

Once your data is loaded, creating a line chart to visualize sales trends is straightforward. This approach showcases how combining Excel's data storage capabilities with Python's advanced visualization tools can enhance your analysis:

```python
fig = px.line(df, x='Date', y='Sales', color='Region', title='Sales Trends Over Time')

fig.show()
```

This code snippet generates an interactive line chart where users can hover over points for detailed information about sales figures by region. The ability to explore trends dynamically distinguishes this visualization from static Excel charts.

As you expand your analysis, you might want to incorporate multiple charts within an Excel sheet for comparative insights. Using Plotly's make_subplots, you can efficiently arrange several plots side by side. Take this example, if you have both regional sales data and product category sales, visualizing them together provides a comprehensive overview:

```python
```

```
from plotly.subplots import make_subplots

fig = make_subplots(rows=1, cols=2,
subplot_titles=("Sales by Region", "Sales by Category"))

\#\# First plot: Sales by Region
fig.add_trace(px.bar(df, x='Region', y='Sales').data[0], row=1,
col=1)

\#\# Second plot: Sales by Category
category_data = df.groupby('Category').sum().reset_index()
fig.add_trace(px.bar(category_data,              x='Category',
y='Sales').data[0], row=1, col=2)

fig.update_layout(title_text="Sales Overview")
fig.show()
` ` `
```

With this setup, viewers can quickly compare sales across regions with those across product categories. This dual visualization not only enhances clarity but also promotes deeper engagement with the data.

Another significant benefit of integrating Python plots into Excel is the ability to automate updates and refreshes. By writing Python scripts that run directly from Excel or in Jupyter Notebooks linked to your workbook, you ensure that your visualizations reflect the most current data without requiring manual intervention.

For example, if new sales figures are added weekly to your Excel file, a simple script could automatically regenerate all relevant plots:

```python
\#\# Assuming 'df' is updated with new data

fig = px.line(df, x='Date', y='Sales', color='Region')

fig.write_html('sales_trends.html')
```

This flexibility enables real-time reporting and continuous analysis—a game-changer for organizations striving to remain agile in their decision-making processes.

It's also worth noting the interactivity that comes with these Python-generated plots. Users can zoom in on specific areas or filter datasets directly within the visualizations. Take this example:

```python
fig.update_traces(hoverinfo='x+y+name')
```

This feature ensures that as users engage with your plots, they receive contextual information tailored to their exploration needs.

As we explore more advanced integrations in the future, remember that effectively combining Python and Excel enhances clarity through design while maximizing interaction through automation. By harnessing these powerful tools together, you'll unlock a new realm of analytical potential—one where insights flow freely and engage users at every level.

With each plot you create and each dashboard you customize using this blend of technologies, you're not just presenting numbers; you're crafting narratives that resonate with stakeholders and drive informed decisions. Embrace this dynamic duo as a cornerstone of your analytical strategy; it will empower you to tell compelling stories through data like never before.

Best Practices for Data Visualization

Creating effective data visualizations is a blend of art and science. When you integrate Python into your Excel workflows, following best practices can greatly enhance the quality and impact of your visual representations. These practices not only improve clarity but also ensure that your insights are communicated effectively, leading to more informed decision-making.

Begin by understanding your audience and their specific needs. Different stakeholders may require varying levels of detail and types of visual representation. For example, a finance team may prefer detailed line graphs to illustrate trends over time, while a marketing team might find bar charts comparing sales across campaigns more useful. By tailoring your visualizations to your audience's expectations, you lay a solid foundation for effective communication.

Simplicity is another fundamental principle of data visualization. Although it might be tempting to present all available data at once, this approach can overwhelm viewers. Instead, concentrate on the most relevant information that supports your narrative. Highlight key trends or anomalies rather than cluttering your charts with excessive detail. Take this example, when plotting sales data, consider showcasing only the top three products or regions, allowing viewers to grasp significant insights without distraction.

Utilizing consistent color schemes can enhance both comprehension and aesthetics. Colors convey meaning; for instance, red often signifies loss while green indicates growth. A uniform color palette across all visualizations in a report not only unifies the presentation but also helps viewers quickly draw connections between different charts.

Python libraries like Matplotlib offer customization options for color palettes, enabling you to align visuals with your branding or specific themes.

When creating interactive plots using libraries like Plotly, it's important to incorporate tooltips that provide additional context without cluttering the main visualization. Tooltips can display precise values or extra information when users hover over specific elements in a graph, adding depth while maintaining clarity.

Automation can significantly streamline your workflow. For datasets that update regularly—such as weekly sales figures —writing scripts to automatically refresh charts can save time and minimize errors associated with manual updates. For example:

```python
\#\# Refresh the plot with new data

def update_plot():

df = pd.read_excel('sales_data.xlsx') \# Load updated data

fig = px.line(df, x='Date', y='Sales', color='Region')

fig.show()


update_plot()
```

This code snippet illustrates how simple automation ensures that stakeholders always have access to current insights.

Accessibility should also be an integral part of your best practices. Consider users with color vision deficiencies; providing alternative text labels or patterns within charts ensures that everyone can interpret the visuals effectively. Tools like Seaborn facilitate the creation of accessible plots by allowing adjustments to contrast ratios and the inclusion of patterns.

Another critical aspect is clear labeling of axes and providing descriptive titles for each visualization. Well-defined axis labels enable viewers to quickly grasp what each axis represents without deciphering abbreviations or jargon. A well-labeled chart reflects professionalism and a commitment to clarity:

```python
fig.update_layout(title='Monthly Sales Trends',

xaxis_title='Month',

yaxis_title='Sales (\()',

legend_title='Region')
```

Incorporating annotations into your visualizations is also valuable for emphasizing key points or trends within the data. Annotations can direct users' attention precisely where you want it—whether highlighting peak sales during a specific month or noting an unexpected dip due to external factors:

```python
fig.add_annotation(x='2023-06-01', y=5000,

text="Peak Sales Month",

showarrow=True,

arrowhead=2)
```

By implementing these best practices, you not only enhance the effectiveness of your visualizations but also foster greater engagement from your audience. This approach transforms static presentations into dynamic dialogues, where insights are actively explored rather than passively observed.

As you refine these techniques over time, remember that every chart represents an opportunity—a chance to narrate compelling stories through data that resonate deeply with stakeholders at all levels of an organization. The combination of Python's capabilities and Excel's familiarity provides an extraordinary platform for transforming raw numbers into impactful narratives that drive action and foster understanding in any business context.

Embrace these best practices as you navigate the intricacies of combining Python and Excel; they will serve as invaluable guidelines on your journey toward masterful data visualization.

CHAPTER 8: STATISTICAL ANALYSIS IN EXCEL USING PYTHON

Basics of Statistical Analysis

Understanding the basics of statistical analysis is essential for effective data-driven decision-making. When we delve into data, our goal is often to extract meaningful insights that can inform our actions, support strategic decisions, or validate hypotheses. This process begins with a solid understanding of key concepts, such as the distinction between population and sample, types of data, and important statistical measures.

A population refers to the entire group of individuals or instances about which we want to draw conclusions. In contrast, a sample is a subset taken from that population. Using a sample makes statistical analysis more manageable and less resource-intensive. However, it's critical to ensure that your sample accurately represents the population to avoid biases in your results. For example, if you conduct a survey on customer satisfaction in a retail store by only sampling frequent shoppers, your findings may be skewed.

Next, grasping the different types of data—nominal, ordinal, interval, and ratio—is foundational for analysis. Nominal data consists of categories without inherent order (like colors or product types), while ordinal data involves rankings where the order matters (such as customer satisfaction ratings ranging from "very dissatisfied" to "very satisfied"). Interval and ratio data focus on numerical values; interval data lacks a true zero point (like temperature), whereas ratio data does (such as height). Understanding these distinctions allows you to apply the appropriate statistical tests effectively.

Descriptive statistics play a crucial role in summarizing and describing the characteristics of your dataset. Measures of central tendency—mean, median, and mode—help identify where most values lie within your data. The mean is calculated by summing all values and dividing by their count; however, it can be heavily influenced by outliers. In contrast, the median represents the middle value when data points are arranged in order and is less affected by extreme values. Knowing when to use each measure can significantly enhance your analysis.

Take this example:

```python
import pandas as pd

\#\# Sample dataset
data = 'Sales': [200, 220, 250, 2750] \# Note the outlier: 2750
df = pd.DataFrame(data)
```

```
mean_sales = df['Sales'].mean()

median_sales = df['Sales'].median()


print(f"Mean Sales: mean_sales")

print(f"Median Sales: median_sales")
```
` ` `

This code snippet demonstrates how to compute both mean and median sales using Python's Pandas library.

Beyond central tendency measures, variability statistics such as range, variance, and standard deviation provide insights into how spread out your data points are. The range calculates the difference between the highest and lowest values; variance quantifies how much individual scores deviate from the mean, while standard deviation expresses that variability in original units.

An important aspect of statistical analysis involves inferential statistics—the process of making predictions or generalizations about a population based on sample data. Key methods in this domain include hypothesis testing and confidence intervals. Hypothesis testing requires formulating a null hypothesis (indicating no effect) and an alternative hypothesis (suggesting that an effect exists). Statistical tests like t-tests or chi-square tests can then be employed to determine which hypothesis is supported by your data.

For example:

` ` `python

from scipy import stats

```
\#\# Sample A/B test results

group_a = [20, 21, 19, 23] \# Conversions for group A
group_b = [18, 22, 21, 20] \# Conversions for group B


t_statistic, p_value = stats.ttest_ind(group_a, group_b)
print(f"T-statistic: t_statistic, P-value: p_value")
```

This code performs an independent t-test comparing conversions between two groups. A low p-value (typically less than 0.05) indicates significant differences between groups.

Mastering these foundational concepts equips you with valuable tools for deeper explorations into more complex analyses like regression analysis or machine learning applications using Python in Excel. As you become proficient in executing basic analyses accurately with libraries like Pandas or SciPy integrated within Excel environments for enhanced productivity and accuracy, you'll be well-positioned to uncover powerful insights that drive informed decision-making.

statistical analysis transcends mere number crunching; it's about crafting narratives from data—stories that reveal trends hidden beneath surface observations or predict outcomes not immediately visible in raw figures. Every dataset holds potential narratives waiting for skilled interpretation through the careful application of these foundational concepts.

Descriptive Statistics with Pandas

Descriptive statistics are fundamental to data analysis,

providing the means to summarize and convey essential characteristics of datasets. When analyzing data, especially within Excel using Python, leveraging these statistics effectively is vital for extracting insights that inform decision-making. The Pandas library in Python offers robust tools for performing descriptive statistics, facilitating the manipulation and analysis of data housed in DataFrames.

A good starting point is understanding measures of central tendency—mean, median, and mode—which help pinpoint the average or most common values in a dataset. The mean is calculated by summing all values and dividing by the number of observations. However, it can be skewed by outliers. For example, in a sales dataset where most figures are around 200 but one outlier jumps to 2,000, the mean could misrepresent typical performance. In contrast, the median, which is the middle value when all observations are ordered, provides a more reliable measure as it is less sensitive to extreme values.

Consider this practical example using Pandas:

```python
import pandas as pd

\#\# Sample dataset representing monthly sales figures
data = 'Sales': [200, 220, 250, 2750] \# Note the outlier: 2750
df = pd.DataFrame(data)

\#\# Calculating mean and median
mean_sales = df['Sales'].mean()
median_sales = df['Sales'].median()
```

```
print(f"Mean Sales: mean_sales")    \# Output: Mean Sales:
717.5
```

```
print(f"Median Sales: median_sales") \# Output: Median
Sales: 220.0
```
` ` `

In this instance, the mean sales figure is significantly influenced by the outlier of 2750, distorting our understanding of average performance. Conversely, the median offers a clearer picture of typical monthly sales.

While measures of central tendency shed light on where most values lie within a dataset, variability statistics such as range, variance, and standard deviation reveal how dispersed those values are. The range, defined as the difference between the highest and lowest values, provides a quick overview of dispersion but may be misleading in the presence of outliers.

Variance delves deeper into how individual data points differ from the mean and is calculated by averaging the squared differences from that mean:

` ` `python

\#\# Calculating variance and standard deviation

variance_sales = df['Sales'].var()

std_dev_sales = df['Sales'].std()

print(f"Variance of Sales: variance_sales")

print(f"Standard Deviation of Sales: std_dev_sales")
` ` `

Grasping these measures equips analysts with essential tools for describing datasets and making inferences about broader populations based on sample data. Descriptive statistics seamlessly lead into inferential statistics—the analysis that seeks to determine whether observed patterns can extend to larger populations.

An important part of inferential statistics is hypothesis testing. Here, we formulate a null hypothesis (suggesting no difference or effect) against an alternative hypothesis (indicating that an effect exists). Statistical tests like t-tests help analysts determine whether differences between groups are significant or merely due to chance.

Here's how you can perform a t-test using Python's SciPy library:

```python
from scipy import stats


\#\# Sample A/B test results for conversion rates from two different campaigns

group_a = [20, 21, 19, 23] \# Conversions for group A

group_b = [18, 22, 21, 20] \# Conversions for group B


t_statistic, p_value = stats.ttest_ind(group_a, group_b)

print(f"T-statistic: t_statistic, P-value: p_value")
```

A low p-value suggests sufficient evidence to reject the null hypothesis in favor of the alternative hypothesis—indicating that one campaign statistically outperforms another.

By mastering descriptive statistics with Pandas, analysts not only summarize data effectively but also build a foundation for more complex analyses such as regression or predictive modeling in Python integrated within Excel environments. These insights are crucial as they guide strategic decisions grounded in empirical evidence rather than assumptions.

To wrap things up, descriptive statistics transform raw data into actionable insights that drive critical business strategies. By utilizing tools like Pandas in Python alongside Excel's visualization capabilities—such as graphs or dashboards—you can create compelling narratives that resonate with stakeholders while uncovering trends hidden within mere numbers. This combination of technology and statistical expertise distinguishes you as an analyst capable of extracting meaningful value from every dataset encountered.

Hypothesis Testing in Python

Hypothesis testing is a fundamental aspect of inferential statistics, allowing analysts to draw meaningful conclusions about populations based on sample data. The process typically begins with the formulation of two opposing hypotheses: the null hypothesis, which asserts that no significant difference or effect exists, and the alternative hypothesis, which posits the presence of a difference or effect. This framework is crucial for informed decision-making across various fields, including marketing strategies and scientific research.

To illustrate how hypothesis testing works in practice, consider an example where you aim to evaluate the effectiveness of two different marketing campaigns on conversion rates. You would start by collecting conversion data from both campaigns and applying statistical tests to determine whether any observed differences are statistically significant or merely the result of chance.

Using Python's SciPy library simplifies this analysis. Take this example, suppose you have collected conversion rates from two marketing campaigns:

```python
from scipy import stats

\#\# Sample conversion rates for two different campaigns
group_a = [20, 21, 19, 23] \# Campaign A conversions
group_b = [18, 22, 21, 20] \# Campaign B conversions

\#\# Performing a t-test to compare the means of the two groups
t_statistic, p_value = stats.ttest_ind(group_a, group_b)

print(f"T-statistic: t_statistic, P-value: p_value")
```

In this example, the t-test evaluates the means of conversions from both campaigns. The t-statistic measures the distance between the two group means in terms of standard deviations, while the p-value indicates whether these differences are statistically significant. A common threshold for significance is a p-value below 0.05, suggesting evidence against the null hypothesis.

If your analysis yields a low p-value—say, 0.03—you can confidently reject the null hypothesis and conclude that there is a significant difference in effectiveness between the two marketing campaigns. Such insights can inform and refine future marketing strategies.

Beyond t-tests, there are other statistical tests suited for different scenarios. For example, when comparing more than two groups at once, you would use ANOVA (Analysis of Variance):

```python
\#\# Sample data for three different marketing campaigns
group_a = [20, 21, 19]
group_b = [18, 22, 21]
group_c = [23, 24, 22]


f_statistic, p_value = stats.f_oneway(group_a, group_b, group_c)
print(f"F-statistic: f_statistic, P-value: p_value")
```

This approach helps determine whether at least one group mean significantly differs from the others. A low p-value in this context suggests that at least one campaign stands out in performance—a critical insight for decision-makers looking to optimize their strategies.

Effect size is another important consideration in hypothesis testing. While p-values indicate statistical significance, effect sizes provide context about the practical importance of these differences. Calculating Cohen's d can quantify this:

```python
import numpy as np


def cohen_d(group1, group2):
n1 = len(group1)
n2 = len(group2)
mean1 = np.mean(group1)
mean2 = np.mean(group2)
```

```
var1 = np.var(group1)

var2 = np.var(group2)


return (mean1 - mean2) / np.sqrt((((n1 - 1) * var1 + (n2 - 1) *
var2) / (n1 + n2 - 2))


d_value = cohen_d(group_a, group_b)

print(f"Cohen's d: d_value")
```
```

This calculation provides insight into how large or small your observed effects are relative to variability in your data—a crucial aspect in assessing practical significance.

As you become more proficient in hypothesis testing using tools like Python and Excel, think about how these methods can be applied to your own datasets and business contexts. Each statistical analysis reveals not just numbers but narratives—stories that illuminate consumer behavior or operational efficiency.

Harnessing these insights allows you to transition from guesswork to data-driven decision-making. Hypothesis testing equips you with evidence that can validate strategic initiatives and measure their impacts effectively.

Mastering robust statistical analyses not only enhances informed decision-making but also strengthens your role as a trusted advisor within your organization. By grounding your recommendations in empirical evidence derived from hypothesis testing and related techniques, you position yourself as a leader capable of navigating complex challenges with clarity and confidence.

**Regression Analysis in Excel**
```

Regression analysis is a powerful tool in statistics, particularly useful for understanding relationships between variables. In Excel, it enables you to model how a dependent variable changes in response to fluctuations in one or more independent variables. This capability is essential across various fields, from forecasting sales to assessing the impact of marketing expenditures on revenue.

To effectively conduct regression analysis using Python in Excel, it's important to familiarize yourself with its fundamental components. A standard linear regression model can be expressed with the equation: $Y = \beta_0 + \beta_1 X_1 + \beta_2 X_2 + \ldots + \beta_n X_n + \varepsilon$. In this equation, Y represents the dependent variable, X denotes the independent variables, β indicates the coefficients that quantify the influence of each variable, and ε captures the error term.

Let's consider a practical example: analyzing how an advertising budget (X_1) and product price (X_2) affect sales revenue (Y). Begin by gathering relevant data into an Excel workbook, which might look something like this:

| Advertising Budget | Product Price | Sales Revenue |

| 1000 | 10 | 5000 |

| 2000 | 15 | 7000 |

| 1500 | 12 | 6000 |

| ... | ... | ... |

Once your dataset is prepared, you can leverage Python's statsmodels library to conduct the regression analysis. Start by importing the necessary libraries and loading your data from Excel:

```python
import pandas as pd

import statsmodels.api as sm
```

```
\#\# Load data from Excel
data = pd.read_excel('sales_data.xlsx')

\#\# Define independent variables and dependent variable
X = data[['Advertising Budget', 'Product Price']]
Y = data['Sales Revenue']

\#\# Add a constant term for intercept
X = sm.add_constant(X)

\#\# Fit the regression model
model = sm.OLS(Y, X).fit()
print(model.summary())
```

The summary() method provides valuable insights into your regression model, including R-squared values that reveal how well your independent variables explain variability in the dependent variable. A high R-squared value close to 1 suggests a strong relationship between your predictors and the outcome.

Beyond understanding relationships, regression analysis empowers you to make predictions based on new input values. Take this example, if you want to forecast sales for an advertising budget of)2,500 and a product price of (13, you can do so with the following code:

```python
new_data = pd.DataFrame('const': [1], 'Advertising Budget':
```

[2500], 'Product Price': [13])

predicted_sales = model.predict(new_data)

print(f"Predicted Sales Revenue: predicted_sales[0]")
` ` `

This predictive capability transforms your findings from simple observations into actionable insights that can guide strategic decision-making.

However, it's vital to assess your model's assumptions— such as linearity, independence of errors, homoscedasticity (constant variance of errors), and normality of residuals—to ensure reliable results. You can visualize these aspects using residual plots or Q-Q plots:

` ` `python
import matplotlib.pyplot as plt

import seaborn as sns

\#\# Residuals vs Fitted values plot

plt.figure(figsize=(10,5))

sns.residplot(x=model.fittedvalues, y=model.resid)

plt.axhline(0, linestyle='--', color='red')

plt.xlabel('Fitted Values')

plt.ylabel('Residuals')

plt.title('Residuals vs Fitted Values')

plt.show()
` ` `

This visualization helps identify any patterns that might indicate violations of regression assumptions. Recognizing such patterns is crucial for making necessary adjustments and achieving more reliable results.

As you become more proficient with regression analysis in Python and Excel, consider exploring multiple regression models or even polynomial regressions for non-linear relationships. The realm of statistical modeling is vast; mastering these tools can significantly enhance your analytical skills.

Grounding your decision-making processes in solid statistical evidence derived from thorough regression analysis not only elevates the quality of insights but also enhances their potential impact on business outcomes. This approach equips you with knowledge and confidence—an invaluable asset in any professional environment where data-driven decisions take precedence.

Time Series Analysis with Python

Time series analysis plays a vital role in understanding how data points evolve over time. In fields such as finance, economics, and environmental science, recognizing patterns, seasonal effects, and trends can significantly influence strategic decision-making. While Excel offers basic tools for handling time series data, utilizing Python greatly enhances these capabilities through advanced statistical techniques and powerful libraries.

Here's a glimpse of what such data might look like in Excel:

Month	Sales
2021-01	2000
2021-02	2200
2021-03	2500
2021-04	2700
2021-05	3000
...	...

To analyze this time series data using Python, you can take advantage of libraries like pandas and statsmodels. First, load your Excel dataset:

```python
import pandas as pd

\#\# Load sales data from Excel

data = pd.read_excel('monthly_sales.xlsx')


\#\# Convert 'Month' column to datetime format

data['Month'] = pd.to_datetime(data['Month'])

data.set_index('Month', inplace=True)
```

With the data prepared, visualizing it can yield valuable insights into its structure. Plotting helps reveal visible trends or seasonality:

```python
import matplotlib.pyplot as plt

\#\# Plotting the time series

plt.figure(figsize=(12, 6))

plt.plot(data.index, data['Sales'], marker='o')

plt.title('Monthly Sales Over Time')

plt.xlabel('Month')

plt.ylabel('Sales')

plt.grid()
```

```
plt.show()
```
` ` `

From the graph, you may notice patterns such as an upward trend during certain months, suggesting seasonal influences. To quantify these observations further, we can apply decomposition techniques available in statsmodels. This process breaks down the time series into its components: trend, seasonality, and residuals.

` ` `python

```
from statsmodels.tsa.seasonal import seasonal_decompose

\#\# Decompose the time series

decomposed       =       seasonal_decompose(data['Sales'], model='additive')

decomposed.plot()

plt.show()
```
` ` `

This decomposition visualizes how much variance in your sales figures is attributed to each component. Understanding these elements is crucial; for instance, if a significant portion of the variation stems from seasonality, businesses can adjust their strategies to capitalize on expected demand peaks.

Beyond visualization and decomposition lies the essential task of forecasting future values. One effective method for making predictions based on past values is the ARIMA (AutoRegressive Integrated Moving Average) model. Here's how you can implement it:

First, ensure your dataset is stationary—meaning its statistical properties remain constant over time. The Dickey-

Fuller test from statsmodels is commonly used to check for stationarity.

```python
from statsmodels.tsa.stattools import adfuller


result = adfuller(data['Sales'])

print(f'Statistic: result[0]')

print(f'p-value: result[1]')
```

If the p-value falls below a predetermined threshold (typically set at 0.05), you can reject the null hypothesis that the series has a unit root—indicating stationarity.

Assuming your data meets this criterion, you can fit an ARIMA model:

```python
from statsmodels.tsa.arima.model import ARIMA


\#\# Fit ARIMA model (p=1,d=1,q=1)

model = ARIMA(data['Sales'], order=(1, 1, 1))

model_fit = model.fit()

print(model_fit.summary())
```

The output summary provides key statistics about your fitted model—essential for assessing its effectiveness.

Once fitted successfully, forecasting future values becomes straightforward:

```python
```

```
\#\# Forecasting next 12 months

forecast = model_fit.forecast(steps=12)

forecast_index = pd.date_range(start=data.index[-1] + pd.DateOffset(months=1), periods=12, freq='M')


\#\# Visualizing forecasted values along with historical data

plt.figure(figsize=(12, 6))

plt.plot(data.index[-36:], data['Sales'][-36:], label='Historical Sales', marker='o')

plt.plot(forecast_index, forecast, label='Forecasted Sales', marker='o', color='orange')

plt.title('Sales Forecast for Next Year')

plt.xlabel('Month')

plt.ylabel('Sales')

plt.axvline(x=data.index[-1], color='grey', linestyle='--') \# Indicate end of historical data

plt.legend()

plt.grid()

plt.show()
` ` `
```

This predictive modeling enables businesses to strategically prepare for anticipated changes in demand based on historical performance.

Engaging with time series analysis through Python not only enhances accuracy but also deepens insights into temporal dynamics within datasets. By understanding trends and making informed forecasts, organizations can develop actionable business strategies—an essential skill set in today's fast-paced environment where timely decisions are paramount.

Monte Carlo Simulations

Monte Carlo simulations offer a robust framework for analyzing uncertainty and variability in complex systems. By harnessing randomness and statistical sampling, these simulations allow practitioners to predict potential outcomes and evaluate risks across various scenarios. This technique is particularly valuable in fields such as finance, project management, and engineering, where making informed decisions under uncertainty is crucial.

To illustrate the effectiveness of Monte Carlo simulations, let's consider a financial scenario: estimating the future value of an investment portfolio over time. Suppose you start with an initial investment of)10,000, anticipating an average annual return of 7% and a standard deviation of 15%. However, market conditions can fluctuate significantly from year to year. By simulating numerous possible future paths for this investment using Python, we can uncover insights into the range of potential outcomes.

First, we need to install and import the necessary libraries. Ensure you have numpy and matplotlib ready:

```bash
pip install numpy matplotlib
```

Now we can set up our Monte Carlo simulation:

```python
import numpy as np

import matplotlib.pyplot as plt
```

```
\#\# Parameters for the simulation
initial_investment = 10000 \# Initial investment amount
annual_return = 0.07     \# Expected annual return
annual_volatility = 0.15    \# Expected annual volatility
years = 30             \# Investment duration in years
num_simulations = 1000     \# Number of simulations


\#\# Run Monte Carlo simulation
np.random.seed(42) \# For reproducibility
simulations = np.zeros((num_simulations, years))


for i in range(num_simulations):
    yearly_returns     =     np.random.normal(annual_return,
annual_volatility, years)
    portfolio_value    =    initial_investment    *    (1    +
yearly_returns).cumprod()
    simulations[i] = portfolio_value


\#\# Plotting results
plt.figure(figsize=(12, 6))
plt.plot(simulations.T, color='lightblue', alpha=0.1)    \#
Transpose to plot each simulation on y-axis
plt.title('Monte Carlo Simulations: Future Value of
Investment Portfolio')
```

```python
plt.xlabel('Years')

plt.ylabel('Portfolio Value (\()')

plt.grid()

plt.show()
```
` ` `

In this code snippet, we generate random returns based on a normal distribution defined by our expected return and volatility. Each simulation creates a unique trajectory for the portfolio value over the specified period.

The resulting plot showcases the wide range of potential outcomes from this investment strategy. While some simulations indicate substantial growth, others may reveal significant losses or lower-than-expected returns.

To derive meaningful insights from our simulations, we can calculate statistics such as mean outcomes and confidence intervals:

` ` `python

```python
\#\# Calculate mean and confidence intervals

mean_outcomes = simulations.mean(axis=0)

lower_bound = np.percentile(simulations, 2.5, axis=0)

upper_bound = np.percentile(simulations, 97.5, axis=0)


\#\# Plotting mean outcomes with confidence intervals

plt.figure(figsize=(12, 6))

plt.plot(mean_outcomes, label='Mean Outcome', color='blue')

plt.fill_between(range(years), lower_bound, upper_bound,
```

```
color='lightgreen', alpha=0.5,

label='95% Confidence Interval')

plt.title('Mean Outcome with Confidence Intervals')

plt.xlabel('Years')

plt.ylabel('Portfolio Value (\))')

plt.legend()

plt.grid()

plt.show()
```
` ` `

This visualization not only highlights the average expected growth but also delineates a confidence interval around this mean outcome—providing insights into the level of risk associated with the investment strategy.

Monte Carlo simulations are a dynamic tool for risk assessment and decision-making. They enable us to explore numerous potential futures rather than relying solely on static estimates or deterministic models. When integrated with Excel through Python scripts or tools like PyXLL or xlwings, these powerful analyses enhance reporting capabilities within familiar environments.

As professionals navigate complex financial landscapes or evaluate projects fraught with uncertainty, mastering Monte Carlo simulations equips them to make informed decisions grounded in data-driven insights rather than intuition alone. The ability to visualize risks and rewards fosters clearer strategies essential for thriving in today's unpredictable economic environment.

Machine Learning Models in Excel

Machine learning models have transformed data analysis,

offering tools that can learn from data and deliver predictions with impressive accuracy. By integrating these models into Excel, users who are already familiar with the platform can enhance their analytical capabilities without the need for extensive programming knowledge. This combination leverages Python's advanced machine learning libraries alongside Excel's intuitive interface.

To establish a solid foundation, we'll utilize Python's popular machine learning library, scikit-learn. This library simplifies the implementation of various algorithms, such as regression, classification, and clustering. Consider a dataset containing historical sales data for a retail store, featuring variables like advertising spend, store location, and sales figures. Our objective is to predict future sales based on this information.

First, ensure you have the necessary libraries installed:

```bash
pip install pandas scikit-learn openpyxl
```

Next, let's set up a straightforward linear regression model using this dataset:

```python
import pandas as pd

from sklearn.model_selection import train_test_split

from sklearn.linear_model import LinearRegression


\#\# Load your dataset from Excel

data = pd.read_excel('sales_data.xlsx')


\#\# Define features and target variable
```

```
X = data[['Advertising_Spend', 'Store_Location']] \# Features
y = data['Sales']                    \# Target

\#\# Split the dataset into training and testing sets
X_train, X_test, y_train, y_test = train_test_split(X, y,
test_size=0.2, random_state=42)

\#\# Create and fit the model
model = LinearRegression()
model.fit(X_train, y_train)

\#\# Making predictions on the test set
predictions = model.predict(X_test)
` ` `
```

This simple approach illustrates how we can train a linear regression model on our sales data. The train_test_split function divides the dataset into training and testing subsets to allow for accurate evaluation of the model's performance.

To gauge how effectively our model predicts sales, we can calculate metrics such as Mean Absolute Error (MAE) or R-squared:

```
` ` `python
from sklearn.metrics import mean_absolute_error, r2_score

mae = mean_absolute_error(y_test, predictions)
r2 = r2_score(y_test, predictions)
```

```python
print(f'Mean Absolute Error: mae')
```

```python
print(f'R-squared: r2')
```
```
` ` `
```

These metrics provide valuable insights into our model's accuracy. A lower MAE signifies better performance in predicting sales figures, while R-squared indicates how well our independent variables explain the variability in the dependent variable.

Now comes an exciting aspect: integrating this predictive capability back into Excel for easy access and reporting. By using tools like xlwings, we can call Python functions directly from Excel cells. Here's how to implement a function that predicts future sales based on new advertising spend values:

```python
` ` `python
import xlwings as xw


@xw.func

def predict_sales(ad_spend):

\#\# Assuming Store Location is fixed or represented numerically

location_value = 1  \# Example value for "Store Location


\#\# Make prediction using the trained model

return model.predict([[ad_spend, location_value]])[0]
` ` `
```

With this function set up, any user can enter a new

advertising spend amount directly into an Excel cell and receive an instant sales prediction by simply calling =predict_sales(cell_reference).

This integration not only enhances reporting but also empowers decision-makers who may not possess deep technical expertise to engage with complex predictive analytics seamlessly within their established workflows.

Beyond linear regression, scikit-learn offers a variety of more sophisticated algorithms—such as decision trees and random forests—that may yield even better results depending on your specific dataset characteristics. Each algorithm has unique strengths and weaknesses; exploring them will enrich your understanding of machine learning applications.

As professionals increasingly rely on data-driven decisions in today's fast-paced environment, mastering these machine learning techniques within familiar tools like Excel becomes invaluable. Blending Python's capabilities with Excel's accessibility leads to innovative solutions that can uncover insights previously hidden in raw data.

The ability to analyze trends dynamically not only enhances operational efficiency but also fosters a culture of informed decision-making across teams and organizations— ultimately making you an indispensable asset in any data-driven landscape.

Presenting Statistical Findings

Statistical analysis is essential to data-driven decision-making, providing insights that can influence strategies and drive success across various industries. To effectively communicate statistical findings, clarity and precision are crucial. Transforming complex data into compelling narratives can elevate a presentation from a simple collection of numbers to an engaging story that informs and motivates action.

Start by structuring your findings around a clear objective. What primary question or hypothesis are you addressing? Take this example, if your analysis focuses on sales trends over time, outline the key metrics that will support your narrative. These may include averages, medians, or trends identified through time series analysis.

Consider a scenario in which you've analyzed quarterly sales data to assess the impact of marketing efforts on revenue. Your findings may indicate a consistent increase in sales following specific marketing campaigns. To convey this effectively, use visuals such as line charts or bar graphs, which illustrate changes over time more intuitively than tables of numbers.

For example, here's how you can create a simple visualization using Python's Matplotlib library:

```python
import pandas as pd

import matplotlib.pyplot as plt


\#\# Load your quarterly sales data

data = pd.read_excel('quarterly_sales_data.xlsx')


\#\# Plotting the sales trend

plt.figure(figsize=(10, 6))

plt.plot(data['Quarter'], data['Sales'], marker='o')

plt.title('Quarterly Sales Trend')

plt.xlabel('Quarter')

plt.ylabel('Sales (\()')
```

```
plt.grid()

plt.xticks(rotation=45)

plt.tight_layout()

plt.show()
```
` ` `

This code snippet generates a line chart that effectively illustrates sales trends over the quarters. Visuals like these not only enhance engagement but also improve information retention among stakeholders who may not be deeply familiar with statistical nuances.

Providing context for your findings is also vital. Explain what the statistics mean in relation to your business objectives. If your analysis reveals a spike in sales following a campaign launch, explore potential reasons—was there increased brand awareness? Did customer engagement rise? By connecting the numbers to real-world implications, you underscore their relevance and encourage decisive action.

The interpretation phase is where statistical significance comes into play. Techniques such as hypothesis testing help determine whether observed effects are genuine or merely due to random chance. Take this example:

` ` `python

from scipy import stats

\#\# Example data: Sales before and after marketing campaign

before_campaign = [1000, 1200, 1100]

after_campaign = [1500, 1700, 1600]

\#\# Perform t-test

t_statistic, p_value = stats.ttest_ind(before_campaign, after_campaign)

print(f'T-statistic: t_statistic, P-value: p_value')

` ` `

If the p-value falls below a predetermined threshold (commonly set at 0.05), you can confidently assert that there is statistically significant evidence supporting the effectiveness of your marketing efforts.

When compiling your report or presentation on these findings, consider incorporating storytelling techniques to further engage your audience. Start with an introduction that sets the stage—what prompted this analysis? What questions were you hoping to answer? Then transition smoothly into your methodology; succinctly explain how you collected data and which statistical methods were used.

After presenting key findings and interpretations supported by visuals and statistics, conclude with actionable recommendations based on your insights. You might suggest reallocating budget toward successful campaigns or increasing resources for areas showing potential for growth.

Finally, anticipate questions from stakeholders by preparing well-founded answers grounded in your analysis. This approach not only demonstrates thoroughness but also reassures decision-makers of the credibility of your conclusions.

In summary, effectively presenting statistical findings involves more than simply displaying numbers; it requires clear communication through structured narratives supported by strong visuals and rigorous analytical methods. Engaging presentations foster informed decision-making, ultimately propelling organizations toward their strategic goals with confidence rooted in robust statistical evidence. By mastering these skills within Python and Excel environments, you are well-equipped to lead impactful discussions that resonate across teams and drive meaningful change within your organization.

CHAPTER 9: EXCEL AND PYTHON: TIPS AND TRICKS

Time-Saving Python Scripts for Excel

Harnessing the power of Python to automate tasks in Excel can significantly cut down the time spent on repetitive activities. Picture a scenario where you frequently generate reports by pulling data from multiple sheets, performing calculations, and formatting results. Rather than manually executing each step—a process that is often tedious and prone to errors—a well-crafted Python script can complete these tasks in mere seconds. This allows you to redirect your focus toward more strategic analysis.

To illustrate this, let's consider a practical example: compiling sales data from various regional spreadsheets into a master workbook. By using Python, particularly libraries like Pandas and OpenPyXL, you can easily create a script that automates this entire process. First, ensure you have the necessary libraries installed:

```bash
```

```
pip install pandas openpyxl
```
` ` `

Now, let's write a simple script that consolidates sales data from multiple Excel files located in a specific directory. The process unfolds as follows:

` ` `python

```python
import pandas as pd

import os


\#\# Set the directory containing your Excel files

directory = 'path/to/your/excel/files'

sales_data = []


\#\# Iterate through each file in the directory

for filename in os.listdir(directory):

if filename.endswith('.xlsx'):

\#\# Read each Excel file into a DataFrame

file_path = os.path.join(directory, filename)

df = pd.read_excel(file_path)

sales_data.append(df)


\#\# Concatenate all DataFrames into a single DataFrame

consolidated_data = pd.concat(sales_data)


\#\# Save the consolidated data to a new Excel file
```

```
consolidated_data.to_excel('consolidated_sales_data.xlsx',
index=False)
```

This script accomplishes several key tasks: it reads each Excel file in the specified directory, aggregates the data into a single DataFrame, and finally saves that aggregated data as a new Excel file. Each component of the script is modular, allowing you to easily make adjustments based on specific requirements—whether that means filtering certain columns or applying transformations before saving.

Beyond simple consolidation, Python offers extensive customization options for processing your data. For example, if you want to calculate total sales per region and generate a summary report automatically, you can extend the script with just a few additional lines:

```python
\#\# Assuming 'Region' and 'Sales' are columns in your DataFrame

summary_report = consolidated_data.groupby('Region')['Sales'].sum().reset_index()

summary_report.to_excel('sales_summary_report.xlsx',
index=False)
```

With these two lines of code, you've not only consolidated your sales data but also created an insightful summary that highlights performance across different regions. This example demonstrates how Python transforms Excel from a simple spreadsheet tool into a powerful data processing engine.

The advantages of such automation go beyond mere time savings; they also enhance accuracy. Manual processes are often susceptible to oversight or input errors, while scripts execute predetermined instructions consistently every time they run. Imagine presenting reports free from discrepancies because you've transitioned laborious calculations to automated scripts.

Additionally, automating repetitive tasks fosters innovation within your role. With less time consumed by mundane activities, you gain the opportunity to delve deeper into data analysis or strategic planning. By leveraging Python scripts for basic operations like these, you position yourself not just as an analyst but as a proactive problem-solver capable of driving significant improvements within your organization.

As workflows evolve and demands increase across industries, integrating Python with Excel will become crucial for maintaining productivity and competitiveness. Embracing this approach today sets the stage for continuous improvement tomorrow.

In summary, we've explored how Python can save time by efficiently automating standard Excel tasks. The adaptability and power of this integration not only revolutionize our approach to data management but also equip us with tools for ongoing innovation in our roles. This journey enhances individual productivity while elevating organizational capability—a transformative shift that is well worth embracing.

Optimizing Excel Performance with Python

Maximizing Excel's performance with Python not only streamlines tasks but also significantly enhances the efficiency of your data workflows. Working with large datasets or complex calculations can often lead to performance bottlenecks in Excel, resulting in frustrating delays. This is where Python can become a game-changer. By offloading heavy computational tasks to Python scripts, you can maintain speed and responsiveness while still utilizing

Excel's intuitive interface.

Consider a typical scenario involving financial data that requires extensive calculations across thousands of rows. Performing these operations directly in Excel may slow down your workbook and hinder responsiveness. However, by leveraging Python for these computations, you can process data more quickly and return results to Excel without the sluggishness often encountered. Take this example, if you're tasked with financial forecasting based on historical sales data, a Python script can efficiently handle large datasets.

Here's a practical example of using Python to calculate moving averages—a common requirement in financial analysis:

```python
import pandas as pd

\#\# Load your dataset
data = pd.read_excel('sales_data.xlsx')

\#\# Calculate the moving average over a specified window
data['Moving_Average'] = data['Sales'].rolling(window=3).mean()

\#\# Save the updated DataFrame back to Excel
data.to_excel('sales_data_with_moving_average.xlsx', index=False)
```

In this code snippet, we load sales data from an Excel file, compute a three-period moving average of the sales figures, and then save the updated dataset back into a new Excel file. This method alleviates the computational burden on Excel while ensuring that calculations remain accurate and current.

When automating such processes, it's crucial to include error handling in your scripts, especially when working with external data sources or performing operations reliant on the integrity of input data. Incorporating try-except blocks can safeguard against unexpected issues:

```python
try:

\#\# Load your dataset

data = pd.read_excel('sales_data.xlsx')

except FileNotFoundError:

print("The specified file was not found.")

except Exception as e:

print(f"An error occurred: e")
```

This attention to detail ensures that your scripts are robust and capable of managing unexpected situations gracefully, preventing crashes or erroneous outputs.

Another significant advantage of using Python is its ability to conduct complex statistical analyses that would be cumbersome within Excel alone. For example, if you're tasked with performing regression analysis on sales trends over time, libraries like statsmodels can provide powerful insights quickly:

```python
import pandas as pd
```

```
import statsmodels.api as sm

\#\# Load the dataset
data = pd.read_excel('sales_data.xlsx')

\#\# Define your independent (X) and dependent (Y) variables
X = data[['Marketing_Spend']]
Y = data['Sales']

\#\# Add a constant to the model (required for statsmodels)
X = sm.add_constant(X)

\#\# Fit the regression model
model = sm.OLS(Y, X).fit()

\#\# Print out the statistics
print(model.summary())
` ` `
```

This example illustrates how straightforward it is to establish a linear regression model using Python. The detailed output regarding coefficients, R-squared values, and other statistics aids decision-making far more efficiently than traditional spreadsheet methods.

Integrating Python into your Excel workflows unlocks improved performance and advanced analytical capabilities that transform mundane tasks into streamlined operations.

By offloading intensive calculations to Python while still interacting with Excel for presentation purposes, you create a powerful hybrid solution.

And, optimizing workflows enhances productivity and allows you to concentrate on higher-value activities—an invaluable shift for anyone involved in data analysis or reporting. As organizations increasingly rely on real-time decision-making driven by accurate insights, mastering these integrations positions you as an essential asset capable of navigating complex challenges with agility.

In today's evolving landscape of data management, remember that optimizing performance goes beyond mere speed; it's also about making informed decisions quickly and effectively. Embracing Python alongside Excel not only revolutionizes your workflow but amplifies your potential impact within your organization—ensuring you are not just keeping pace but leading from the front in this digital age of analytics.

Python Shortcuts for Excel Users

Navigating the complex landscape of Excel can often feel overwhelming, especially when your goal is to optimize data handling. Fortunately, Python offers a wealth of shortcuts that can significantly streamline your workflows, transforming tedious tasks into seamless processes. These shortcuts not only save valuable time but also enhance your overall experience with Excel, allowing you to shift your focus from the mechanics of data entry and management to insightful analysis.

One of the most compelling advantages of integrating Python with Excel is its capability to automate repetitive tasks. For example, if you regularly generate weekly reports that involve pulling data from multiple sheets, performing calculations, and formatting the output, you can replace the manual execution of these steps with a Python script. This approach enables you to complete the work in a fraction of the time. Using libraries like openpyxl, you can easily read and write Excel files:

```python
from openpyxl import Workbook, load_workbook

\#\# Load an existing workbook
workbook = load_workbook('weekly_report_template.xlsx')
sheet = workbook.active

\#\# Perform your calculations or data manipulations here
\#\# Example: Adding a total to a specific cell
total_sales = sum(sheet['B2:B10'])  \# Assuming sales data is in column B
sheet['C1'] = total_sales  \# Writing total to cell C1

\#\# Save the modified workbook
workbook.save('updated_weekly_report.xlsx')
```

This snippet illustrates how Python can directly interact with Excel files, allowing you to automate what would otherwise be a labor-intensive task. By programming this functionality, you not only enhance speed but also minimize human error—an essential benefit when accuracy is critical.

In addition to automation, Python excels at data cleaning and preparation, which can often be bottlenecks in your workflow. Dealing with inconsistencies such as missing values or incorrect formatting can be cumbersome in Excel.

However, Python's pandas library offers powerful functions that simplify these processes and transform messy datasets into structured formats ready for analysis. Consider this example:

```python
import pandas as pd

\#\# Load your dataset
data = pd.read_excel('raw_data.xlsx')

\#\# Drop rows with missing values
cleaned_data = data.dropna()

\#\# Convert column types if necessary
cleaned_data['Date'] = pd.to_datetime(cleaned_data['Date'])

\#\# Save cleaned data back to Excel
cleaned_data.to_excel('cleaned_data.xlsx', index=False)
```

In this case, Python efficiently handles missing values and date conversions—tasks that would require several steps in Excel are condensed into just a few lines of code.

And, Python's ability to utilize external libraries for specialized tasks further enhances its utility. When conducting exploratory data analysis (EDA), tools like matplotlib and seaborn provide robust visualization options that can be easily integrated into your Excel reporting:

```python
```

```
import matplotlib.pyplot as plt

\#\# Load cleaned data for visualization
data = pd.read_excel('cleaned_data.xlsx')

\#\# Create a simple line plot for sales trends over time
plt.figure(figsize=(10, 5))
plt.plot(data['Date'], data['Sales'])
plt.title('Sales Trends Over Time')
plt.xlabel('Date')
plt.ylabel('Sales')
plt.grid(True)
plt.savefig('sales_trends.png') \# Save the figure as an image
` ` `
```

This code not only visualizes sales trends but also generates an image file that can be seamlessly embedded into your Excel reports. The ability to create high-quality visualizations without the need for manual chart formatting in Excel adds another layer of efficiency.

Finally, when it comes time to share insights from your analyses, Python simplifies the creation of visually appealing reports. Libraries like ReportLab allow you to generate PDFs or HTML reports that encapsulate your findings along with visual aids—all while keeping your original Excel files organized and intact.

By incorporating these Python shortcuts into your daily Excel routines, you can transform mundane tasks into streamlined processes. This empowers you with more time for strategic thinking and analysis. The direct interaction between Python and Excel not only boosts your productivity but also significantly expands what you can achieve with your datasets.

Embracing these powerful integrations positions you at the forefront of modern data analysis practices. As organizations increasingly seek professionals who blend technical skills with analytical insight, mastering Python shortcuts for Excel will undoubtedly make you an invaluable asset capable of driving innovation and efficiency across projects.

Troubleshooting Common Issues

As you explore the integration of Python and Excel, you may encounter various challenges that can disrupt your workflow. Recognizing these common issues and knowing how to troubleshoot them is vital for maintaining productivity and achieving smooth functionality. Whether you're automating processes or analyzing data, resolving problems efficiently can save you both time and frustration.

One of the most prevalent challenges is file compatibility. When using Python libraries like pandas or openpyxl, it's essential to ensure that your Excel files are in a suitable format. Take this example, if you attempt to read an older .xls file with a library that supports only .xlsx, you may face errors. The solution often involves converting these files into a compatible format, which can be accomplished through Excel or with a straightforward script:

```python
import pandas as pd


\#\# Convert an older .xls file to .xlsx format

data = pd.read_excel('old_file.xls')

data.to_excel('converted_file.xlsx', index=False)
```

` ` `

This snippet illustrates how quickly you can resolve file format issues, allowing for smoother data manipulation.

Another common hurdle is handling missing values. If your dataset contains gaps in critical areas, calculations can produce inaccurate results or even crash your script. To avoid this risk, always check for missing data before performing operations. With pandas, you can easily identify and manage these gaps:

` ` `python

\#\# Check for missing values

if data.isnull().values.any():

print("Missing values detected!")

\#\# Handle missing values by dropping or filling

data = data.fillna(method='ffill')   \# Forward fill as an example

` ` `

By proactively addressing missing values, you not only enhance the integrity of your analyses but also streamline the debugging process.

Type mismatches can also be a source of frustration when manipulating Excel data with Python. For example, if a numeric column is mistakenly interpreted as a string, operations like summation will fail. To prevent such issues, it's wise to conduct type checks and conversions explicitly:

` ` `python

\#\# Ensure 'Sales' column is numeric

data['Sales'] = pd.to_numeric(data['Sales'], errors='coerce')

` ` `

Using the errors='coerce' argument converts non-numeric entries into NaN, allowing you to manage potential inaccuracies from the outset.

Additionally, scripting errors can occur due to syntax mistakes or logical flaws in your code. The Python traceback feature is invaluable for diagnosing such problems, providing a detailed error message along with the line number where the issue arose. When faced with an error message, take a moment to review the traceback carefully; it often leads directly to the source of the problem.

To further enhance your troubleshooting capabilities, consider implementing robust logging within your scripts. This practice captures errors and tracks script performance over time:

```python
import logging

logging.basicConfig(filename='app.log', level=logging.INFO)

try:
\#\# Your processing logic here
logging.info('Data processed successfully.')
except Exception as e:
logging.error(f'Error encountered: e')
```

This code snippet establishes basic logging capabilities that document both successful actions and exceptions, making it easier to identify issues in future runs.

Finally, keeping your Python environment updated can help

prevent compatibility issues with libraries and functions. Regular updates ensure access to new features and bug fixes that improve overall stability.

By mastering these troubleshooting techniques, you will not only tackle common issues as they arise but also cultivate a proactive mindset toward resolving potential setbacks in your workflow. This skill set enhances your confidence and competence in using Python alongside Excel, ultimately preparing you for more complex tasks and analyses without falling prey to recurring technical obstacles.

As you continue integrating these tools into your work routine, remember that each resolved issue is not merely a problem solved; it represents a step toward greater efficiency and innovation in your analytical capabilities.

Improving Excel Accessibility

Enhancing accessibility in Excel is not merely about improving usability; it's about ensuring that everyone, regardless of ability, can effectively interact with data. As you utilize Python to streamline your Excel workflows, consider how these integrations can help bridge accessibility gaps and promote inclusivity.

A key element of accessibility is a clear and structured layout. When programming Excel files, it's crucial to maintain logical organization within your data. Using meaningful headers and consistent formatting can guide users through the spreadsheet. Take this example, instead of labeling a column simply as "Data," opt for "Sales Figures for Q1 2023." This provides necessary context and clarity, making navigation easier for all users.

In addition to organized layouts, incorporating descriptive metadata can significantly enhance accessibility. With Python, you can add comments or notes that clarify the purpose of specific cells or ranges. This is especially beneficial for complex datasets or when sharing files with individuals who may not be familiar with the content. Here's how you can add comments using openpyxl:

```python
from openpyxl import Workbook

\#\# Create a workbook and select the active worksheet
wb = Workbook()
ws = wb.active

\#\# Adding a comment to a cell
cell = ws['A1']
cell.value = "Sales Data
cell.comment = "This column contains sales figures for Q1 2023.

wb.save("accessible_data.xlsx")
```

By annotating your data effectively, you provide users with insights into what they're viewing, reducing the need for extensive external documentation.

Visual elements also play a vital role in accessibility. Color contrast is critical for readability, especially for users who rely on screen readers or have visual impairments. It's important to choose colors that are easily distinguishable and comfortable to read. Python libraries can assist in automating color adjustments according to accessibility guidelines. For example, using xlsxwriter, you can implement conditional formatting that alters colors based on cell values:

```python
import xlsxwriter

workbook = xlsxwriter.Workbook('accessible_colors.xlsx')
worksheet = workbook.add_worksheet()

\#\# Define formats for high contrast
red_format = workbook.add_format('bg_color': '\#FF0000', 'font_color': '\#FFFFFF')

green_format = workbook.add_format('bg_color': '\#00FF00', 'font_color': '\#000000')

\#\# Apply conditional formatting
worksheet.conditional_format('A1:A10', 'type': 'cell',
'criteria': '<=',
'value': 50,
'format': red_format)

worksheet.conditional_format('A1:A10', 'type': 'cell',
'criteria': '>',
'value': 50,
'format': green_format)

workbook.close()
```

This example highlights low values in red and high values in green, drawing attention to critical areas while ensuring legibility.

Keyboard navigation is another important consideration. Users with mobility impairments often depend on keyboard shortcuts rather than a mouse. Thus, making sure your Python scripts facilitate this experience is essential. You can streamline tasks like navigating between sheets or triggering macros through keyboard shortcuts programmed into your scripts:

```python
import win32com.client as win32

\#\# Open an existing Excel workbook
excel_app = win32.gencache.EnsureDispatch('Excel.Application')
workbook = excel_app.Workbooks.Open(r'path.xlsx')

\#\# Create a simple macro that moves to the next sheet
excel_app.Application.OnKey("^+m", "NextSheet")  \# Ctrl + Shift + M to move to next sheet

def NextSheet():
excel_app.ActiveSheet.Next.Select()

excel_app.Visible = True
```

In this snippet, we use the win32com library to create a

shortcut that allows easy switching between sheets.

It's equally important to ensure compatibility with assistive technologies. Screen readers should be able to interpret your data accurately. Using appropriate naming conventions for ranges and tables within Excel aids screen reader software in reading data correctly. Python libraries can enable you to name ranges dynamically:

```python
import pandas as pd

data = pd.DataFrame(
'Product': ['A', 'B', 'C'],
'Sales': [200, 300, 150]
)


with pd.ExcelWriter('named_ranges.xlsx') as writer:
data.to_excel(writer, sheet_name='Sales Data')
writer.sheets['Sales Data'].name_columns('Product Sales Data') \# Naming the range
```

Using named ranges enhances access and understanding of specific datasets for all users.

And, ongoing feedback from users is crucial in enhancing accessibility efforts. Engaging stakeholders about their experiences can reveal valuable insights into necessary improvements. A user-centric approach not only aligns with ethical practices but also enriches the overall quality of your data presentation.

Improving accessibility in Excel through Python transcends

mere compliance; it empowers individuals by creating an environment where everyone has equal access to information and tools vital for success. By thoughtfully applying these techniques, you will not only enhance usability but also foster a more inclusive workplace where data-driven decisions benefit all users equally.

Effective Documentation Practices

Effective documentation practices are vital in any data-driven environment, especially when integrating Python with Excel. As you automate tasks and develop complex workflows, the significance of clear and concise documentation becomes increasingly apparent. It acts as a roadmap, guiding both your current self and anyone who may engage with your code or Excel files in the future.

To start, it's beneficial to establish a consistent structure for your documentation. This can encompass sections like purpose, usage instructions, and examples. Take this example, when writing a Python function designed to manipulate Excel data, it's essential to include not only the code but also a brief description of its purpose, parameters, and expected outputs. Here's an example using Python docstrings:

```python
def read_excel_file(file_path):
    "
```

Reads an Excel file and returns a DataFrame.

Parameters:

file_path (str): The path to the Excel file to be read.

Returns:

pd.DataFrame: A DataFrame containing the data from the Excel file.

Example:

df = read_excel_file('data.xlsx')

"

import pandas as pd

return pd.read_excel(file_path)

` ` `

This format allows others, or even your future self, to quickly understand the function's purpose and how to use it effectively.

In addition to structured documentation, incorporating inline comments within your code can greatly enhance clarity. While meaningful variable names and organized structure should ideally make the code self-explanatory, comments can clarify complex logic or specific decisions made during development. For example:

` ` `python

\#\# Iterate through each row in the DataFrame to apply sales tax

for index, row in df.iterrows():

\#\# Calculate tax only for sales over \)100

if row['Sales'] > 100:

df.at[index, 'Sales Tax'] = row['Sales'] * 0.07 \# 7% sales tax

` ` `

Such comments not only aid understanding but also

simplify future modifications.

Documentation should extend beyond your scripts to include details about the overall project architecture. A README file can outline the project's purpose, list any dependencies required for execution, and summarize how various components interact. This is especially useful when sharing your work with colleagues or revisiting projects after some time.

And, maintaining a changelog is another valuable practice. This log tracks changes over time—whether bug fixes, new features, or optimizations—keeping collaborators informed about the project's evolution. Here's a simple format for a changelog:

```
` ` `

Changelog
[1.0.1] - 2023-10-01
        · Fixed issue with reading empty cells.

        · Updated function names for clarity.

[1.0.0] - 2023-09-25
        · Initial release of the data processing script.

` ` `
```

Incorporating visual documentation can also enhance understanding when appropriate. Flowcharts or diagrams can effectively represent processes or data flows that might be challenging to explain through text alone. Tools like Lucidchart or draw.io can help you create these visuals easily.

Consider using Jupyter Notebooks as an interactive documentation tool. Notebooks allow you to blend executable code with rich text annotations and visualizations seamlessly. This format is particularly effective for demonstrating data analyses or workflows that benefit from both code execution and narrative

explanations.

Here's an example of how you might structure a notebook:

Sales Analysis

This notebook performs analysis on sales data extracted from our database.

Step 1: Load Data

``` `python

import pandas as pd

Load sales data from an Excel file

sales_data = pd.read_excel('sales_data.xlsx')
```

Step 2: Data Summary

``` `python

sales_data.describe()
```
```

By merging narratives with code snippets and visual outputs directly into Jupyter Notebooks, you create an accessible resource that others can easily follow.

Finally, don't underestimate the benefits of collaborative documentation tools like Confluence or Google Docs. These platforms allow team members to contribute insights or suggestions in real time, fostering collaboration and ensuring that everyone is aligned on processes and practices.

While documentation may sometimes seem tedious, it lays a strong foundation for collaboration and personal growth within your projects. Embracing effective documentation leads to smoother handovers, quicker onboarding for new
```

team members, and reduced friction when revisiting old projects. As you refine your workflows integrating Python with Excel, remember that clear documentation transforms complexity into clarity—making it easier for everyone involved to navigate the intricacies of your work with confidence and understanding.

Case Studies of Python-Excel Integration

Integrating Python with Excel has led to a variety of innovative applications that can significantly streamline workflows and enhance data analysis. Real-world case studies reveal the practical implications of this integration, illustrating how different industries harness Python to extend Excel's capabilities. Each example offers insights into specific challenges faced and the effective solutions implemented, providing valuable lessons for your own projects.

Take, for instance, a financial services company that aimed to automate its monthly reporting process. Traditionally, analysts spent several days compiling data from multiple sources, entering it into Excel, and formatting reports manually. By incorporating Python scripts with Excel, they were able to automate this labor-intensive task. Using the Pandas library, they seamlessly pulled data from various databases and APIs. This automation allowed them to aggregate sales data, calculate key performance indicators, and generate comprehensive reports in just minutes instead of days.

Here's a script that illustrates how they automated the data pull directly into an Excel file:

```python
import pandas as pd


\#\# Load sales data from a SQL database
```

```python
def fetch_sales_data():
\#\# Assuming we have a connection established
query = "SELECT * FROM sales_data WHERE date >= '2023-01-01'
return pd.read_sql(query, connection)

\#\# Write to an Excel file
def write_to_excel(data):
data.to_excel('monthly_report.xlsx', index=False)

sales_data = fetch_sales_data()
write_to_excel(sales_data)
```

The time saved allowed analysts to concentrate on deriving insights from the data rather than merely compiling it.

In another scenario within the marketing sector, a digital marketing firm utilized Python's web scraping capabilities alongside Excel to gather competitive intelligence. By employing libraries such as BeautifulSoup and Requests, they scraped pricing and promotional strategies from competitor websites. This information was processed and visualized in Excel for use during strategic planning sessions.

Here's a snippet demonstrating how they scraped pricing information:

```python
import requests
from bs4 import BeautifulSoup
```

```
\#\# Function to scrape product prices
def scrape_prices(url):
response = requests.get(url)
soup = BeautifulSoup(response.text, 'html.parser')

\#\# Example: Extracting price information
prices = soup.find_all(class_='product-price')
return [price.get_text() for price in prices]

product_prices = scrape_prices('https://competitor.com/products')
```

This automation not only provided timely insights but also empowered teams to adapt their strategies quickly based on real-time market conditions.

A healthcare organization showcased the power of Python integration in managing patient data. They struggled with analyzing large datasets stored in numerous Excel files scattered across various departments. Leveraging Python's OpenPyXL library, they developed scripts that consolidated these disparate files into a centralized database format within Excel. This not only improved accessibility but also facilitated compliance with regulatory requirements by ensuring all patient data was organized and up-to-date.

Here's an example of how they merged multiple Excel files:

```python
import openpyxl
```

```
import os

def merge_excel_files(directory):
combined_wb = openpyxl.Workbook()
combined_ws = combined_wb.active

for filename in os.listdir(directory):
if filename.endswith('.xlsx'):
wb    =    openpyxl.load_workbook(os.path.join(directory,
filename))
ws = wb.active

for row in ws.iter_rows(values_only=True):
combined_ws.append(row)

combined_wb.save('merged_patient_data.xlsx')

merge_excel_files('path_to_directory_with_excel_files')
```
` ` `

This approach drastically reduced errors associated with manual entry while ensuring that all departments operated off the same dataset.

Another notable example comes from an educational institution that harnessed Python for its grading systems while using Excel as their primary tool for recording student performance. By developing automated scripts that processed grades and generated feedback reports directly from raw score spreadsheets, they minimized human error and saved countless hours spent on manual calculations and reporting.

Here's a simple illustration of how they calculated average scores:

```python
def calculate_average(grades):

return sum(grades) / len(grades)


student_grades = [88, 92, 79]

average_score = calculate_average(student_grades)

print(f"Average Score: average_score")
```

This automated approach ensured accuracy while allowing educators more time to focus on teaching rather than administrative tasks.

These case studies not only highlight the effectiveness of integrating Python with Excel but also encourage innovative thinking about your own workflow challenges. Each organization demonstrated that through strategic automation and efficient use of available tools, significant time savings can be realized while maintaining high standards of accuracy and reliability. The potential for future applications is vast; the question remains—how will you leverage this powerful combination in your work?

Exploring New Opportunities

Integrating Python with Excel unlocks a wealth of opportunities for professionals across various sectors, enabling them to automate tedious tasks and enhance data analysis. As we've seen in previous examples, the practical applications of this combination are both diverse and transformative. Organizations increasingly recognize that adopting these technologies can lead to substantial efficiency gains and improved decision-making.

Take the retail sector, for instance, where effective inventory management is crucial. A major retail chain struggled with tracking inventory and managing restocking processes. To address these challenges, they implemented Python scripts that connected directly to their Excel inventory sheets, automating restocking alerts based on real-time sales data. By leveraging libraries like Pandas and OpenPyXL, they established a system that not only updated stock levels in Excel but also notified managers when items needed replenishment. This proactive strategy significantly reduced stockouts and enhanced customer satisfaction.

Here's a glimpse into their inventory update process:

```python
import pandas as pd

\#\# Load current inventory data
def load_inventory():
return pd.read_excel('inventory.xlsx')

\#\# Update inventory based on sales
def update_inventory(sales_data):
inventory = load_inventory()
for item, sold_quantity in sales_data.items():
if item in inventory.index:
inventory.at[item, 'Stock'] -= sold_quantity
```

```
inventory.to_excel('updated_inventory.xlsx')
```

```
sales_data = 'item_a': 5, 'item_b': 3
```

```
update_inventory(sales_data)
```

```
` ` `
```

The outcome was not only a more streamlined operation but also a marked decrease in lost sales due to stock shortages.

In another example, a human resources department sought to enhance its recruitment process through Python and Excel integration. They automated candidate screening by developing scripts that analyzed resumes stored in Excel format. By applying natural language processing techniques using libraries like NLTK or spaCy, they extracted relevant skills and experiences from candidates' resumes, automatically scoring them against job requirements.

Here's a basic illustration of how they processed resumes:

```
` ` `python
```

```
import pandas as pd
```

```
\#\# Load candidate data
```

```
def load_candidates():
```

```
return pd.read_excel('candidates.xlsx')
```

```
\#\# Simple keyword matching for scoring
```

```
def score_candidates(candidates):
```

```
scores =
```

```python
for index, row in candidates.iterrows():

score = sum(keyword in row['Resume'] for keyword in ['Python', 'Excel', 'Data Analysis'])

scores[row['Name']] = score


return scores


candidates_df = load_candidates()

candidate_scores = score_candidates(candidates_df)

print(candidate_scores)
```
```

This approach allowed HR teams to efficiently identify top candidates without the need to sift through countless resumes manually.

The educational sector has also embraced this integration to manage student records more effectively. An academic institution developed a comprehensive system using Python scripts to automate grade entry from multiple sources into a centralized Excel file. By connecting directly with their student information system via APIs, they significantly reduced administrative workload while ensuring grades were promptly updated.

Here's an example script demonstrating how grades could be pulled from an API:

```python
import requests

import pandas as pd
```
```

```
\#\# Function to fetch grades from an API

def fetch_grades(api_url):

response = requests.get(api_url)

return response.json()


grades_data                =                fetch_grades('https://
api.educationinstitution.edu/grades')

grades_df = pd.DataFrame(grades_data)

grades_df.to_excel('student_grades.xlsx', index=False)
```
```

This automation not only improved accuracy but also provided timely insights into student performance metrics.

As we've explored these examples across various industries —from retail to HR and education—it's clear that the integration of Python with Excel empowers organizations to unlock new efficiencies and capabilities. This flexibility means that no matter your field or specific challenges, innovative solutions are waiting to be discovered.

Reflect on your own workflows. Are there areas where repetitive tasks consume valuable time, or where manual processes might introduce errors? Embracing Python's capabilities can enable you to streamline operations while enhancing overall productivity. The tools are readily available; now is the time to explore how you can leverage them effectively in your context. What new opportunities will you uncover by integrating Python into your Excel workflows?
```

CHAPTER 10:
WEB SCRAPING
AND EXCEL

Introduction to Web Scraping

Web scraping has become a vital technique in data analysis, enabling users to effortlessly extract large volumes of information from websites. Its true value lies in the ability to access data that may be challenging or even impossible to gather otherwise. Many organizations now rely on web scraping to inform strategic decisions, enhance market research, and monitor competitor activities.

Take this example, imagine a financial analyst tasked with tracking daily stock prices from various sources. Manually checking multiple websites can be time-consuming and prone to errors. By automating this process with Python scripts, analysts can save hours each week and improve accuracy. Utilizing libraries such as BeautifulSoup and Requests, they can establish a robust pipeline for collecting and processing real-time data.

Consider this simple example that fetches stock prices from a hypothetical finance website:

```python
import requests
from bs4 import BeautifulSoup

\#\# Function to scrape stock price
def get_stock_price(symbol):
url = f'https://www.examplefinance.com/stocks/symbol'
response = requests.get(url)
soup = BeautifulSoup(response.text, 'html.parser')

price = soup.find('div', class_='stock-price').text
return price.strip()

\#\# Get stock price for a specific company
stock_symbol = 'AAPL'
current_price = get_stock_price(stock_symbol)
print(f'The current price of stock_symbol is current_price')
```

This script offers a straightforward method for acquiring live stock data. By integrating such tools into their workflows, analysts can remain informed without the burden of manual checks.

Web scraping's utility extends well beyond finance; businesses in various industries harness it for numerous purposes. For example, e-commerce platforms often track competitor pricing and product availability through automated scraping processes. This capability allows them to adapt their strategies in real time based on market fluctuations or competitor actions. By consistently collecting and analyzing this data in Excel, businesses can maintain a competitive edge and respond swiftly to changing conditions.

Here's an example that demonstrates how to collect product prices from an e-commerce site:

```python
import requests

from bs4 import BeautifulSoup


def get_product_prices(category_url):

response = requests.get(category_url)

soup = BeautifulSoup(response.text, 'html.parser')


products = soup.find_all('div', class_='product')

prices =


for product in products:

name = product.find('h2', class_='product-name').text.strip()

price        =        product.find('span',        class_='product-price').text.strip()

prices[name] = price


return prices
```

```
category_url    =    'https://www.exampleecommerce.com/
category/laptops'

product_prices = get_product_prices(category_url)

print(product_prices)
```
```

Once the data is extracted using these scripts and stored in Excel, businesses can analyze trends over time or visualize pricing strategy changes through charts and graphs.

And, web scraping finds its place in academia as well. Research scholars frequently scrape articles from online databases to compile literature reviews or bibliographies efficiently. This technique enables them to track relevant publications quickly without getting bogged down by repetitive tasks.

For example, here's how one could scrape academic article titles from a research database:

```python
import requests

from bs4 import BeautifulSoup


def scrape_academic_titles(url):

response = requests.get(url)

soup = BeautifulSoup(response.text, 'html.parser')


titles = []

for title in soup.find_all('h3', class_='article-title'):
```
```

```
titles.append(title.text.strip())

return titles

research_url = 'https://www.exampleacademic.com/recent-papers'
titles_list = scrape_academic_titles(research_url)
print(titles_list)
```
` ` `

Once these titles are collected, they can be organized and analyzed in Excel to identify trends or gaps in current research topics.

As we explore web scraping techniques throughout this guide, our focus will remain on seamlessly integrating these practices with Python and Excel workflows. The potential applications are vast; whether you're looking to enhance business intelligence, streamline research projects, or keep tabs on industry movements, mastering web scraping equips you with the tools to access information efficiently.

the power of web scraping lies not just in data collection but in transforming that data into actionable insights that drive decision-making. As you reflect on your objectives—whether monitoring trends or automating report generation—the possibilities expand beyond traditional methods. Embrace the innovations at your fingertips; leverage Python's capabilities alongside Excel's analytical features to maximize your impact in your professional endeavors.

Setting Up BeautifulSoup and Requests

To fully harness the power of web scraping, setting up the right tools is essential. Two libraries that stand out in the

Python ecosystem for this purpose are BeautifulSoup and Requests. These libraries are fundamental for anyone serious about extracting data from the web, offering intuitive interfaces for handling HTML and making HTTP requests.

Let's begin with the installation process. If you haven't installed these libraries yet, using pip is a straightforward approach. Simply open your terminal or command prompt and run:

```bash
pip install beautifulsoup4 requests
```

This command installs both BeautifulSoup and Requests, making them available for use in your Python scripts. With these libraries ready to go, you can start leveraging their functionalities to extract data from websites.

The Requests library plays a pivotal role in sending HTTP requests to retrieve web content. Its user-friendly design allows you to focus on what matters most: obtaining the data you need. For example, fetching a webpage's HTML can be accomplished with just a single line of code:

```python
import requests

response = requests.get('https://www.example.com')

html_content = response.text
```

In this snippet, we fetch the HTML content of the specified URL. If the request is successful (indicated by a status code of 200), the variable html_content will contain the website's markup, ready to be parsed by BeautifulSoup.

Next, we turn to BeautifulSoup, which transforms this raw HTML into a more navigable structure. This transformation allows you to easily search for elements using various methods such as .find() and .find_all(). Here's how to use it alongside Requests:

```python
from bs4 import BeautifulSoup

\#\# Fetch HTML content
response = requests.get('https://www.example.com')
soup = BeautifulSoup(response.text, 'html.parser')

\#\# Find a specific element
element = soup.find('h1')
print(element.text)
```

In this example, we retrieve the text of the first <h1> element found on the page. BeautifulSoup's ability to query elements based on tags, classes, and other attributes is one of its significant strengths.

While scraping, it's important to consider ethical guidelines and legal restrictions. Always check a website's robots.txt file to understand its scraping policies. Take this example, if you're interested in scraping data from 'https://www.example.com', you can visit 'https://www.example.com/robots.txt' to see if this action is permitted.

Now, let's take our exploration a step further by looking at a practical example where we combine both libraries to scrape product details from an e-commerce website. Suppose you're tasked with gathering information about laptops listed on a site:

```python
import requests
from bs4 import BeautifulSoup

def scrape_laptops(url):
response = requests.get(url)
soup = BeautifulSoup(response.text, 'html.parser')

laptops = []
for item in soup.find_all('div', class_='product-item'):
name = item.find('h2', class_='product-title').text.strip()
price = item.find('span', class_='price').text.strip()
laptops.append('name': name, 'price': price)

return laptops

laptop_url    =    'https://www.exampleecommerce.com/laptops'
laptop_data = scrape_laptops(laptop_url)
print(laptop_data)
```

In this function, we send a GET request to the specified laptop URL, parse the returned HTML using BeautifulSoup, and extract each product's name and price. The results are stored in a list of dictionaries—an excellent format for further analysis or export to Excel.

After you've scraped your desired data, you might want to save it for future use or analysis. Converting the collected information into an Excel file is seamless with Python's Pandas library. Here's how to do that:

```python
import pandas as pd


\#\# Assuming laptop_data holds our scraped laptop details

df = pd.DataFrame(laptop_data)

df.to_excel('laptop_prices.xlsx', index=False)
```

This code snippet creates a DataFrame from the list of dictionaries and exports it as an Excel file named laptop_prices.xlsx. Having your scraped data in Excel allows you to leverage additional analysis or visualizations using Excel's powerful features.

As we delve deeper into web scraping throughout this guide, mastering BeautifulSoup and Requests will serve as your foundation. These tools empower you not only to gather data but also to convert that information into meaningful insights that can influence strategic decisions across various fields—from business intelligence and marketing analytics to academic research.

Taking the time to understand these libraries will set you on a path toward developing sophisticated web scraping solutions tailored to your needs. As opportunities arise for automating data collection or enhancing research methodologies, your skills in using Python alongside these libraries will become invaluable. Embrace the learning process; each scrape brings you closer to becoming proficient at efficiently harnessing web data.

Fetching Live Data to Excel

Fetching live data from the web into Excel opens up a wealth of opportunities for data analysis and informed decision-making. With the ability to extract real-time information, professionals can quickly adapt to market fluctuations, monitor competitors, and gather valuable insights for research. By harnessing the power of BeautifulSoup and Requests, we can seamlessly tap into this potential.

To illustrate this process, let's say you're interested in tracking stock prices from a financial news website. The first step is to fetch the HTML content of the webpage that displays the stock data. This can be accomplished using the Requests library, as demonstrated in the following example:

```python
import requests

url = 'https://www.examplefinancialnews.com/stocks'

response = requests.get(url)

if response.status_code == 200:

html_content = response.text

else:

print("Failed to retrieve data")
```

In this code snippet, we begin by checking whether our request was successful by looking at the status code. A status code of 200 indicates success; any other code suggests an issue with retrieving the data. Once we have access to the HTML content, we can move on to parsing it with BeautifulSoup.

Next, we use BeautifulSoup to navigate through the fetched HTML and extract relevant stock information. Take this example, if each stock's details are contained within a <div> element with a specific class name, we can proceed as follows:

```python
from bs4 import BeautifulSoup

soup = BeautifulSoup(html_content, 'html.parser')

stocks = []
for item in soup.find_all('div', class_='stock-item'):
name = item.find('h2', class_='stock-name').text.strip()
price = item.find('span', class_='stock-price').text.strip()
stocks.append('name': name, 'price': price)
```

Here, we loop through all <div> elements representing individual stocks. By utilizing .find() methods on each item, we efficiently extract both the stock name and its price. This structured approach organizes our scraped data into a list of dictionaries—a format that's perfect for further analysis.

Once you've gathered your desired stock information, consider how best to store it for analysis or reporting purposes. Converting your list of dictionaries into an Excel file using Pandas simplifies this task:

```python
import pandas as pd

df = pd.DataFrame(stocks)
df.to_excel('stock_prices.xlsx', index=False)
```

This code snippet creates a DataFrame from our scraped stock data and saves it as stock_prices.xlsx. The resulting Excel file allows for additional manipulation or visualization using Excel's built-in features—ideal for presenting findings during meetings or reporting sessions.

This entire process showcases how accessible web scraping can be when paired with Python libraries like Requests and BeautifulSoup. With these tools at your disposal, you can automate data collection tasks that would otherwise be time-consuming and prone to errors if done manually.

As you refine your web scraping techniques, it's important to remain mindful of ethical considerations. Always check a website's terms of service before scraping their content and respect any limitations specified in their robots.txt files. This mindfulness not only safeguards your efforts but also nurtures trust between data collectors and website owners.

Through diligent practice and experimentation with different sites and types of data, you'll develop robust skills that transform your approach to information gathering in your professional environment. Whether you're tracking live stock prices or collecting product details from e-commerce platforms, each successful scrape empowers you with timely insights that facilitate informed decision-making.

As you embark on this journey of fetching live data into Excel via Python, take pride in mastering these techniques—your ability to convert real-time web information into actionable intelligence will distinguish you as a leader in your field.

Cleaning Web Data with Python

Cleaning web data is an essential step in the data analysis workflow, particularly after collecting live data. Raw data acquired through web scraping often contains inconsistencies, irrelevant information, and formatting issues that can obstruct effective analysis. By utilizing Python's robust data manipulation libraries, you can refine and cleanse this data efficiently, making it ready for deeper insights.

Let's explore the cleaning process with practical examples. After gathering stock prices, you may discover that some entries contain extraneous characters or are missing values entirely. For example, stock prices might include currency symbols or commas (like "(1,234.56")), which need to be removed to convert them into a numeric format suitable for calculations. Here's how you can achieve this using Pandas:

```python
import pandas as pd


\#\# Assume 'stocks' is your list of dictionaries collected from web scraping
df = pd.DataFrame(stocks)


\#\# Clean the stock price column
df['price'] = df['price'].replace('\\)': ", ',': ", regex=True).astype(float)
```

In this code snippet, we use regular expressions to replace dollar signs and commas before converting the 'price' column to a float data type. This transformation allows for numerical operations such as calculations or aggregations later in your analysis workflow.

Another common issue you may encounter is missing values within your dataset. To address these gaps effectively, you can either fill them with a default value or drop any rows that contain nulls, depending on your specific needs:

```python
\#\# Fill missing prices with the average price

average_price = df['price'].mean()

df['price'].fillna(average_price, inplace=True)


\#\# Alternatively, drop rows with missing values

df.dropna(subset=['name', 'price'], inplace=True)
```

This example showcases two strategies: one that fills in missing price entries with the average of available prices and another that removes rows lacking essential information altogether. The choice of approach depends on the context of your analysis and how you prefer to handle incomplete records.

In addition to addressing missing values and formatting issues, it's crucial to eliminate duplicates from your dataset. When scraping multiple pages or websites for information, it's easy to inadvertently capture repeated entries. Removing duplicates ensures that each data point is unique and reliable:

```python
\#\# Remove duplicate stock entries based on name

df.drop_duplicates(subset='name',                    keep='first',
```

inplace=True)

` ` `

With this command, we remove duplicate stocks while retaining the first occurrence of each entry based on their names. This process not only preserves data integrity but also simplifies subsequent analysis stages.

Once your data is cleaned and organized in Pandas, exporting it back to Excel is straightforward. You can easily save DataFrames as Excel files using to_excel(), allowing you to specify additional options for formatting and organization that enhance readability when presenting your findings.

Beyond cleaning techniques, it's also important to emphasize documentation during this process. Keeping track of changes—whether through comments in your code or a separate log—can be invaluable for future reference or collaboration with others.

As you refine your cleaning techniques further, remember that each dataset presents unique challenges and idiosyncrasies. Developing an intuition for recognizing potential pitfalls will empower you to handle varying formats and structures with confidence.

By mastering the art of cleaning web-sourced data through Python's extensive libraries like Pandas, you not only set yourself up for successful analyses but also enhance decision-making capabilities across projects. these efforts will elevate your skills and contribute to more robust insights drawn from high-quality datasets.

Updating Excel with Real-time Data

Updating Excel with real-time data can significantly enhance your analysis and decision-making capabilities. Imagine needing to track stock prices, weather updates, or social media metrics; having that information automatically reflected in your spreadsheets not only saves time but also ensures accuracy. This integration can be seamlessly achieved using Python.

To get started, you'll want to utilize the pandas library along with requests, which allows you to fetch data from APIs. Take this example, in the financial sector, access to live stock price data can make or break investment decisions. A straightforward way to illustrate this is by using the Alpha Vantage API for stock market data. First, if you haven't already, install the necessary packages:

```bash
pip install pandas requests
```

Once installed, you can write a script that pulls in real-time stock data. Below is a practical code snippet demonstrating how to retrieve current stock prices:

```python
import pandas as pd

import requests


\#\# Replace 'YOUR_API_KEY' with your actual Alpha Vantage API key

API_KEY = 'YOUR_API_KEY'

symbol = 'AAPL' \# Example: Apple Inc.

url = f'https://www.alphavantage.co/query?function=TIME_SERIES_INTRADAY&symbol=symbol&interval=1min&apikey=API_KEY'


response = requests.get(url)

data = response.json()
```

```
\#\# Extracting the latest price information
latest_time = list(data['Time Series (1min)'].keys())[0]
latest_data = data['Time Series (1min)'][latest_time]
latest_price = float(latest_data['1. open'])

print(f'The latest price of symbol is: \(latest_price')
```

This simple program retrieves the current price of Apple Inc. stocks from the Alpha Vantage API and prints it out. Now that we have real-time data flowing in, let's explore how to update an Excel sheet with this information.

For manipulating Excel files easily, you can use the openpyxl library. If you're not familiar with it yet, install it using:

```bash
pip install openpyxl
```

Next, let's create a function that updates our Excel workbook with the fetched stock price:

```python
from openpyxl import Workbook


def update_excel(price):
\#\# Creating a new workbook and activating the current sheet
workbook = Workbook()
sheet = workbook.active
```

```
\#\# Setting headers
sheet['A1'] = 'Stock Symbol'
sheet['B1'] = 'Current Price'

\#\# Inserting the data
sheet['A2'] = symbol
sheet['B2'] = price

\#\# Saving the workbook
workbook.save('Stock_Price_Updates.xlsx')

update_excel(latest_price)
```

In this code, we create a new Excel workbook, set up headers for stock symbols and prices, insert our fetched price, and save the workbook. Running this script repeatedly updates your Excel file with the latest stock price each time.

For applications that require continuous updates—such as tracking prices every minute—you might want to introduce a loop with delays:

```python
import time

while True:
    response = requests.get(url)
```

```
data = response.json()

latest_time = list(data['Time Series (1min)'].keys())[0]

latest_data = data['Time Series (1min)'][latest_time]

latest_price = float(latest_data['1. open'])

update_excel(latest_price)

print(f'Updated symbol price: \)latest_price')

\#\# Sleep for 60 seconds before fetching new data

time.sleep(60)
` ` `
```

This code continuously fetches and updates your Excel file every minute with live data.

Incorporating real-time updates can transform your workflow from static reporting to dynamic analytics. However, be mindful of API limits; many services restrict the number of calls per minute or day, so keep this in mind when designing your application.

Using Python for real-time updates not only enhances your efficiency but also provides a competitive edge in making timely decisions based on accurate data. As you integrate these techniques into your projects, consider how other types of real-time data—such as weather forecasts or sales metrics—can enrich your analyses and improve responsiveness within your organization.

Handling API Data and Excel

APIs, or Application Programming Interfaces, act as vital connections between different software applications, enabling seamless communication. This capability allows you to access extensive data sources for your Excel applications, ranging from financial metrics to social media analytics. However, working with API data does require some technical skills, especially when integrating that information directly into Excel.

Once you familiarize yourself with the basics of API interaction, you can utilize libraries like requests in Python to facilitate the data retrieval process. Take this example, let's revisit our earlier example involving stock prices from Alpha Vantage. We'll delve into how to effectively parse that data and incorporate it into your workflows.

Understanding the JSON format is essential since most APIs return data structured in this way. After fetching the response using requests, you'll need to navigate through the JSON object to extract the relevant information. In our case, once you have the latest price data, you can refine it for analysis in Excel.

Here's an improved version of our previous script that includes robust handling of API responses:

```python
import json

response = requests.get(url)

\#\# Checking if the response was successful
if response.status_code == 200:
data = response.json()
```

```python
\#\# Check for error messages in the response

if 'Error Message' in data:

print(f"Error fetching data: data['Error Message']")

else:

latest_time = list(data['Time Series (1min)'].keys())[0]

latest_data = data['Time Series (1min)'][latest_time]

latest_price = float(latest_data['1. open'])

print(f'The latest price of symbol is: \(latest_price')

else:

print(f"Failed to retrieve data: response.status_code")
```
` ` `

This code snippet introduces error-checking features to ensure that your application behaves predictably, even when issues arise during the API request—such as invalid requests or exceeded rate limits. Building resilient applications like this is essential for long-term automation.

Next, let's consider a critical aspect: efficiently updating existing Excel files instead of creating new ones each time. The openpyxl library enables you to manipulate existing workbooks effectively, allowing you to append new data without losing previously entered information:

` ` `python

```python
from openpyxl import load_workbook


def update_existing_excel(price):

try:
```

HAYDEN VAN DER POST

```
\#\# Load an existing workbook
workbook = load_workbook('Stock_Price_Updates.xlsx')
sheet = workbook.active

\#\# Find the next empty row
next_row = sheet.max_row + 1

\#\# Inserting new data
sheet[f'Anext_row'] = symbol
sheet[f'Bnext_row'] = price

\#\# Saving the workbook with updates
workbook.save('Stock_Price_Updates.xlsx')

except FileNotFoundError:
print("Workbook not found, creating a new one.")
update_excel(price)  \# Create new file if not found

update_existing_excel(latest_price)
```
```

In this updated function, we first attempt to load an existing workbook. If that fails due to the file's absence, we revert to a previous function that creates a new workbook. This dual approach provides flexibility in managing your data storage.

As you become more proficient at handling API data and integrating it into Excel, consider exploring
```

additional libraries such as pandas. This powerful library can significantly simplify your data handling and offer functionalities for more complex analyses. Take this example, imagine fetching multiple stock prices simultaneously and compiling them into a structured DataFrame before exporting everything into Excel.

```python
import pandas as pd


def fetch_multiple_stocks(symbols):

prices =


for symbol in symbols:

url = f'https://www.alphavantage.co/query?function=TIME_SERIES_INTRADAY&symbol=symbol&interval=1min&apikey=API_KEY'


response = requests.get(url)


if response.status_code == 200:

data = response.json()

if 'Time Series (1min)' in data:

latest_time = list(data['Time Series (1min)'].keys())[0]

latest_data = data['Time Series (1min)'][latest_time]

prices[symbol] = float(latest_data['1. open'])

else:

print(f"Error fetching symbol: data.get('Error Message',
```

'Unknown error')")

return prices

\#\# Example usage

symbols_to_track = ['AAPL', 'GOOGL', 'MSFT']

stock_prices = fetch_multiple_stocks(symbols_to_track)

print(stock_prices)

` ` `

With this function, you can easily collect real-time prices for various stocks and store them in a dictionary for further manipulation or display.

Integrating these dynamic capabilities will undoubtedly enhance your analytical prowess within Excel. The flexibility offered by Python not only streamlines the handling of live API data but also empowers you to create sophisticated reporting tools tailored to your analytical needs. As you explore these techniques further, think about how they can be adapted across various domains—whether finance, e-commerce, or social media metrics—and consider the insights that could be unlocked through timely and accurate analysis.

Automating Web Scraping Tasks

Web scraping is an invaluable skill that can greatly enhance your data analysis capabilities in Excel. By automating the extraction of data from websites, you can efficiently gather large volumes of information and integrate it directly into your Excel models. This not only saves time but also uncovers new opportunities for insights.

To streamline the automation of web scraping tasks,

Python's libraries provide robust tools. A commonly used combination includes BeautifulSoup for parsing HTML and requests for fetching web pages. Let's walk through setting up a basic web scraper that retrieves data from a website and stores it in Excel.

First, make sure you have the necessary libraries installed:

```bash
pip install requests beautifulsoup4 openpyxl
```

For our example, we'll scrape product prices from an e-commerce site. While this scenario is hypothetical, it effectively demonstrates how you can adapt these techniques for practical applications. Here's how to get started:

```python
import requests

from bs4 import BeautifulSoup


def scrape_product_prices(url):

response = requests.get(url)

soup = BeautifulSoup(response.text, 'html.parser')


products = []


\#\# Assume each product is contained within a specific HTML structure

for item in soup.find_all('div', class_='product-item'):

name = item.find('h2', class_='product-title').text
```

```
price = item.find('span', class_='product-price').text

products.append((name, price))


return products


\#\# Example URL (replace with an actual e-commerce site)

url = 'https://www.example.com/products'

product_data = scrape_product_prices(url)

print(product_data)
```
```

In this script, we send a request to the target URL and use BeautifulSoup to parse the HTML content. The loop searches for all product items based on their class names, which may vary depending on the website's design. The gathered product names and prices are stored as tuples in a list.

After obtaining the scraped data, the next step is to save it in Excel. Building on our earlier functions with openpyxl, here's how to write that data into an Excel file:

```python
from openpyxl import Workbook


def save_to_excel(data):

workbook = Workbook()

sheet = workbook.active


\#\# Adding headers

sheet['A1'] = 'Product Name'
```
```

```
sheet['B1'] = 'Price'

\#\# Inserting product data into rows

for idx, (name, price) in enumerate(data, start=2):

sheet[f'Aidx'] = name

sheet[f'Bidx'] = price


workbook.save('Product_Prices.xlsx')


\#\# Saving scraped data to Excel

save_to_excel(product_data)
` ` `
```

This function initializes a new workbook, writes headers for product names and prices, and populates each row with the scraped information. The final result is saved as 'Product_Prices.xlsx'.

To ensure your scraper operates efficiently over time, consider implementing scheduling with tools like cron on Linux or Task Scheduler on Windows. This setup allows your script to run at specified intervals—whether daily or weekly—keeping your datasets current without manual effort.

While automating web scraping can yield impressive results, it's essential to respect ethical guidelines and legal restrictions surrounding these practices. Always check if a website permits scraping by reviewing its robots.txt file or terms of service. Adhering to these boundaries not only protects your work but also promotes responsible data practices.

With these automation strategies at your disposal, you will

be well-equipped to effectively harness real-time data from various online sources. This flexibility empowers you to stay ahead in a rapidly changing landscape where timely insights are often the key to success.

CHAPTER 11:
DATABASE INTEGRATION WITH PYTHON AND EXCEL

*Introduction to Databases
and Excel*

Web databases are essential in data management and analysis, especially when combined with Excel. By learning how to connect databases to Excel, you unlock a wealth of opportunities for efficient data manipulation and reporting. Whether you're accessing historical sales data, customer information, or real-time transaction records, this integration simplifies processes and enhances analytical capabilities.

Excel transcends its role as a mere spreadsheet tool; it also acts as a front-end interface for complex database systems like SQL. This connection allows users to execute queries directly, retrieve data, and analyze extensive datasets that would otherwise be challenging to manage within Excel alone. That's why, decision-makers can quickly and efficiently access the information they need.

To begin integrating databases with Excel, it's crucial to understand the common types of databases used alongside it. Relational databases such as MySQL, PostgreSQL, and Microsoft SQL Server are particularly popular due to their structured data storage and robust querying capabilities. For example, let's explore how to establish a connection between Python and a SQL database using SQLAlchemy, a powerful library designed for object-oriented interaction with relational databases.

First, you'll need to install the necessary libraries. If you haven't done so yet, run the following command:

```bash
pip install sqlalchemy pymysql openpyxl
```

In this example, we'll connect to a MySQL database to extract sales data. Here's how to initiate that connection and perform basic operations like querying:

```python
from sqlalchemy import create_engine

import pandas as pd


\#\# Replace with your actual credentials and database details
DATABASE_TYPE = 'mysql'

DBAPI = 'pymysql'

USER = 'your_username'

PASSWORD = 'your_password'

HOST = 'localhost' \# or your database host
```

```
PORT = '3306' \# default port for MySQL

DATABASE = 'your_database'


\#\# Creating the connection string

connection_string      =      f"DATABASE_TYPE+DBAPI://
USER:PASSWORD@HOST:PORT/DATABASE

engine = create_engine(connection_string)


\#\# Example query to fetch sales data

query = "SELECT * FROM sales_data


\#\# Fetching data into a DataFrame

sales_data = pd.read_sql(query, engine)

print(sales_data.head())
` ` `
```

This code snippet establishes a connection using your database credentials and retrieves sales data into a Pandas DataFrame. The convenience of pd.read_sql() allows you to execute any valid SQL query directly from Python while automatically managing the connection lifecycle.

After retrieving your data into a DataFrame, integrating it with Excel is straightforward. Building on our earlier discussions about openpyxl, you can easily export this DataFrame to an Excel workbook:

```
` ` `python

def save_to_excel(dataframe):

filename = 'Sales_Data.xlsx'
```

```
dataframe.to_excel(filename, index=False)


save_to_excel(sales_data)
` ` `
```

This method creates an Excel file containing all your queried sales data—ready for further analysis or reporting in Excel's familiar environment.

To streamline your workflow even more, consider automating these queries based on schedules or triggers using Python scripts along with task scheduling tools. Automation enables periodic updates of datasets without manual intervention, ensuring your reports remain current with minimal effort.

As you harness these capabilities, it's important to prioritize data integrity and security best practices when working with databases. Always handle sensitive information in compliance with regulations such as GDPR or HIPAA if applicable. This not only safeguards your organization but also fosters trust in the data-driven processes you implement.

As you enhance your skills in integrating Python with databases and Excel, reflect on the insights that this powerful combination can provide. Effectively analyzing large volumes of structured data empowers stakeholders across various departments—from finance to marketing—to make informed decisions based on real-time analytics.

By mastering these techniques, you position yourself at the forefront of modern data management strategies where agility and insight generation are crucial. The collaboration between Python and Excel evolves from simple convenience into a formidable toolkit tailored for today's fast-paced business environment.

Setting Up SQLAlchemy and SQLite

Integrating SQLAlchemy with SQLite unlocks a wealth of opportunities for managing and analyzing data directly within Python, making it a crucial skill for any data analyst. SQLite's simplicity and lightweight design make it especially beneficial for smaller projects or scenarios where a full database server isn't necessary. Fortunately, setting up SQLAlchemy to work with SQLite involves just a few straightforward steps.

To begin, you'll need to install SQLAlchemy if you haven't already. This can easily be accomplished using pip:

```bash
pip install sqlalchemy
```

After the library is installed, you can create an SQLite database. Unlike traditional database systems that require a server setup, SQLite allows you to create a database file directly on your filesystem. Let's explore how to create a simple SQLite database and connect to it using SQLAlchemy.

```python
from sqlalchemy import create_engine


\#\# Create an SQLite database (this will create 'example.db' in your current directory)

engine = create_engine('sqlite:///example.db')
```

This line of code establishes a connection to an SQLite database named example.db. If the file doesn't already exist, it will be created automatically.

Next, we'll set up a table in this database to store sample data.

For our demonstration, we will use the following schema for a sales data table:

```python
from sqlalchemy import Column, Integer, String, Float
from sqlalchemy.ext.declarative import declarative_base
from sqlalchemy.orm import sessionmaker

Base = declarative_base()

class SalesData(Base):
    __tablename__ = 'sales_data'

    id = Column(Integer, primary_key=True)
    product_name = Column(String)
    quantity_sold = Column(Integer)
    revenue = Column(Float)

\#\# Create all tables in the engine (this will create the 'sales_data' table)
Base.metadata.create_all(engine)

\#\# Create a session
Session = sessionmaker(bind=engine)
session = Session()
```

In this snippet, we've defined a SalesData class that

represents the structure of our table. The create_all method then creates the specified table within our SQLite database.

With our table set up, let's proceed to populate it with some sample data. You can add records using the session object as follows:

```python
```python
\#\# Adding sample data

new_sale        =        SalesData(product_name='Widget', quantity_sold=100, revenue=299.99)

session.add(new_sale)


\#\# Committing the transaction

session.commit()
```
```

This code inserts a new record for 'Widget' into our sales data table and commits the transaction. You can easily add multiple records by repeating this process or utilizing a loop for batch entries.

Once your data is safely stored in the SQLite database, retrieving it is equally straightforward. Here's how you can query this data and load it into a Pandas DataFrame for analysis:

```python
```python
import pandas as pd


\#\# Querying data from sales_data table

query_result = session.query(SalesData).all()
```
```

\#\# Converting query result to DataFrame

sales_df = pd.DataFrame([(d.id, d.product_name, d.quantity_sold, d.revenue) for d in query_result],

columns=['ID', 'Product Name', 'Quantity Sold', 'Revenue'])

print(sales_df)

` ` `

This snippet fetches all records from the sales_data table and converts them into a Pandas DataFrame for easier manipulation and visualization.

Integrating this workflow with Excel can significantly enhance your reporting capabilities. Exporting your DataFrame to Excel is simple:

` ` `python

def export_to_excel(dataframe):

filename = 'Sales_Data.xlsx'

dataframe.to_excel(filename, index=False)

export_to_excel(sales_df)

` ` `

With just this function call, you can generate an Excel file containing your sales data, ready for further analysis or presentation.

As you deepen your understanding of SQLAlchemy and SQLite alongside Excel integration, consider automating these tasks through scripts that manage repetitive actions —such as scheduled exports or periodic dataset updates. Automation reduces manual effort while ensuring timely access to insights derived from your databases.

While using databases like SQLite through SQLAlchemy streamlines many processes in Excel-based analysis, it's essential to maintain best practices regarding security and data integrity. Make sure sensitive information is handled appropriately and comply with relevant regulations to protect your organization's data.

In today's rapidly evolving landscape of data management tools and techniques, mastering SQLAlchemy with SQLite provides you with vital skills that elevate your analytical capabilities beyond basic spreadsheet operations. By leveraging these tools alongside Python and Excel, you'll position yourself at the forefront of innovative solutions tailored to address complex business challenges effectively.

Connecting Python to SQL Databases

Connecting Python to SQL databases opens up a wealth of opportunities for data management and analysis, enabling you to leverage the strengths of both Python and SQL in your projects. This integration allows for seamless data retrieval, manipulation, and storage, enhancing your workflow efficiency significantly. With tools like SQLAlchemy, engaging with databases becomes both straightforward and effective.

To begin connecting Python with a SQL database, the first step is to ensure that SQLAlchemy is installed. If you haven't done so yet, you can easily install it using pip:

```bash
pip install sqlalchemy
```

After installing SQLAlchemy, establishing a connection to your database of choice is simple. Whether you're working with SQLite for smaller projects or opting for more robust systems like PostgreSQL or MySQL for larger applications, the process remains intuitive. For example, here's how to connect to an SQLite database:

```python
from sqlalchemy import create_engine

\#\# Establishing a connection to the SQLite database

engine = create_engine('sqlite:///example.db')
```

This command sets up a connection to example.db, creating it if it doesn't already exist. Understanding this foundational step is crucial as it serves as the gateway for all subsequent operations on your database.

Next, let's outline the data structure you'll be working with by creating a table. For illustration purposes, we'll define a simple user table to store user information. This involves creating a class that inherits from SQLAlchemy's declarative base:

```python
from sqlalchemy.ext.declarative import declarative_base

from sqlalchemy import Column, Integer, String

Base = declarative_base()

class User(Base):
    __tablename__ = 'users'

    id = Column(Integer, primary_key=True)
    username = Column(String)
```

```
email = Column(String)
```

\#\# Create all tables in the engine (this will create the 'users' table)

```
Base.metadata.create_all(engine)
```

` ` `

In this snippet, we've created a User class that defines the structure of our users table. Using Base.metadata.create_all(engine), we efficiently construct this table within your SQLite database.

Populating the table with data is just as straightforward. You can leverage session objects to add records seamlessly:

` ` `python

```
from sqlalchemy.orm import sessionmaker
```

\#\# Creating a session

```
Session = sessionmaker(bind=engine)
session = Session()
```

\#\# Adding sample users

```
new_user              =              User(username='john_doe',
email='john@example.com')
session.add(new_user)
```

\#\# Committing the transaction

```
session.commit()
```

` ` `

This example illustrates how to insert a new user record into the users table. You can follow this pattern to add multiple entries or handle batch processes efficiently.

Retrieving data from your database introduces another layer of functionality. Take this example, let's fetch user records and convert them into a Pandas DataFrame for easier manipulation:

```python
import pandas as pd


\#\# Querying all users from the users table

query_result = session.query(User).all()


\#\# Converting query result to DataFrame

user_df    =    pd.DataFrame([(user.id,    user.username, user.email) for user in query_result],

columns=['ID', 'Username', 'Email'])

print(user_df)
```

This code collects all user records and converts them into a Pandas DataFrame named user_df, enabling convenient analysis and reporting.

To further enhance your reporting capabilities, integrating this process with Excel can be incredibly beneficial. Exporting your DataFrame directly into an Excel file is seamless:

```python
def export_to_excel(dataframe):
```

```
filename = 'Users_Data.xlsx'

dataframe.to_excel(filename, index=False)


export_to_excel(user_df)
```
` ` `

By simply invoking this function, you generate an Excel file containing all user data—ready for distribution or further analysis.

As you dive deeper into using SQLAlchemy with databases like SQLite alongside Python and Excel, think about how automation could streamline your workflows. Automate repetitive tasks such as periodic data updates or scheduled exports using tailored scripts that meet your specific requirements.

It's also important to remain mindful of best practices regarding data integrity and security when managing databases. Ensure sensitive information is properly protected and adhere to compliance regulations relevant to your organization's needs.

Mastering connections between Python and SQL databases significantly enriches your skill set—empowering you not only to manipulate large datasets effectively but also providing insights that drive business decisions forward. By blending these technologies with Excel's familiar interface, you position yourself at the forefront of modern data analysis techniques that can greatly influence your professional landscape.

Importing Database Data to Excel

Integrating database data into Excel significantly enhances the functionality of both platforms, enabling users to leverage extensive datasets while taking advantage of Excel's intuitive interface for analysis and reporting. This synergy allows for the transformation of raw data into actionable insights, streamlining the often cumbersome processes associated with manual entry.

To start importing data from a SQL database into Excel, we can utilize Python's powerful libraries in conjunction with a connection established using SQLAlchemy. After setting up your SQL connection and populating your database with the necessary data, the next step is to execute effective queries.

For example, let's consider you have a table named sales in your database that records transaction details. You can construct a structured query to retrieve this information:

```python
\#\# Importing the required library

from sqlalchemy import select


\#\# Defining a class for the sales table

class Sale(Base):

__tablename__ = 'sales'


id = Column(Integer, primary_key=True)

product_name = Column(String)

quantity_sold = Column(Integer)

sale_date = Column(String)


\#\# Executing a query to fetch sales records

query_sales = select(Sale)

sales_data = session.execute(query_sales).scalars().all()
```

` ` `

In this code snippet, we define our Sale class to represent the sales table and run a query to retrieve all records. The method scalars().all() efficiently gathers all results.

Next, we can convert this data into a Pandas DataFrame, which simplifies manipulation and prepares it for export to Excel:

` ` `python

\#\# Creating a DataFrame from sales records

sales_df = pd.DataFrame([(sale.id, sale.product_name, sale.quantity_sold, sale.sale_date) for sale in sales_data],

columns=['ID', 'Product Name', 'Quantity Sold', 'Sale Date'])

print(sales_df)

` ` `

Once the DataFrame is ready, exporting this information to an Excel file is straightforward:

` ` `python

def export_sales_to_excel(dataframe):

filename = 'Sales_Data.xlsx'

dataframe.to_excel(filename, index=False)

export_sales_to_excel(sales_df)

` ` `

Running this function generates an Sales_Data.xlsx file containing all transaction details from your SQL database— ideal for further analysis or distribution. The combination of Python's processing power with Excel's reporting capabilities significantly boosts productivity.

Now imagine automating this entire workflow: you could set up Python scripts to run on a schedule, pulling fresh data from your database and exporting it directly into updated Excel reports. Libraries like schedule or APScheduler allow you to specify times or intervals for these scripts to run automatically.

Also, consider how visualizations can enhance your reports. By utilizing libraries such as Matplotlib or Seaborn within Python, you can create engaging charts based on your DataFrame before exporting them directly into Excel:

```python
import matplotlib.pyplot as plt


\#\# Example visualization: total quantity sold by product

quantity_sold_summary = sales_df.groupby('Product Name')['Quantity Sold'].sum()

quantity_sold_summary.plot(kind='bar')

plt.title('Total Quantity Sold by Product')

plt.ylabel('Quantity Sold')

plt.xlabel('Product Name')

plt.tight_layout()

plt.savefig('quantity_sold_summary.png') \# Save the figure


\#\# This image can be integrated into your exported Excel file if needed.
```

This snippet generates a visual summary of quantities sold per product. Saving the figure enables later integration into any Excel report—transforming your data from merely informative to visually compelling.

To ensure smooth integration across these various steps—querying the database, manipulating data in Pandas, and exporting results—it's crucial to maintain modular code. This practice not only facilitates maintenance but also enhances readability by isolating distinct functionalities within functions or classes.

By adopting best practices—such as routinely validating data integrity and ensuring code efficiency—you position yourself as a proficient user capable of swiftly transforming complex datasets into organized insights. This skill is vital in today's fast-paced work environment where timely decision-making relies heavily on accurate and accessible information. Mastering these techniques not only boosts personal productivity but also significantly contributes to broader organizational goals.

Exporting Excel Data to Databases

Exporting data from Excel to databases marks a significant transformation in how businesses manage information, converting static spreadsheets into dynamic data management systems. As organizations increasingly depend on databases for storing and analyzing large volumes of data, the need for seamless integration between Excel and these systems has become crucial. This integration not only improves data accuracy but also streamlines workflows, facilitating more efficient decision-making.

To start exporting Excel data to a database, it's essential to have a solid understanding of your target database system—be it MySQL, PostgreSQL, or SQLite. Knowing how to connect and authenticate with your database is fundamental. Python's SQLAlchemy library greatly simplifies this process. Below is a basic example demonstrating how to establish your connection and prepare for the export:

```python
from sqlalchemy import create_engine

\#\# Setting up the database connection
DATABASE_TYPE = 'postgresql' \# Change as per your DB
USER = 'username'
PASSWORD = 'password'
HOST = 'localhost'
PORT = '5432'
DB_NAME = 'your_database'


\#\# Creating the connection string
connection_string          =          f"DATABASE_TYPE://
USER:PASSWORD@HOST:PORT/DB_NAME
engine = create_engine(connection_string)
```

Once you have established the connection, you can proceed to export data directly from an Excel file into your database. Take this example, consider you have an Excel file named Sales_Data.xlsx containing sales records. The next step is to read this file using Pandas and write its contents to your database.

Here's how you can achieve that:

```python
import pandas as pd

\#\# Reading the Excel file
```

```
excel_data = pd.read_excel('Sales_Data.xlsx')
```

\#\# Exporting DataFrame to SQL Database

```
excel_data.to_sql('sales',  con=engine,  if_exists='replace',
index=False)
```

` ` `

In this code snippet, the to_sql() method converts the DataFrame into a SQL table. The if_exists='replace' argument indicates that any existing table named sales will be replaced by the new data from the DataFrame. If you want to keep existing records while adding new ones, you can change this argument to append.

This flexible approach lends itself well to automation. Consider regularly scheduled reports generated in Excel that need to be uploaded back to your database. You can encapsulate this logic within a Python script that runs at specified intervals, ensuring your database remains current with the latest information.

And, it's prudent to implement validation steps before exporting data. You might want to confirm that all required fields are populated in your DataFrame and that their data types align with those defined in your database schema. A simple validation check can help prevent potential issues later on:

` ` `python

\#\# Validating required columns before export

```
required_columns = ['ID', 'Product Name', 'Quantity Sold',
'Sale Date']

missing_columns    =    set(required_columns)    -
set(excel_data.columns)
```

if missing_columns:

print(f"Missing columns: missing_columns")

else:

excel_data.to_sql('sales', con=engine, if_exists='replace', index=False)

` ` `

This snippet checks for any missing columns prior to export, offering immediate feedback so you can rectify issues before making updates to the database.

Beyond simple exports, consider leveraging SQL queries within Python for more complex operations. Instead of directly exporting raw data, you could aggregate or transform it first:

` ` `python

\#\# Example: Grouping sales data by product name and summing quantities sold

aggregated_data = excel_data.groupby('Product Name').agg('Quantity Sold': 'sum').reset_index()

\#\# Exporting aggregated results to the database

aggregated_data.to_sql('aggregated_sales', con=engine, if_exists='replace', index=False)

` ` `

This code snippet groups sales by product names and sums their quantities sold, providing a concise summary of key insights before storing them in your database.

As you further develop these export functionalities, keep performance considerations in mind. Large datasets can be unwieldy; optimizing read and write operations—such as chunking data or utilizing bulk inserts—can significantly enhance efficiency when handling extensive records.

By mastering these techniques, you'll not only streamline workflows but also uphold accuracy and integrity within your organization's data ecosystem. The interplay between Python and databases transcends mere data transfer; it fosters an environment where data-driven decisions can flourish seamlessly. By continually honing these skills, you position yourself as an invaluable asset in any analytical landscape, capable of harnessing the full potential of data across platforms.

Data Mapping and Transformation

Data mapping and transformation play a crucial role in optimizing the flow of information between systems. When integrating Excel with databases, it's essential not only to transfer data but also to translate it into formats that preserve its utility and accuracy. Whether handling sales figures, customer information, or inventory records, maintaining the meaning and relevance of data during this transfer is vital.

A solid understanding of both your Excel files and the target database schema is the first step in effective data mapping. This involves identifying which columns in Excel correspond to fields in the database. Take this example, consider an Excel file containing customer details with fields like CustomerID, Name, Email, and PurchaseDate. In your database, these fields may align with a similar schema or may require slight adjustments—such as converting date formats or ensuring names are properly capitalized.

Using Pandas can significantly streamline this mapping process. Imagine you have an Excel sheet structured like this:

| CustomerID | Name | Email | PurchaseDate |

| 1 | John Smith | john@example.com | 2023-10-01 |

| 2 | Jane Doe | jane@example.com | 2023-10-02 |

When loading this data into a DataFrame, it's crucial to ensure that each field matches the expected type in your database. For example, if your database requires PurchaseDate to be in datetime format, you should convert it upon import:

```python
import pandas as pd

\#\# Loading data from Excel
df = pd.read_excel('Customer_Data.xlsx')

\#\# Ensuring PurchaseDate is a datetime type
df['PurchaseDate'] = pd.to_datetime(df['PurchaseDate'])
```

This conversion not only aligns the data types but also helps prevent potential errors when executing SQL commands later.

After verifying that the data is correctly formatted, the next step is to transform it as needed before exporting it to your database. This might involve aggregating data or deriving new columns based on existing ones. Take this example, if you want to calculate how many days have passed since each customer's last purchase date and include this information in a new column:

```python
from datetime import datetime
```

\#\# Adding a new column for Days Since Last Purchase

df['DaysSinceLastPurchase'] = (datetime.now() - df['PurchaseDate']).dt.days
``` ` ` ` ```

Such transformations enrich your datasets, providing deeper insights once they are stored in a relational database.

Once your data is prepared, mapping it into the target tables becomes straightforward. Continuing with our customer example, suppose you wish to export this DataFrame into a table named Customers. Using SQLAlchemy alongside Pandas makes this process seamless:

` ` `python

from sqlalchemy import create_engine

\#\# Setting up the database connection

DATABASE_TYPE = 'postgresql'

USER = 'username'

PASSWORD = 'password'

HOST = 'localhost'

PORT = '5432'

DB_NAME = 'your_database'

connection_string = f"DATABASE_TYPE://USER:PASSWORD@HOST:PORT/DB_NAME

engine = create_engine(connection_string)
```

\#\# Exporting DataFrame to SQL Database

df.to_sql('Customers', con=engine, if_exists='replace', index=False)

` ` `

In this case, using if_exists='replace' means any existing table will be replaced—an important consideration for keeping your data fresh. If you frequently update records rather than replacing them entirely, using if_exists='append' ensures continuity without loss.

Validation after transformation but before exporting is often necessary. Checking for duplicates or confirming that all required columns have valid entries can prevent issues down the line:

` ` `python

\#\# Validating for duplicate CustomerIDs before export

if df['CustomerID'].duplicated().any():

print("Duplicate CustomerIDs found!")

else:

df.to_sql('Customers', con=engine, if_exists='replace', index=False)

` ` `

This proactive approach helps avoid complications from invalid entries entering your database.

As businesses grow and evolve, their datasets and schemas do as well. Regularly revisiting your mappings and transformations ensures they remain relevant; even small changes in source structures may necessitate larger adjustments downstream.

Mapping and transforming data between Excel and databases isn't merely about technical execution; it's about creating relationships between different systems while maintaining integrity throughout. As organizations increasingly depend on accurate insights derived from unified datasets across platforms, mastering these techniques empowers you to navigate complex workflows efficiently.

proficiency in mapping and transforming data solidifies your role as an essential contributor within any organization. It's not just about getting numbers right; it's about understanding their story and ensuring they drive meaningful action across teams.

Ensuring Data Integrity

Ensuring data integrity is a crucial aspect of working with Excel and Python, particularly when transferring information between systems or manipulating datasets. The accuracy and consistency of your data can profoundly influence decision-making processes; even a single erroneous entry can trigger a chain reaction of failures in reporting, analysis, and strategic initiatives.

To start, it's essential to establish clear protocols for validating data before processing or exporting it. This validation process should include checking for common issues such as duplicates, missing values, and incorrect formats. Take this example, when managing a customer database in Excel, ensuring that each CustomerID is unique is vital to prevent duplication across records. The Pandas library in Python can simplify this task significantly:

```python

import pandas as pd
```

```
\#\# Load data from Excel

df = pd.read_excel('Customer_Data.xlsx')


\#\# Check for duplicates

if df['CustomerID'].duplicated().any():

print("Warning: Duplicate CustomerIDs detected!")
```
` ` `

This code snippet effectively identifies duplicate entries, allowing you to address these issues before further processing the data. Maintaining unique identifiers is critical for preserving relational integrity when exporting to databases.

Next, it's important to tackle missing values—an issue that can compromise analyses if not addressed properly. In your customer information dataset, you may find rows lacking essential fields like Email or PurchaseDate. You can use Pandas to either intelligently fill these gaps or drop the affected entries entirely:

` ` `python
```
\#\# Drop rows where critical information is missing

df.dropna(subset=['Email', 'PurchaseDate'], inplace=True)
```
` ` `

In some scenarios, it may be more appropriate to fill in missing values rather than deleting entire rows. If your dataset permits, you could replace empty purchase dates with a default date or even today's date if it fits the context:

` ` `python
```
\#\# Filling missing PurchaseDate with today's date
```

```python
df['PurchaseDate'].fillna(pd.Timestamp('today'),
inplace=True)
```

Once you've addressed duplicates and missing values, validating the data types of each column becomes essential. This step ensures that data formats are compatible with any systems they will interact with later—such as databases that require specific field types.

Take this example, if your PurchaseDate needs to be in datetime format for SQL queries, confirming this alignment before uploading the dataset is crucial:

```python
\#\# Converting PurchaseDate to datetime format if not
already

df['PurchaseDate']    =    pd.to_datetime(df['PurchaseDate'],
errors='coerce')
```

Using errors='coerce' will convert invalid dates into NaT (Not a Time), making it easier to identify problematic entries.

After validating your dataset's integrity through these checks, consider implementing logging mechanisms to track changes made during data preparation. Maintaining logs helps trace modifications should questions arise about the dataset's history:

```python
\#\# Logging changes made during validation

with open('data_validation_log.txt', 'a') as log_file:

log_file.write(f"Processed    len(df)    records    on
pd.Timestamp.now()")
```

```
` ` `
```

This straightforward logging mechanism provides an ongoing record of actions taken—a valuable resource for audits or quality checks.

Another vital aspect is ensuring that all relevant business rules have been correctly applied to your dataset before final exportation. For example, if certain customers should only be included based on specific criteria—such as those who made purchases in the last year—you need to filter accordingly before transferring this refined dataset into your database:

```python
` ` `python

\#\# Filtering out customers who haven't made purchases in the last year

last_year = pd.Timestamp.now() - pd.DateOffset(years=1)

df = df[df['PurchaseDate'] >= last_year]

` ` `
```

Such filtering guarantees that only pertinent information flows into analytical models or reporting systems.

Finally, regularly revisiting your validation strategies fosters continuous improvement as new datasets evolve and organizational requirements change. Staying agile means being prepared to adapt your validation processes in response to shifts in business needs or emerging data quality standards.

Ensuring data integrity isn't merely a procedural step; it represents a commitment to excellence that enhances the overall reliability of insights generated from your datasets. By meticulously validating every aspect of your data —from uniqueness and completeness to formatting—you position yourself as an essential contributor who safeguards organizational accuracy and informs sound decision-making based on trustworthy information. Your diligence in upholding these standards not only elevates your personal proficiency but also strengthens your organization's operational foundation.

Automating Database-Excel Workflows

Automating workflows between databases and Excel can significantly streamline operations, boost efficiency, and reduce the risk of human error. By creating a seamless connection for data exchange, you enable real-time updates and simplify reporting tasks.

To begin, you'll need to establish a connection between your database and Excel. This often involves utilizing libraries like SQLAlchemy in Python, which facilitates communication with various database engines. Take this example, here's a simple setup to pull data from a SQL database into an Excel file:

```python
from sqlalchemy import create_engine

import pandas as pd


\#\# Create a database engine (replace with your actual database URL)

engine = create_engine('sqlite:///my_database.db')


\#\# Load data from a specific table into a DataFrame

df = pd.read_sql('SELECT * FROM my_table', con=engine)


\#\# Write the DataFrame to an Excel file
```

```python
df.to_excel('output.xlsx', index=False)
```
` ` `

This code snippet connects to your SQLite database, retrieves data from my_table, and exports it to an Excel file named output.xlsx. This automation alleviates the need for manual data exports, allowing you to focus more on analysis.

Once your data is in Excel, think about additional processes you may want to automate. Take this example, if you need to generate regular reports—like monthly sales summaries —you can create scripts that run at specified intervals. The Python schedule library is particularly useful for this:

` ` `python

```python
import schedule

import time


def job():

\#\# Code for pulling updated data and generating report

df = pd.read_sql('SELECT * FROM sales WHERE date >= date("now", "-1 month")', con=engine)

df.to_excel('monthly_sales_report.xlsx', index=False)


\#\# Schedule the job every month

schedule.every(30).days.do(job)


while True:

schedule.run_pending()

time.sleep(1)
```

```
` ` `
```

In this example, the job() function is set to execute every 30 days. It pulls updated sales data from the previous month and saves it as an Excel file, thereby automating what could otherwise be a tedious task.

It's essential to also incorporate error handling into your automation process. Unexpected issues such as connectivity problems or missing data entries can occur during execution. By implementing robust error-catching mechanisms, you ensure that your automation remains resilient:

```python
try:

df = pd.read_sql('SELECT * FROM sales', con=engine)

except Exception as e:

print(f"An error occurred: e")
```

In this case, if retrieving data from the database fails, the exception will be caught and logged instead of halting the entire script. This approach allows your automation to continue running smoothly even when challenges arise.

Another crucial aspect of automating workflows is maintaining consistent formatting when exporting data back into Excel or databases. Formatting discrepancies can lead to processing errors later on. For example, ensuring uniform date formats before export is essential:

```python
df['date_column']                                    =
pd.to_datetime(df['date_column']).dt.strftime('%Y-%m-%d')
```

By standardizing your datasets prior to export or further analysis, you reduce the risks associated with incompatible formats.

And, documenting each step of your automated workflow is vital. This documentation serves several purposes: it acts as a reference for troubleshooting any issues that might come up and provides clarity on processes for team members who may take over these tasks in the future.

automation is not just about enhancing efficiency; it's about creating systems that empower teams with timely and accurate insights. By effectively automating your database-Excel workflows, you're not only saving time but also boosting productivity across operations while ensuring quality control over critical datasets.

To wrap things up, establishing automated connections between databases and Excel requires careful planning and execution but yields substantial rewards: time savings, improved accuracy, and streamlined processes that facilitate better decision-making within organizations. Your commitment to refining these workflows demonstrates not only technical skill but also strategic foresight in leveraging technology for maximum organizational impact.

CHAPTER 12: TROUBLESHOOTING AND DEBUGGING

Common Errors in Python-Excel Integration

Integrating Python with Excel can be a rewarding yet challenging endeavor, often fraught with unexpected pitfalls. For anyone looking to leverage Python's capabilities within an Excel environment, understanding common errors is essential. By identifying and addressing these issues early on, you can save valuable time and reduce frustration, leading to more efficient workflows.

A frequent challenge users encounter is library compatibility. Many find themselves grappling with version mismatches, particularly when working with packages like Pandas or OpenPyXL. For example, if a new feature in the latest version of Pandas isn't supported by your installed version of OpenPyXL, you may face cryptic error messages that impede progress. To avoid such complications, it's crucial to ensure your libraries are both up-to-date and compatible. You can easily check your installed packages and their versions using the command pip list, which helps verify compatibility.

Another common issue stems from data type mismatches. Excel and Python handle data types differently, which can lead to errors during the reading and writing of Excel files. Take this example, a cell formatted as a date in Excel might be interpreted as a string in Python if not managed correctly. Attempting arithmetic operations on this string without converting it to a date object first will result in a TypeError. A practical approach is to use Pandas' pd.to_datetime() function when importing date columns, ensuring that your data is correctly typed for analysis.

File path issues also frequently disrupt seamless interactions between Python and Excel. Users often overlook the need for proper formatting, especially when switching between different operating systems. Take this example, Windows uses backslashes for file paths while macOS employs forward slashes; mixing these can lead to FileNotFoundError exceptions. To avoid this, leverage Python's built-in os module to construct file paths dynamically with os.path.join(), which adjusts path separators based on the operating system.

Permission errors can catch even seasoned users off guard. When attempting to access or modify an Excel file that is open in another application or lacks appropriate permissions, Python will raise an IOError. To mitigate this issue, ensure that files are closed before executing scripts and double-check permission settings.

Handling large datasets introduces its own set of challenges. Importing extensive data can lead to memory errors if your machine lacks sufficient RAM, especially when loading entire spreadsheets into memory using Pandas' read_excel() function. A practical solution is to utilize chunking by specifying the chunksize parameter during reading, allowing you to process the data piece by piece instead of all at once.

As projects grow in complexity, effective debugging becomes increasingly important. Tools such as Jupyter Notebook's cell-by-cell execution facilitate easier identification of problematic code sections while integrating Python with Excel. Strategically placing print statements throughout your code can help track variable values and execution paths effectively.

Lastly, it's vital not to overlook the importance of error handling within your scripts. Implementing try-except blocks ensures that your program doesn't crash unexpectedly due to unhandled exceptions; instead, it allows you to log errors or provide meaningful feedback without disrupting the user's experience.

By proactively recognizing these common pitfalls and applying best practices in error management and debugging techniques, you can enhance your efficiency and foster a more resilient integration process between Python and Excel —ultimately positioning yourself for success in managing complex data workflows with ease.

Using Python's Debugging Tools

Debugging is a vital aspect of programming, especially when integrating Python with Excel. Having effective debugging tools can greatly enhance your workflow and ensure that your scripts execute smoothly in the Excel environment.

One of the most important tools at your disposal is the built-in pdb module, which stands for Python Debugger. This powerful utility allows you to set breakpoints in your code, step through execution line by line, and inspect variables at any point during runtime. To start debugging, simply insert import pdb; pdb.set_trace() at the desired point in your script. When execution reaches this line, you will enter an interactive mode where you can execute commands like n to move to the next line or c to continue until the next breakpoint. This hands-on approach helps pinpoint exactly where issues arise in your logic or data handling.

In addition to pdb, utilizing logging is an effective way to track down problems. By replacing print statements with Python's logging module, you can capture detailed information about your program's execution without cluttering your output. The logging module allows you to set different levels (DEBUG, INFO, WARNING, ERROR), enabling you to filter messages based on their significance. For example:

```python
import logging


logging.basicConfig(level=logging.DEBUG)

logging.debug("This is a debug message.")
```

This method not only aids in identifying bugs but also provides a historical record of your program's behavior over time.

Understanding exceptions that occur during runtime is another critical aspect of debugging. Python offers a range of built-in exceptions that indicate various types of errors—such as an IndexError when accessing elements outside a list or a ValueError when converting incompatible data types. To handle these exceptions gracefully and provide meaningful feedback, strategically employ try-except blocks around your code:

```python
try:
```

\#\# Code that may raise an exception

result = 10 / user_input \# Assuming user_input comes from Excel

except ZeroDivisionError:

logging.error("User input cannot be zero.")

except ValueError as e:

logging.error(f"Value error occurred: e")

` ` `

This approach allows you to manage errors without crashing the application while offering insights into what went wrong.

When working specifically with Excel files, using libraries like Pandas can add complexity to your debugging process. If you encounter errors related to file reading or writing operations, it's essential to validate file paths and ensure accessibility before executing any read/write commands. A common practice is to confirm a file's existence using os.path.exists(file_path) before attempting operations on it:

` ` `python

import os

if os.path.exists("data.xlsx"):

df = pd.read_excel("data.xlsx")

else:

logging.error("File does not exist.")

` ` `

Additionally, if you are manipulating large datasets from

Excel, memory management becomes crucial. Techniques like lazy loading—using the iterator parameter in Pandas' read_excel() function—can help prevent memory overload by processing data in manageable chunks.

debugging is not just about fixing errors; it's also about learning and refining your coding practices over time. Regularly revisiting and refactoring older scripts based on insights gained from debugging can lead to more efficient and readable code.

By incorporating these debugging strategies into your workflow, you'll streamline the process of integrating Python with Excel. With practice and patience, you'll gain confidence in troubleshooting issues quickly and effectively —transforming potential obstacles into opportunities for greater productivity and innovation in your projects. Mastering these tools positions you not only as a user of technology but as a skilled problem-solver capable of navigating complexities with ease and precision.

Fixing Workbook and Sheet Issues

When addressing workbook and sheet issues in Excel, you may encounter challenges that range from minor annoyances to major roadblocks that can hinder productivity. These problems often emerge while working with large datasets or complex formulas. Fortunately, there are systematic strategies to resolve these issues effectively.

One common concern is dealing with corrupt or damaged workbooks, which may present as error messages upon opening files or missing data within sheets. To tackle this, begin by trying to open the workbook in a different version of Excel or utilize Excel's built-in repair feature. If those methods prove unsuccessful, you can leverage Python to create backups of your important data. The openpyxl library is particularly effective for reading and writing Excel files safely.

```python
from openpyxl import load_workbook

try:
workbook = load_workbook('your_file.xlsx')
except Exception as e:
print(f"Error loading workbook: e")
```

This approach allows you to handle exceptions gracefully while safeguarding your data.

Another prevalent issue involves formatting inconsistencies within sheets or across multiple sheets. For example, numerical values stored as text can lead to calculation errors and misinterpretation of data. A practical solution is to iterate through your dataset and explicitly convert these values using Python's pandas library.

```python
import pandas as pd

df = pd.read_excel('data.xlsx')
df['ColumnName'] = pd.to_numeric(df['ColumnName'], errors='coerce') \# Converts strings to numbers
df.to_excel('corrected_data.xlsx', index=False)
```

This script corrects formatting issues while handling errors by converting problematic entries into NaN (Not a Number).

Effective management of worksheets can also prevent many common issues. Renaming sheets and organizing them logically enhances navigation and minimizes confusion. Take this example, if you frequently use specific sheets for reporting or analysis, consider prefixing these names for easier identification.

```python
for sheet in workbook.sheetnames:

if 'Report' in sheet:

new_name = f"Report_sheet

workbook[sheet].title = new_name
```

Although this organizational step may seem minor, it significantly boosts workflow efficiency, particularly in collaborative environments where multiple users access the same files.

Cell references in formulas often break after copying between sheets or workbooks, creating additional headaches. Using named ranges can help stabilize references, ensuring they remain consistent regardless of where they're utilized. You can create named ranges through Python for added control:

```python
from openpyxl import Workbook

wb = Workbook()

ws = wb.active

ws['A1'] = 10

ws['A2'] = 20

ws['A3'] = '=SUM(A1:A2)'
```

```python
wb.create_named_range('SumRange', ws['A1:A2'])
```

By establishing these stable references, you mitigate issues even if the underlying data shifts.

Finally, it's essential to handle user inputs from Excel effectively. Incorrect input types often lead to errors that disrupt calculations or script execution. To avoid this, validate inputs right away within your Python script:

```python
user_input = input("Enter a number: ")

try:

value = float(user_input)

except ValueError:

print("Invalid input; please enter a numeric value.")
```

By checking inputs before further processing in your workflow, you reduce the risk of encountering errors that could derail your entire process.

In summary, resolving workbook and sheet issues requires both strategic organization and effective coding practices. By implementing techniques such as safeguarding against corruption with backups, correcting formatting through conversions, managing worksheets wisely, utilizing named ranges for stability, and validating user inputs, you equip yourself with the tools necessary to maintain control over your Excel environment. This proactive approach transforms potential hurdles into opportunities for enhancing productivity and accuracy in your projects, allowing you to focus on analysis rather than troubleshooting glitches.

Handling Data Errors in Excel

Data errors in Excel can be a significant source of frustration, affecting both the integrity of your information and the efficiency of your workflows. These errors can manifest in various ways, including incorrect calculations, misformatted entries, or missing values. By mastering effective strategies to handle these issues, you can enhance your data management skills and streamline your overall productivity.

One prevalent type of data error occurs when data types are incorrectly assigned. Take this example, if numerical values are inadvertently formatted as text, Excel may struggle to perform calculations accurately. A straightforward way to address this issue is by using Python's Pandas library to identify and rectify these discrepancies efficiently. With just a few lines of code, you can convert entire columns to the correct data type:

```python
import pandas as pd


\#\# Load your Excel file

df = pd.read_excel('data.xlsx')


\#\# Convert a specific column to numeric, coercing errors into NaN

df['ColumnName'] = pd.to_numeric(df['ColumnName'], errors='coerce')


\#\# Save the corrected DataFrame back to an Excel file
```

```python
df.to_excel('corrected_data.xlsx', index=False)
```

This method not only resolves formatting issues but also maintains the integrity of your dataset by converting problematic entries into NaN (Not a Number), which you can address later in your analysis.

Another challenge you may encounter involves missing values. In large datasets, it's common for some entries to be blank or unrecorded. Effectively managing these gaps is crucial, and employing techniques such as imputation or removal can be helpful. For example, if you wish to fill missing values with the mean of a column, you could use the following code:

```python
mean_value = df['ColumnName'].mean()

df['ColumnName'].fillna(mean_value, inplace=True)
```

This snippet calculates the mean of the specified column and replaces any missing values accordingly. It's important to evaluate whether this method suits your specific dataset and analysis goals.

In addition to addressing individual errors, it's essential to ensure that formulas across sheets function correctly. Changes in references can disrupt calculations when formulas point to cells in other sheets or workbooks. One effective practice is to use named ranges for critical references:

```python
from openpyxl import Workbook
```

```
wb = Workbook()

ws = wb.active

\#\# Create named ranges for better stability in formulas

ws['A1'] = 10

ws['A2'] = 20

ws.create_named_range('Total', ws['A1:A2'])


\#\# Use named range in a formula

ws['A3'] = '=SUM(Total)'
```
` ` `

Using named ranges simplifies formula management and ensures that references remain intact even when modifications occur elsewhere.

When processing user inputs from Excel files, validating input types beforehand is crucial for preventing execution errors later on. Implementing input checks directly in your Python script helps ensure that users provide acceptable data formats:

` ` `python

```python
user_input = input("Please enter a number: ")

try:

value = float(user_input)

except ValueError:

print("Invalid input; please enter a numeric value.")
```

` ` `

This proactive validation step minimizes disruption by catching potential errors early on.

Lastly, maintaining an organized approach when working with Excel files is vital. Adopting logical naming conventions for sheets and consistent formatting practices enhances clarity and reduces confusion—especially in collaborative environments where multiple users access shared documents. For example:

` ` `python

for sheet in wb.sheetnames:

if 'Data' not in sheet:

wb[sheet].title = f"Report_sheet

` ` `

By systematically renaming sheets based on their content or purpose, you create an environment that fosters efficiency.

Addressing data errors in Excel through Python not only sharpens your technical skills but also empowers you to take control over your analytical processes. By implementing strategies such as correcting data types with Pandas, managing missing values effectively, utilizing named ranges for stable formulas, validating user inputs promptly, and maintaining organized workflows, you can turn potential setbacks into opportunities for growth within your projects. This foundational approach significantly elevates the quality and reliability of your data analysis efforts.

Reading Python Error Logs

When working with Python and Excel, encountering errors is an inevitable aspect of the process. However, understanding how to interpret Python error logs can significantly enhance your ability to diagnose and resolve issues efficiently during data analysis or automation tasks. Think of error logs as a roadmap that guides you through the nature of the problem and often points toward potential solutions.

Python's traceback system provides detailed information whenever an error occurs. Each traceback outlines the sequence of function calls leading up to the error, making it an invaluable tool for debugging. Take this example, encountering a KeyError indicates that you're trying to access a key in a dictionary or DataFrame that doesn't exist. Consider this simple example:

```python
import pandas as pd


\#\# Sample DataFrame
data = 'Name': ['Alice', 'Bob', 'Charlie'], 'Age': [25, 30, 35]
df = pd.DataFrame(data)


\#\# Attempting to access a non-existent column
try:
print(df['Height'])
except KeyError as e:
print(f"Error: e")
```

In this case, running the code generates an error log that indicates KeyError: 'Height'. This message provides clear insight into what went wrong—attempting to access a column that hasn't been defined.

Another common error is the ValueError, which arises when

a function receives an argument of the correct type but an inappropriate value. For example, if you try to convert user input into an integer:

```python
user_input = "abc

try:

number = int(user_input)

except ValueError as e:

print(f"ValueError: e")
```

This snippet captures the exception and provides an informative message explaining why the conversion failed.

In addition to understanding error types, utilizing Python's logging module can greatly enhance your ability to monitor scripts and catch errors in real time. By configuring logging in your application, you can record both errors and informational messages during execution. Here's a basic setup for logging:

```python
import logging

\#\# Set up logging configuration

logging.basicConfig(level=logging.INFO)


def process_data(data):

try:

\#\# Simulated processing step
```

```
result = data / 0 \# This will raise a ZeroDivisionError

except ZeroDivisionError as e:

logging.error(f"ZeroDivisionError occurred: e")


process_data(10)
` ` `
```

In this example, when process_data encounters a division by zero, it logs an error message instead of crashing the program. This approach allows you to maintain awareness of what went wrong while preserving the context of your application's state.

Reading logs not only aids in immediate error resolution but also supports long-term improvements. By analyzing patterns in errors, you can identify persistent issues within your code or workflow. Are there specific types of inputs that consistently lead to problems? Do certain functions frequently break down? Engaging in this reflective practice enables you to make iterative enhancements in your coding practices.

And, using Integrated Development Environments (IDEs) can streamline debugging through built-in error highlighting and suggestions. IDEs provide real-time feedback about potential issues while coding, allowing for proactive adjustments before running scripts.

Finally, consider implementing unit tests within your Python scripts to catch errors early in the development cycle. Writing tests ensures that individual components behave as expected before they are integrated into larger workflows:

```python
def add_numbers(a, b):
```

```
return a + b

\#\# Unit test example
def test_add_numbers():
    assert add_numbers(2, 3) == 5
    assert add_numbers(-1, 1) == 0

test_add_numbers()
```
` ` `

If any assertions fail during testing, you receive immediate feedback on what went wrong—making it easier to address issues before they escalate.

By honing your skills in reading Python error logs and employing effective debugging techniques, you empower yourself to navigate challenges more adeptly. This capability not only boosts your productivity but also instills confidence in tackling complex projects involving Python and Excel integration. Embrace these practices as essential components of your workflow; they form foundational steps toward mastering effective data analysis and automation with Python.

Optimizing Script Performance

Optimizing script performance in Python, particularly when working with Excel, requires a comprehensive approach. Enhancing performance not only speeds up your scripts but also ensures they operate efficiently, especially when dealing with large datasets or complex calculations.

A key initial step in this optimization process is to identify bottlenecks in your code. The built-in cProfile module is invaluable for pinpointing which sections of your code consume the most time. For example, if you're processing a large DataFrame and suspect certain operations are causing delays, you can set up a profiling session as follows:

```python
import pandas as pd

import cProfile


def process_data(df):
\#\# Simulated data processing
return df.sum()


\#\# Sample DataFrame
data = 'A': range(1000000), 'B': range(1000000)

df = pd.DataFrame(data)


\#\# Profiling the function
cProfile.run('process_data(df)')
```

Executing this code will generate a detailed report that highlights where time is being spent in the process_data function. This information allows you to target inefficiencies and refactor those areas for improved performance.

Once you've identified bottlenecks, consider employing vectorization as a powerful technique to accelerate operations on DataFrames. Instead of relying on loops to iterate through rows, take advantage of Pandas' built-in functions that work on entire columns simultaneously. This method reduces Python overhead and utilizes optimized C libraries. For example, when calculating the sum of two columns, you can choose the more efficient vectorized approach:

```python
\#\# Inefficient loop method

df['C'] = 0

for i in range(len(df)):

df['C'][i] = df['A'][i] + df['B'][i]


\#\# Efficient vectorized method

df['C'] = df['A'] + df['B']
```

The vectorized operation not only simplifies your code but also significantly enhances execution speed.

Another important strategy is to minimize unnecessary data copies during processing. Every time you slice or modify a DataFrame, Pandas may create a new copy rather than altering the original object in place. This can lead to increased memory usage and slower performance. To address this issue, use methods that modify the DataFrame directly whenever possible:

```python
\#\# Modifying in place

df.drop(columns=['B'], inplace=True)
```

By setting inplace=True, you reduce memory overhead by modifying the existing DataFrame instead of creating a new one.

As datasets continue to grow larger, effective memory

management becomes increasingly critical. Opt for data types that consume less memory whenever feasible. Take this example, if you're handling integer values within a specific range, using smaller data types like np.int8 or np.int16 can result in significant memory savings compared to the default int64. Here's how to specify data types when creating a DataFrame:

```python
import numpy as np

data = 'A': np.array(range(1000000), dtype=np.int16)
df = pd.DataFrame(data)
```

In addition, consider implementing caching strategies for results that involve repetitive calculations or data retrievals. Storing frequently accessed results helps reduce redundant processing time. You can use Python's built-in functools.lru_cache for this purpose:

```python
from functools import lru_cache

@lru_cache(maxsize=None)
def expensive_function(x):
\#\# Simulate an expensive calculation
return x ** 2

result1 = expensive_function(10)
result2 = expensive_function(10) \# This call will be faster
```

due to caching

` ` `

In this example, the second call to expensive_function(10) retrieves the result from cache instead of recalculating it.

Lastly, don't underestimate the benefits of parallel processing for computationally intensive tasks. The multiprocessing module enables you to distribute workloads across multiple CPU cores, significantly speeding up execution for large operations:

```python
from multiprocessing import Pool


def square(x):

return x ** 2


with Pool(processes=4) as pool:

results = pool.map(square, range(10))
```

By distributing tasks among several processes, you can fully leverage your machine's capabilities.

In summary, optimizing script performance requires careful analysis and strategic enhancements throughout your codebase. By utilizing profiling tools, embracing vectorization, managing memory efficiently, implementing caching techniques, and adopting parallel processing, you can significantly improve the responsiveness of your Python scripts. This meticulous attention to detail not only enhances integration with Excel but also elevates your workflow from functional to exceptional—leading to quicker insights and more efficient automation processes that empower your data-driven initiatives.

Best Practices for Error Handling

Error handling in Python, especially when working with Excel, is essential for developing robust and reliable applications. As you process data—particularly large datasets or complex calculations—unexpected issues may arise. By anticipating potential errors and implementing effective handling strategies, you can prevent crashes and enhance the overall user experience.

A good starting point is to utilize Python's built-in exception handling using try-except blocks. This approach allows you to catch and manage errors gracefully without interrupting the flow of your script. For example, when reading an Excel file, it's important to prepare for situations where the file might not exist or could be corrupted:

```python
import pandas as pd


try:

df = pd.read_excel('data.xlsx')

except FileNotFoundError:

print("The specified file was not found.")

except pd.errors.EmptyDataError:

print("No data found in the file.")

except Exception as e:

print(f"An unexpected error occurred: e")
```

In this snippet, the script attempts to read the Excel file while capturing specific errors that may occur during the operation. By providing clear, meaningful messages, users are informed about what went wrong rather than being confronted with a confusing traceback.

Validating input data before processing it is another crucial aspect of error handling. Ensuring that your data meets expected criteria can help prevent runtime errors. Take this example, if your analysis requires numeric values, you can validate the data type using assertions or conditional checks:

```python
if not pd.api.types.is_numeric_dtype(df['A']):

raise ValueError("Column 'A' must contain numeric values.")
```

This proactive approach minimizes the risk of unexpected behavior during data operations.

Logging is also a vital tool for effective error management. Instead of simply printing error messages to the console, consider using Python's logging module to record errors in a file. This method is particularly useful for debugging and tracking issues over time:

```python
import logging


\#\# Configure logging

logging.basicConfig(filename='app.log',
level=logging.ERROR)


try:

df = pd.read_excel('data.xlsx')

except Exception as e:
```

```python
logging.error("Error occurred", exc_info=True)
```

By documenting errors along with their stack traces in a log file, you gain valuable insights into recurring issues that may need to be addressed.

In addition to catching and logging errors, implementing fallback mechanisms is important. These mechanisms provide alternative solutions when a primary operation fails. For example, if a specific Excel function encounters an issue, you might revert to a simpler calculation:

```python
try:

result = df['A'].mean()

except Exception as e:

logging.error("Failed to calculate mean", exc_info=True)

result = df['A'].sum() / len(df) \# Fallback to manual mean calculation
```

This strategy ensures that your application remains functional even in adverse conditions.

When deploying applications in production environments, consider enhancing your error handling strategies by incorporating user notifications. If users need to be alerted about failures—perhaps through a graphical user interface—libraries like tkinter can significantly improve usability:

```python
import tkinter as tk

from tkinter import messagebox
```

```python
def show_error(message):
root = tk.Tk()
root.withdraw() \# Hide the main window
messagebox.showerror("Error", message)
root.destroy()

try:
df = pd.read_excel('data.xlsx')
except Exception as e:
show_error(str(e))
```

With this approach, users receive clear messages via dialog boxes when errors occur, greatly enhancing their experience.

Lastly, rigorous testing plays a crucial role in preventing errors before they arise. Writing unit tests for your functions ensures they behave as expected under various conditions. Using frameworks like unittest, you can create test cases that simulate both normal and erroneous scenarios:

```python
import unittest

class TestExcelFunctions(unittest.TestCase):

def test_file_not_found(self):
with self.assertRaises(FileNotFoundError):
```

```
pd.read_excel('non_existent_file.xlsx')

if __name__ == '__main__':

unittest.main()
```
` ` `

Testing not only helps identify errors early but also ensures that future modifications do not introduce new issues.

In summary, effective error handling hinges on anticipating potential problems and implementing structured responses to maintain application integrity. By utilizing try-except blocks, validating inputs, logging errors, providing fallbacks, notifying users, and conducting thorough testing, you lay the groundwork for a robust error management strategy. Prioritizing these practices in your Python scripts integrated with Excel will lead to smoother operations and heightened reliability—ultimately creating a more effective and user-friendly experience.

CHAPTER 13: PYTHON FOR FINANCIAL MODELING IN EXCEL

Introduction to Financial Modeling

Financial modeling is a crucial skill in data analysis and business decision-making, enabling professionals to create representations of a company's financial performance and make informed projections for the future. This process typically involves making assumptions based on historical data and utilizing various inputs to forecast outcomes. As the financial landscape continues to evolve, the demand for more sophisticated modeling techniques has increased. One effective approach is integrating Python with Excel, which offers powerful tools that enhance financial models by streamlining processes and improving accuracy.

Traditionally, financial modeling requires a combination of complex calculations, data manipulation, and scenario analysis—all of which can become cumbersome when relying solely on Excel. However, Python simplifies these tasks through libraries like Pandas, NumPy, and SciPy. These libraries provide advanced statistical functions and array operations that can be seamlessly incorporated into your modeling workflows, allowing for more efficient handling of large datasets compared to Excel's built-in capabilities.

For example, imagine you need to project revenue growth over the next five years based on historical sales data. Rather than manually inputting formulas for each year's forecast in Excel, you can automate this process using Python:

```python
import pandas as pd

\#\# Load historical sales data

sales_data = pd.read_excel('historical_sales.xlsx')


\#\# Calculate annual growth rates

sales_data['Growth Rate'] = sales_data['Sales'].pct_change()


\#\# Forecast future sales based on average growth rate

average_growth = sales_data['Growth Rate'].mean()

future_years = pd.DataFrame('Year': range(2023, 2028))

future_years['Projected Sales'] = sales_data['Sales'].iloc[-1] * (1 + average_growth) ** (future_years['Year'] - 2023)


\#\# Save the forecast to an Excel file

with pd.ExcelWriter('projected_sales.xlsx') as writer:

sales_data.to_excel(writer, sheet_name='Historical Data', index=False)
```

```python
future_years.to_excel(writer,        sheet_name='Forecast',
index=False)
```

` ` `

In this script, you load historical data from Excel, calculate growth rates using Pandas' powerful capabilities, and then project future sales into a new worksheet. This example illustrates how Python can significantly enhance your financial modeling efforts by saving time and reducing the potential for errors.

Additionally, incorporating visualizations into your financial models can provide clearer insights for stakeholders. By using libraries such as Matplotlib or Seaborn alongside Pandas, you can create dynamic graphs that visualize trends in real-time rather than relying solely on static charts within Excel:

` ` `python

import matplotlib.pyplot as plt

\#\# Plot historical sales data

plt.figure(figsize=(10, 6))

plt.plot(sales_data['Year'],   sales_data['Sales'],   marker='o', label='Historical Sales')

plt.plot(future_years['Year'], future_years['Projected Sales'], marker='x', linestyle='--', label='Projected Sales')

plt.title('Sales Forecast')

plt.xlabel('Year')

plt.ylabel('Sales Amount')

plt.legend()

plt.grid()

plt.savefig('sales_forecast.png')

` ` `

These visual elements not only enhance presentations but also facilitate more effective communication of complex data stories.

Risk assessment is another critical component of financial modeling where Python truly shines. Running simulations that would be tedious in Excel becomes straightforward with Python's capabilities. Take this example, Monte Carlo simulations are particularly useful for evaluating the probability of different outcomes in uncertain scenarios. Utilizing the numpy library makes it easy to run multiple iterations:

```python
import numpy as np

\#\# Define parameters for simulation
mean_sales = future_years['Projected Sales'].mean()

std_dev_sales = future_years['Projected Sales'].std()

num_simulations = 1000

\#\# Run Monte Carlo simulation
simulated_sales    =    np.random.normal(mean_sales, std_dev_sales, num_simulations)

\#\# Analyze results (e.g., percentiles)
lower_bound = np.percentile(simulated_sales, 5)
```

```python
upper_bound = np.percentile(simulated_sales, 95)

print(f"95%    Confidence    Interval:    (lower_bound,
upper_bound)")
```

This code generates random variables based on your projected sales' mean and standard deviation, allowing you to predict a range of possible outcomes—insights that are invaluable for budget preparation or project viability assessments.

For example, you might set up scheduled scripts that pull updated financial data from APIs or databases to refresh existing models without manual intervention. By automating these tasks with libraries like schedule, you can ensure decision-makers always have access to the latest information:

```python
import schedule

import time


def update_financial_model():

\#\# Your code to refresh model goes here...

print("Financial model updated.")


schedule.every().monday.at("09:00").do(update_financial_model)


while True:

schedule.run_pending()
```

```
time.sleep(60)
```
` ` `

This script illustrates how Python can foster a proactive work environment where crucial updates occur automatically.

mastering financial modeling through Python enhances both accuracy and efficiency while providing flexibility in your analyses. With this knowledge at your fingertips, you elevate your own capabilities and empower those around you by delivering insights that drive informed decisions. In today's fast-paced finance environment, combining Python with Excel positions you strategically at the forefront of innovation within your organization.

Constructing Financial Models with Python

Financial modeling is more than a technical skill; it serves as a strategic tool that informs decision-making within organizations. As businesses confront uncertainty, the ability to predict and analyze financial outcomes becomes increasingly valuable. By integrating Python into this process, you can enhance your capabilities, transforming traditional models into dynamic frameworks that accommodate complexity and variability.

To create effective financial models using Python, begin by establishing your key assumptions. These assumptions —such as growth rates, cost structures, and economic indicators—form the backbone of any financial projection. With Python's powerful data handling capabilities, you can easily manipulate these assumptions in real time, allowing you to see how changes impact your outcomes.

Consider a scenario where you want to evaluate the effects of different growth scenarios on your company's revenue. You can build a flexible model that enables you to adjust growth rates and immediately observe changes in projected revenues over multiple years. Here's how you can set it up:

```python
import pandas as pd

## Define assumptions
base_year_sales = 100000 # Starting sales
growth_scenarios = [0.03, 0.05, 0.07] # Different growth rates

## Create an empty DataFrame to store results
results = pd.DataFrame(columns=['Year', 'Growth Rate', 'Projected Sales'])

## Calculate projected sales for each scenario over five years
for growth_rate in growth_scenarios:
for year in range(1, 6):
projected_sales = base_year_sales * (1 + growth_rate) ** year
results = results.append('Year': year + 2023, 'Growth Rate': growth_rate, 'Projected Sales': projected_sales, ignore_index=True)

## Save results to Excel
results.to_excel('financial_model.xlsx', index=False)
```

This script defines various growth rates and calculates projected sales over five years based on those rates. The resulting data is saved in an Excel file for easy sharing with stakeholders.

Following this step, evaluating these projections through sensitivity analysis is crucial. This analysis helps determine how sensitive your model's outputs are to changes in key inputs. By adjusting one variable at a time while keeping others constant, you can observe how fluctuations affect overall performance.

Here's an example that utilizes the previously defined model:

```python
import numpy as np


\#\# Define ranges for sensitivity analysis

growth_range = np.arange(0.01, 0.11, 0.01) \# Growth rates from 1% to 10%

sensitivity_results = pd.DataFrame(columns=['Growth Rate', 'Projected Sales'])


for rate in growth_range:

future_sales = base_year_sales * (1 + rate) ** 5

sensitivity_results = sensitivity_results.append('Growth Rate': rate, 'Projected Sales': future_sales, ignore_index=True)


\#\# Save sensitivity analysis results to Excel

sensitivity_results.to_excel('sensitivity_analysis.xlsx', index=False)
```

This code snippet illustrates how varying the growth rate impacts projected sales after five years. Analyzing these outcomes provides valuable insights into which variables significantly influence your forecasts.

Visualization also plays a vital role in constructing financial models; it transforms numbers into narratives that resonate with stakeholders. By utilizing libraries like Matplotlib or Seaborn, you can create compelling visuals that highlight key trends and insights derived from your model:

```python
import matplotlib.pyplot as plt


plt.figure(figsize=(10, 6))

plt.plot(results['Year'], results['Projected Sales'], marker='o', label='Projected Sales')

plt.title('Sales Projections under Different Growth Rates')

plt.xlabel('Year')

plt.ylabel('Projected Sales')

plt.legend()

plt.grid()

plt.savefig('sales_projection_chart.png')
```

This visualization captures projections over time and simplifies the communication of complex data.

And, incorporating risk assessment through Monte Carlo simulations further enhances your understanding of potential outcomes under uncertainty. Unlike deterministic forecasts—which rely on fixed inputs—this approach accounts for variability in key assumptions by simulating thousands of scenarios:

```python
```

```
num_simulations = 10000

simulated_growth_rates = np.random.choice(growth_range,
num_simulations)


\#\# Simulate sales projections based on random growth
rates

simulated_sales_projections = base_year_sales * (1 +
simulated_growth_rates) ** 5


\#\# Calculate statistics from simulations

mean_projection = np.mean(simulated_sales_projections)

lower_bound = np.percentile(simulated_sales_projections,
5)

upper_bound = np.percentile(simulated_sales_projections,
95)


print(f"Mean Projected Sales: mean_projection")

print(f"95% Confidence Interval: (lower_bound,
upper_bound)")
    ` ` `
```

By running this simulation code snippet, you generate a distribution of possible future sales figures rather than a single point estimate—allowing for the presentation of confidence intervals that inform better decision-making.

The culmination of these techniques underscores the importance of automation within financial modeling workflows. Implementing scripts that refresh data or conduct regular analyses enables proactive management of insights throughout the financial cycle.

Embracing Python for constructing financial models establishes a robust framework where accuracy meets agility—empowering organizations to navigate complexities confidently while enhancing their strategic decision-making capabilities. This integration modernizes traditional practices and ensures they keep pace with today's fast-evolving business landscape.

Cash Flow Analysis in Excel

Cash flow analysis is fundamental to effective financial management, allowing businesses to evaluate their liquidity, assess operational efficiency, and make informed investment decisions. Integrating Python with Excel can significantly enhance the depth and agility of these analyses. With Python's powerful data manipulation capabilities, you can automate repetitive tasks, streamline calculations, and create compelling visualizations that resonate with stakeholders.

Start by familiarizing yourself with the key components of cash flow: operating activities, investing activities, and financing activities. Each element plays a crucial role in painting a comprehensive picture of a company's financial health. When incorporating Python into your cash flow analysis, begin by gathering historical data from your Excel sheets to establish a baseline for future projections.

Take this example, if you have monthly cash flow data in an Excel file, you can utilize Python's Pandas library to read this data and perform calculations efficiently:

```python
import pandas as pd


\#\# Load cash flow data from Excel

cash_flow_data = pd.read_excel('cash_flow_data.xlsx')
```

\#\# Display the first few rows of the dataset

print(cash_flow_data.head())

` ` `

This snippet reads your historical cash flows into a DataFrame, enabling you to compute metrics such as net cash flow for each month by summing up cash inflows and outflows.

Next, you can project future cash flows based on historical trends. If you've identified average growth rates for your inflows from past performance, you can create a projection model. Here's how:

` ` `python

\#\# Assume average growth rate for inflows is 5% per month

growth_rate = 0.05

\#\# Create a new DataFrame for projections

projected_cash_flows = pd.DataFrame(columns=['Month', 'Projected Cash Inflow', 'Projected Cash Outflow', 'Net Cash Flow'])

\#\# Generate projections for the next 12 months

for i in range(1, 13):

month = f'Month i'

projected_inflow = cash_flow_data['Cash Inflow'].mean() * (1 + growth_rate) ** i

projected_outflow = cash_flow_data['Cash Outflow'].mean() *

```python
(1 + growth_rate) ** i
net_cash_flow = projected_inflow - projected_outflow


projected_cash_flows = projected_cash_flows.append(
'Month': month,
'Projected Cash Inflow': projected_inflow,
'Projected Cash Outflow': projected_outflow,
'Net Cash Flow': net_cash_flow
, ignore_index=True)


\#\# Save projections to Excel
projected_cash_flows.to_excel('projected_cash_flows.xlsx',
index=False)
```

This code snippet generates a straightforward projection model for the coming year based on historical averages adjusted by a designated growth rate. The resulting DataFrame contains estimates for both inflow and outflow alongside net cash flow calculations.

Once you've established projections, it's valuable to conduct variance analysis to compare actual results against your forecasts. This process highlights discrepancies that may indicate operational inefficiencies or shifts in market conditions. For example:

```python
\#\# Load actual results from another Excel file for comparison
actual_results                                          =
```

```
pd.read_excel('actual_cash_flow_results.xlsx')
```

\#\# Merge actual results with projected data for variance analysis

```
variance_analysis = pd.merge(projected_cash_flows, actual_results, on='Month', suffixes=('_Projected', '_Actual'))
```

\#\# Calculate variances

```
variance_analysis['Inflow Variance'] = variance_analysis['Projected Cash Inflow'] - variance_analysis['Cash Inflow_Actual']
```

```
variance_analysis['Outflow Variance'] = variance_analysis['Projected Cash Outflow'] - variance_analysis['Cash Outflow_Actual']
```

```
variance_analysis.to_excel('variance_analysis.xlsx', index=False)
```
` ` `

This approach quantifies how well your predictions align with reality while pinpointing specific areas that may require attention.

In addition to these analyses, visualization enhances clarity in your cash flow assessment. Utilizing libraries like Matplotlib or Seaborn allows you to create charts that illustrate trends over time. For example:

` ` `python

```
import matplotlib.pyplot as plt
```

```
plt.figure(figsize=(12, 6))
```

```
plt.plot(projected_cash_flows['Month'],
```

```
projected_cash_flows['Net     Cash     Flow'],     marker='o',
label='Projected Net Cash Flow')

plt.title('Projected Net Cash Flow Over Next Year')

plt.xlabel('Month')

plt.ylabel('Net Cash Flow')

plt.xticks(rotation=45)

plt.legend()

plt.grid()

plt.savefig('projected_net_cash_flow.png')
` ` `
```

Such visualizations enable stakeholders to quickly comprehend future cash positions at a glance.

Lastly, integrating scenario analysis into your model increases its robustness by allowing assessments of potential outcomes under various conditions—such as best-case and worst-case scenarios—based on varying inflow and outflow assumptions. This method equips decision-makers with insights essential for strategic planning and risk management.

As you implement these techniques within your organization, remember that automation through Python not only boosts efficiency but also enhances accuracy in financial forecasting. The synergy of historical data analysis with predictive modeling lays the foundation for informed decision-making processes—transforming how businesses navigate their financial strategies in today's complex landscape. Embracing this integration modernizes traditional practices and empowers organizations to approach uncertainty with confidence and precision.

Valuation Models Using Python

Valuation models form the cornerstone of financial decision-making, enabling analysts to evaluate the worth of assets, companies, or investment opportunities. By integrating these models with Python's robust capabilities, they become more dynamic and easier to manipulate and analyze. Utilizing Python's libraries and tools allows you to automate tedious valuation tasks, freeing you to focus on interpreting results that inform strategic decisions.

To start building a valuation model in Python, it's crucial to understand the different approaches available. The three primary methods are Discounted Cash Flow (DCF), Comparable Company Analysis (Comps), and Precedent Transactions. Each method offers unique insights, but the DCF approach is particularly noteworthy for its emphasis on future cash flows and the time value of money—concepts that align seamlessly with Python's data-handling capabilities.

Let's explore how to construct a simple DCF model. Begin by gathering your data, specifically historical financials from Excel that include revenue figures, operating expenses, and capital expenditures. For example, suppose you have a spreadsheet named 'financial_data.xlsx' containing this information. The first step is to load this data using Pandas:

```python
import pandas as pd

\#\# Load financial data

financial_data = pd.read_excel('financial_data.xlsx')

\#\# Display the first few rows

print(financial_data.head())
```

` ` `

With your historical data ready, you can calculate free cash flow (FCF), which is crucial for the DCF calculation. FCF is derived from operating cash flow minus capital expenditures. You can calculate it in Python as follows:

` ` `python

\#\# Calculate Free Cash Flow (FCF)

financial_data['Free Cash Flow'] = financial_data['Operating Cash Flow'] - financial_data['Capital Expenditures']

` ` `

Next, project future cash flows based on historical trends. Using a growth rate derived from past performance, you can create projections for several years:

` ` `python

\#\# Define growth rates

growth_rate = 0.07 \# 7% annual growth rate

\#\# Project future cash flows for the next five years

for i in range(1, 6):

projected_fcf = financial_data['Free Cash Flow'].iloc[-1] * (1 + growth_rate) ** i

financial_data.loc[len(financial_data)]   =   [None]   * len(financial_data.columns) \# Add empty row for new year

financial_data.at[len(financial_data)-1, 'Year'] = f'Year i'

financial_data.at[len(financial_data)-1, 'Free Cash Flow'] = projected_fcf

` ` `

After projecting these cash flows, you'll need to discount them back to their present value using a discount rate—often the company's weighted average cost of capital (WACC). This discounting reflects the principle that money today holds more value than the same amount in the future:

```python
\#\# Assume a discount rate (WACC)
discount_rate = 0.10 \# 10%


\#\# Calculate present value of future cash flows
financial_data['Present Value FCF'] = financial_data['Free Cash Flow'] / ((1 + discount_rate) ** financial_data.index)
```

Once you've calculated the present value of projected cash flows, sum them up to determine the total enterprise value (EV) of the business:

```python
enterprise_value = financial_data['Present Value FCF'].sum()

print(f'Total Enterprise Value: enterprise_value')
```

This figure provides an estimate of what investors might be willing to pay for the business based on its future cash-generating potential.

Another vital component of valuation models is sensitivity analysis. This technique helps analysts understand how changes in assumptions—such as growth rates or discount rates—impact enterprise value. By creating a simple function that varies these inputs and recalculates EV accordingly, you can visualize potential outcomes:

```python
import matplotlib.pyplot as plt

def sensitivity_analysis(base_growth_rate):
    growth_rates = [base_growth_rate - 0.02 * i for i in range(5)] + [base_growth_rate + 0.02 * i for i in range(6)]
    values = []

    for rate in growth_rates:
        projected_fcf = base_fcf * (1 + rate)
        pv_fcf = projected_fcf / ((1 + discount_rate) ** year_index)
        values.append(pv_fcf)

    plt.figure(figsize=(12, 6))
    plt.plot(growth_rates, values)
    plt.title('Sensitivity Analysis: Impact of Growth Rate on Enterprise Value')
    plt.xlabel('Growth Rate')
    plt.ylabel('Enterprise Value')
    plt.grid()
    plt.show()

sensitivity_analysis(0.07)  \# Base growth rate of 7%
```

This function generates a graph that illustrates how

fluctuations in growth rates influence enterprise value, providing stakeholders with clearer insights into investment risks.

While DCF models are comprehensive tools on their own, it's advantageous to complement them with other valuation techniques like Comparable Company Analysis and Precedent Transactions. Additionally, leveraging Python's web scraping capabilities or APIs can streamline data collection for comparables and benchmarks.

mastering valuation models through Python enhances your analytical skillset and empowers you to deliver actionable insights that inform strategic decisions within your organization. As you develop these models and automate calculations, remember that accuracy is essential—but so is your ability to interpret those numbers effectively to guide stakeholders through uncertainties.

Risk Assessment Techniques

The foundation of risk assessment begins with the identification of risks, which can be categorized into qualitative and quantitative types. Qualitative risks are often subjective, relying on experience or expert judgment, while quantitative risks involve numerical analysis. A useful approach is to classify risks into distinct categories: market risk, credit risk, operational risk, and liquidity risk. For example, market risk refers to fluctuations in market prices that can impact investment returns, whereas credit risk relates to the potential loss from a borrower's failure to repay a loan.

Once risks are identified, the next crucial step is quantification. This process typically employs statistical measures such as standard deviation and Value at Risk (VaR). Standard deviation assesses the volatility of investment returns. Take this example, when evaluating a stock portfolio, you might calculate the standard deviation of historical returns over a specified period. A higher standard deviation indicates greater volatility and thus increased risk. Here's how you can perform this calculation using Python with a Pandas DataFrame containing historical price data:

``` python
import pandas as pd

\#\# Load your data into a DataFrame

data = pd.read_csv('stock_prices.csv')

data['Returns'] = data['Close'].pct_change()

std_dev = data['Returns'].std()

print(f'Standard Deviation of Returns: std_dev')
```

Value at Risk (VaR) is another vital metric in financial modeling. It estimates the potential loss of a set of investments with a specified probability over a given time frame under normal market conditions. For example, if you have a portfolio worth)1 million and a daily VaR of (50, there's a 5% chance that your portfolio could lose more than)50 in one day. You can calculate VaR in Python as follows:

``` python
import numpy as np

\#\# Assuming 'returns' is an array of daily returns

confidence_level = 0.95

var = np.percentile(data['Returns'], 100 * (1 - confidence_level))
```

```python
print(f'Value at Risk (VaR) at confidence_level*100%
confidence level: var')
```
``` `

However, risk assessment extends beyond identification and quantification; it also encompasses scenario analysis and stress testing. These methodologies help gauge how shifts in market conditions can influence financial outcomes. Scenario analysis involves modeling various scenarios—such as economic downturns or sudden interest rate changes—to evaluate their potential impact on investments.

For example, you might create a simple scenario analysis model in Excel by adjusting key inputs like sales growth rates or expense ratios to observe their effects on net income projections. By integrating Python with Excel, you can streamline this process through automated scenario generation and analysis using simulations.

A widely used technique is Monte Carlo simulation, which employs random sampling to model the probability of various outcomes in situations influenced by unpredictable variables. Implementing Monte Carlo simulations in Python is straightforward with libraries like NumPy:

```python
import numpy as np


\#\# Parameters for simulation

num_simulations = 10000

mean_return = 0.07 \# Example mean annual return

std_dev_return = 0.15   \# Example annual standard deviation
```
```

```
\#\# Simulating random returns based on assumed
distributions

simulated_returns = np.random.normal(mean_return,
std_dev_return, num_simulations)


\#\# Analyzing results

expected_value = np.mean(simulated_returns)

risk_of_loss = np.sum(simulated_returns < 0) /
num_simulations

print(f'Expected return: expected_value')

print(f'Probability of loss: risk_of_loss')
```
` ` `

And, effective risk assessment requires continuous monitoring of ongoing risks and adjusting models as new data emerges or market conditions change. This adaptive approach ensures that your models remain relevant and actionable over time.

By incorporating these techniques into your financial modeling process, you will gain a deeper understanding of inherent uncertainties while making informed decisions that align with your organization's risk tolerance and strategic objectives. As you become proficient in utilizing Python alongside Excel for risk assessment, you'll find yourself well-equipped to tackle complex financial challenges with both confidence and precision.

Scenario Analysis and Forecasting

Scenario analysis and forecasting are essential elements of effective financial modeling, providing analysts with the tools to evaluate potential future outcomes based on varying assumptions. By employing these techniques, organizations can better understand the implications of different scenarios —whether optimistic, pessimistic, or neutral—on their financial health. When implemented effectively with Python in Excel, scenario analysis can yield valuable insights that inform strategic decisions and help prepare for uncertainties.

At its essence, scenario analysis involves generating a range of possible futures by adjusting key assumptions in your financial models. For example, consider a company projecting revenue growth. You might establish several scenarios: a base case with moderate growth, a best-case scenario reflecting accelerated sales due to market expansion, and a worst-case scenario that accounts for potential downturns or increased competition. Each scenario produces distinct financial outcomes, enabling decision-makers to evaluate the impact of various external factors.

To begin incorporating scenario analysis using Python, start by defining the key variables you wish to manipulate. Suppose you have a simple financial model in Excel that predicts revenue based on sales volume and price per unit. You can create Python scripts that extract these variables from your Excel workbook, modify them according to your defined scenarios, and write the results back into Excel for further analysis.

Here's a brief example:

```python
import pandas as pd

\#\# Load existing Excel data

data = pd.read_excel('financial_model.xlsx')
```

\#\# Define your scenarios

scenarios =

'Base Case': 'sales_volume': data['Sales Volume'].iloc[0], 'price_per_unit': data['Price per Unit'].iloc[0],

'Best Case': 'sales_volume': data['Sales Volume'].iloc[0] * 1.2, 'price_per_unit': data['Price per Unit'].iloc[0] * 1.1,

'Worst Case': 'sales_volume': data['Sales Volume'].iloc[0] * 0.8, 'price_per_unit': data['Price per Unit'].iloc[0] * 0.9

\#\# Analyze each scenario

results =

for case, values in scenarios.items():

revenue = values['sales_volume'] * values['price_per_unit']

results[case] = revenue

\#\# Convert results to DataFrame and save back to Excel

results_df = pd.DataFrame(list(results.items()), columns=['Scenario', 'Projected Revenue'])

results_df.to_excel('scenario_analysis_results.xlsx', index=False)

` ` `

In this example, three distinct scenarios are established by adjusting sales volume and price per unit. The projected revenue for each case is calculated and saved back into an Excel workbook for easy reference.

Complementing scenario analysis is forecasting, which projects future values based on historical trends and patterns. This process typically utilizes statistical methods such as regression analysis or time series forecasting, with Python's libraries like Statsmodels significantly enhancing these capabilities.

Take this example, if you have historical sales data and wish to forecast future sales using linear regression, consider the following implementation:

```python
import pandas as pd
import statsmodels.api as sm

\#\# Load historical sales data
data = pd.read_csv('historical_sales_data.csv')
X = data[['Year']] \# Independent variable
y = data['Sales'] \# Dependent variable

\#\# Add a constant term for intercept calculation
X = sm.add_constant(X)

\#\# Fit the regression model
model = sm.OLS(y, X).fit()

\#\# Make predictions for future years
future_years = pd.DataFrame('Year': [2023, 2024, 2025])
future_years = sm.add_constant(future_years)
```

predictions = model.predict(future_years)

\#\# Output forecasted sales

forecast_df = pd.DataFrame('Year': future_years['Year'], 'Forecasted Sales': predictions)

forecast_df.to_csv('sales_forecast.csv', index=False)
` ` `

This code demonstrates how to utilize historical sales data to build a linear regression model that predicts future sales figures for specific years. The resulting forecasts are saved in a CSV file that can be easily accessed in Excel for further manipulation or presentation.

By integrating these forecasting techniques into your financial models, you enhance their depth and provide stakeholders with critical insights into potential outcomes based on varying market conditions or business strategies. And, leveraging both scenario analysis and forecasting through Python allows for dynamic updates; as new data emerges or assumptions evolve, models can be recalibrated swiftly.

mastering both scenario analysis and forecasting equips financial analysts to navigate uncertainty proactively rather than reactively. The ability to visualize multiple paths forward enables organizations to align their strategies with their risk appetite while adequately preparing for diverse market dynamics. With Python's capabilities paired with Excel's user-friendly interface, you are well-prepared to translate abstract possibilities into concrete strategies that drive informed decision-making throughout your organization.

Automating Financial Reports

Automating financial reports can transform tedious manual processes into streamlined, efficient workflows. By generating timely and accurate financial statements, organizations can significantly enhance their decision-making capabilities. With Python's extensive ecosystem and its seamless integration with Excel, you can automate report generation, reduce human error, and enable analysts to focus on interpretation rather than data compilation.

To embark on this automation journey, start by defining the key components of your financial report. A typical report may include income statements, balance sheets, and cash flow statements—each of which can be dynamically linked to a central dataset that updates regularly. Utilizing Python libraries such as Pandas for data manipulation and OpenPyXL for Excel interaction allows you to automate both data retrieval and the formatting of these reports.

Begin by creating an Excel template for your financial report. This template should incorporate all necessary sections with predefined formulas where applicable. Take this example, your income statement could include revenue figures derived from sales data stored in a separate worksheet. Once your template is established, you can write a Python script to pull in the latest data and populate the template accordingly.

Here's a practical example to illustrate the process:

```python
import pandas as pd

from openpyxl import load_workbook

\#\# Load the latest financial data

data = pd.read_excel('latest_financial_data.xlsx')
```

```
\#\# Load your Excel template
template = load_workbook('financial_report_template.xlsx')
sheet = template.active


\#\# Update the Income Statement section
sheet['B2'] = data['Total Revenue'].iloc[0]  \# Assuming B2 is where revenue goes
sheet['B3'] = data['Cost of Goods Sold'].iloc[0]  \# B3 for COGS
sheet['B4'] = f'=B2-B3'  \# Gross Profit formula


\#\# Save the populated report
template.save('automated_financial_report.xlsx')
` ` `
```

In this script, we first load our most recent financial data alongside an Excel template designed for our reports. We then specify which cells in the template correspond to specific pieces of financial information—like total revenue or cost of goods sold—and update those cells with values extracted from our dataset. The use of formulas within Excel facilitates dynamic calculations based on updated inputs.

Beyond merely populating numbers into designated cells, consider incorporating visual elements like charts or graphs that provide immediate insights at a glance. For example, by integrating Matplotlib within your reporting framework, you can automate chart creation based on historical performance or predictive metrics:

```python
```

```python
import matplotlib.pyplot as plt

\#\# Example: Visualizing revenue trends over time
revenue_trends = data[['Date', 'Total Revenue']]
plt.figure(figsize=(10,5))
plt.plot(revenue_trends['Date'], revenue_trends['Total Revenue'], marker='o')
plt.title('Revenue Trends Over Time')
plt.xlabel('Date')
plt.ylabel('Total Revenue')
plt.grid()
plt.savefig('revenue_trends.png') \# Save chart image
```

You can then programmatically insert this generated chart into your Excel report using OpenPyXL:

```python
from openpyxl.drawing.image import Image

img = Image('revenue_trends.png')
sheet.add_image(img, 'D5') \# Assume D5 is where we want to place it
```

This approach not only provides stakeholders with quantitative data but also presents visual representations within a consolidated document.

Another crucial aspect of automating financial reports is scheduling regular updates to ensure that the most current information is always reflected. You can use task schedulers like cron jobs (for Unix-based systems) or Windows Task Scheduler to run your Python scripts at predetermined intervals—be it daily, weekly, or monthly—depending on how frequently you need new data incorporated into your reports.

And, implementing robust error handling within your automation scripts ensures that any issues encountered during execution are captured and addressed promptly. Using try-except blocks allows you to manage potential exceptions gracefully:

``` python

try:

\#\# Existing code to generate report...

except Exception as e:

print(f"An error occurred: e")
```

By embedding these practices into your automation strategy, you'll not only enhance efficiency but also maintain high standards of accuracy in your reporting processes.

automating financial reports with Python saves time while improving reliability in critical business operations. In today's fast-paced environment, organizations striving for agility and responsiveness will find that automated financial insights empower teams with essential tools for strategic decision-making—freeing analysts to focus on more analytical tasks rather than repetitive report generation.

Tools for Financial Analysts

Financial analysts operate in a dynamic landscape that demands adeptness in data manipulation, reporting, and analysis. To excel in this environment, a range of tools is available to enhance productivity and streamline workflows. One transformative approach is the integration of Python with Excel, which equips analysts with a powerful toolkit for efficiently tackling complex financial tasks.

Central to any financial analyst's capabilities is the ability to manipulate and visualize data effectively. Python libraries such as Pandas have become indispensable for managing large datasets. With its intuitive DataFrame structure, analysts can perform operations like filtering, grouping, and aggregating data effortlessly. For example, calculating key financial ratios from balance sheet data can be done with just a few lines of code:

```python
import pandas as pd


\#\# Load balance sheet data

balance_sheet = pd.read_excel('balance_sheet.xlsx')


\#\# Calculate current ratio

balance_sheet['Current Ratio'] = balance_sheet['Current Assets'] / balance_sheet['Current Liabilities']

```

This straightforward code allows for rapid liquidity analysis, eliminating the need for manual calculations in Excel.

Equally important is the visual representation of data in finance. Libraries like Matplotlib and Seaborn integrate seamlessly with Python to produce compelling visualizations. These tools enable analysts to illustrate trends or compare metrics over time with ease. Take this example, using Seaborn to create a bar plot can effectively showcase changes in revenue across different quarters:

```python
import seaborn as sns
import matplotlib.pyplot as plt

\#\# Sample data for revenue by quarter
revenue_data = pd.DataFrame(
'Quarter': ['Q1', 'Q2', 'Q3', 'Q4'],
'Revenue': [150000, 200000, 250000, 300000]
)

sns.barplot(x='Quarter', y='Revenue', data=revenue_data)
plt.title('Quarterly Revenue')
plt.xlabel('Quarter')
plt.ylabel('Revenue')
plt.show()
```

The clarity provided by such visualizations is invaluable; they enable stakeholders to quickly grasp complex information.

Another essential tool in an analyst's arsenal is Jupyter Notebook, which offers an interactive environment for coding and documentation. This platform encourages iterative development, allowing analysts to run code snippets and observe immediate results—ideal for experimenting with various modeling techniques without disrupting their workflow. For example, an analyst might use Jupyter to build a forecast model using time series analysis:

```python
\#\# Time series forecast example using statsmodels
import statsmodels.api as sm

\#\# Assuming `data` contains the time series information
model = sm.tsa.ARIMA(data['Sales'], order=(1, 1, 1))
results = model.fit()

forecast = results.forecast(steps=12)
print(forecast)
```

Such capabilities enable analysts to pivot swiftly based on insights gained during exploration.

For those working with databases or larger datasets beyond Excel's limits, SQL (Structured Query Language) proves indispensable. Analysts often need to extract specific data from relational databases before further analysis in Python or Excel. By utilizing SQLAlchemy alongside Pandas, they can seamlessly integrate databases into their analytical workflows:

```python
from sqlalchemy import create_engine

\#\# Create a connection to the database
engine = create_engine('sqlite:///financial_data.db')

\#\# Querying data directly into a DataFrame
```

```
query = "SELECT * FROM sales_data WHERE date >=
'2023-01-01'

sales_data = pd.read_sql(query, engine)
```
` ` `

This combination allows analysts to harness the strengths of SQL for efficient data retrieval while leveraging Python for thorough analysis.

Additionally, automation tools such as Airflow or Prefect help streamline repetitive tasks within financial workflows. By automating report generation and ensuring timely updates, these solutions free analysts from mundane duties and allow them to concentrate on strategic insights instead of routine data entry.

Collaboration tools like GitHub also play a crucial role by facilitating version control in projects that involve multiple team members. Managing script changes through version control systems keeps everyone updated and provides an easy way to roll back if needed.

By equipping themselves with these tools, financial analysts not only enhance their capabilities but also position themselves at the forefront of innovative practices within their organizations. The integration of Python into traditional financial frameworks fosters adaptability and ensures readiness for an ever-evolving landscape where speed and accuracy are essential.

effectively leveraging these technologies—be it through efficient data management with Pandas or automating report generation—grants analysts a significant advantage in making informed decisions based on timely analyses that drive business success.

CHAPTER 14: AUTOMATION AND INTEGRATION OF WORKFLOWS

Benefits of Automation in Excel

Automation in Excel greatly boosts productivity and accuracy, making it an essential tool for professionals in any data-driven field. One of the primary advantages of automation is its ability to reduce manual tasks. Repetitive activities—such as data entry, formatting, and report generation—can consume valuable time that would be better spent on strategic analysis and decision-making. By utilizing Python scripts within Excel, users can automate these tedious processes effectively.

For example, consider a scenario where you need to generate monthly sales reports from multiple worksheets. Instead of manually gathering data from each sheet, a Python script can be developed to automatically extract the necessary information and compile it into a single report. Here's a brief code snippet to illustrate this:

```python
import pandas as pd

\#\# Load multiple sheets from an Excel file
xls = pd.ExcelFile('sales_data.xlsx')

\#\# Initialize an empty DataFrame to store results
combined_data = pd.DataFrame()

\#\# Loop through all sheets and concatenate data
for sheet_name in xls.sheet_names:
    sheet_data = pd.read_excel(xls, sheet_name)
    combined_data = pd.concat([combined_data, sheet_data])

\#\# Save the compiled report
combined_data.to_excel('monthly_sales_report.xlsx',
index=False)
```

This example highlights how automation not only saves time but also reduces errors associated with manual data handling.

Another significant benefit of automation is its ability to enhance consistency across reports and analyses. When repetitive tasks are automated, the risk of human error diminishes considerably. Take this example, consistent formatting of charts or the application of complex formulas is crucial for maintaining professional standards in reporting. Python scripts help ensure that every output adheres to specified formats uniformly.

And, automation simplifies complex calculations that might be cumbersome or impractical to perform manually. For financial analysts, conducting sensitivity analysis often involves adjusting multiple input variables and observing their effects on outputs. With Python, analysts can create functions that streamline these simulations:

```python
import numpy as np


def sensitivity_analysis(base_case):
    variations = np.arange(-0.1, 0.11, 0.01)  \# Change inputs from -10% to +10%
    results = []


    for variation in variations:
        new_case = base_case * (1 + variation)
        \#\# Assume some calculation occurs here
        result = calculate_financial_metrics(new_case)   \# Placeholder for actual calculations
        results.append(result)


    return results
```

By automating such analyses, you not only save time but also gain deeper insights through systematic exploration of outcomes under varying conditions.

Additionally, automation fosters collaboration among team

members. In environments where multiple analysts work on similar projects or reports, using shared scripts ensures alignment on methodologies and outputs. Version control systems like Git enable teams to manage changes efficiently while keeping track of different iterations of their automated scripts.

Finally, the flexibility offered by automation paves the way for new opportunities in analysis. Analysts can allocate more time to exploring advanced techniques without being weighed down by mundane tasks. This shift encourages innovation—whether analyzing trends with machine learning algorithms or developing sophisticated models becomes feasible when routine processes are automated.

By integrating automation into their Excel workflows through Python, professionals unlock a range of benefits that lead to improved efficiency, accuracy, and creativity in their work. As you adopt these practices, you'll find yourself completing tasks more quickly while enhancing the quality and depth of your analyses—ultimately transforming how you tackle data challenges within your organization.

Automating Routine Tasks

Automating routine tasks in Excel can significantly enhance your workflow, allowing you to focus on more complex analysis and strategic initiatives. Many professionals find themselves spending countless hours on repetitive tasks such as data entry, formatting, and report generation. By leveraging Python, you can streamline these processes and substantially cut down the time spent on tedious activities.

Take, for example, a common scenario in finance: generating monthly budget reports from various sources. Manually gathering data from multiple spreadsheets can take hours or even days. However, by automating this process with Python, you can create a script that efficiently pulls data from several files and consolidates it into one comprehensive report. Here's a simple illustration:

```python
import pandas as pd
import glob

\#\# Use glob to find all relevant Excel files
files = glob.glob('budget_data/*.xlsx')

\#\# Initialize an empty DataFrame
combined_budget_data = pd.DataFrame()

for file in files:
df = pd.read_excel(file)
combined_budget_data                            =
pd.concat([combined_budget_data, df])

\#\# Save the consolidated report
combined_budget_data.to_excel('consolidated_budget_repo
rt.xlsx', index=False)
```

This code exemplifies the power of automation. With just a few lines of Python, you can seamlessly combine all relevant data into a single workbook, saving yourself hours of work.

Another area where automation proves beneficial is in formatting reports. The manual adjustment of fonts, colors, and layouts can be both tedious and inconsistent. Python libraries like OpenPyXL and XlsxWriter enable you to automate these formatting tasks effectively. For example, if you want to format a specific range of cells with custom styles in your report, you could use the following code:

```python
from openpyxl import Workbook
from openpyxl.styles import Font

workbook = Workbook()
sheet = workbook.active

\#\# Create headers with bold font
header_font = Font(bold=True)
for col in range(1, 6):  \# Assuming five columns of headers
cell = sheet.cell(row=1, column=col)
cell.font = header_font

\#\# Save the formatted workbook
workbook.save('formatted_report.xlsx')
```

This snippet automatically sets the headers to bold when generating reports, ensuring your documents maintain a professional appearance without the hassle of manual adjustments.

Data validation is another routine task that can be effectively automated. When working under tight deadlines, ensuring data integrity during entry can often be overlooked. With Python's capabilities integrated into Excel, you can enforce rules for valid data entries—such as restricting input types or setting ranges—without manually checking each entry.

Take this example:

```python
import win32com.client

excel_app = win32com.client.Dispatch("Excel.Application")
workbook = excel_app.Workbooks.Open('data_validation.xlsx')
worksheet = workbook.Sheets[1]

\#\# Apply data validation for a range of cells
validation_range = worksheet.Range("A2:A100")
validation_range.Validation.Add(
Type=1,
AlertStyle=1,
Operator=1,
Formula1="100",
Formula2="0",
InCellDropdown=True,
ShowInput=True,
ShowError=True,
)

workbook.Save()
excel_app.Quit()
```

` ` `

By applying validation rules programmatically, you reduce the potential for human error and enhance data quality across your reports.

Additionally, scheduling recurring tasks through automation allows you to free up significant time in your calendar. With Python's built-in libraries like schedule, you can set scripts to run at designated intervals—whether it's daily reports or weekly summaries—ensuring that vital tasks are consistently executed without manual intervention.

Here's how scheduling works:

` ` `python

import schedule

import time

def job():

print("Running scheduled task...")

\#\# Schedule job every day at 10:00 AM

schedule.every().day.at("10:00").do(job)

while True:

schedule.run_pending()

time.sleep(60) \# Wait for one minute before checking again

` ` `

This straightforward setup facilitates unattended execution of essential workflows at specified times—such as generating daily sales updates—enabling you to devote more effort to analytical pursuits rather than becoming bogged down by operational tasks.

automating routine tasks creates opportunities for innovation within your organization. Once repetitive processes are managed through scripts, teams are empowered to experiment with advanced analytics techniques or explore new tools without being constrained by time limitations on basic operations. This transformation not only boosts productivity but also fosters a culture of continuous improvement.

By integrating these automation practices into your daily routine with Python in Excel, you'll not only gain efficiency but also experience the satisfaction that comes from making better use of your time and skills. Embrace this shift toward automation and witness how it enhances both your personal productivity and your organization's overall effectiveness in addressing data challenges.

Triggering Python Scripts in Excel

Triggering Python scripts in Excel opens up a world of possibilities for enhancing your workflow. Running scripts directly within the familiar Excel environment allows for seamless integration of complex data manipulations and analyses, enabling you to derive insights more efficiently. Understanding how to initiate these scripts effectively is crucial for maximizing productivity.

One common approach to triggering Python scripts is by using Excel's built-in features, such as buttons or form controls. For example, you can assign a Python script to a button on your worksheet, allowing anyone using the file to execute complex operations with just a click. Let's explore how this can be accomplished using the PyXLL library, which seamlessly connects Python and Excel.

First, ensure that PyXLL is installed and configured properly in your Excel setup. Once that's done, creating a custom function is straightforward. Here's an example:

```python
from pyxll import xl_func


@xl_func
def calculate_total(sales_range):
total = sum(sales_range)
return total
```

This function calculates the total of a selected range of sales data. To trigger this script from Excel, simply enter =calculate_total(A1:A10) in any cell. This will compute the total of the values in cells A1 through A10 whenever invoked.

For more interactive applications, consider creating buttons that execute specific tasks when clicked. You can insert a button via the Developer tab in Excel and assign it to run a macro that calls your Python script. Here's how you can set this up:

1. Navigate to the Developer tab.
2. Click on "Insert" and select "Button (Form Control)."
3. Draw the button on your worksheet.
4. Assign a macro that links to your Python code.

In this scenario, you'll need to create an intermediate VBA macro that invokes your Python script via PyXLL:

```vba
Sub RunPythonScript()
RunPython                     ("import                     my_module;
```

my_module.my_function()")

End Sub

` ` `

Now, when you click the button, it will execute my_function() from my_module, allowing you to perform whatever actions are defined within that function directly from Excel.

Another powerful method involves leveraging events within Excel—such as opening or saving files—to trigger Python scripts automatically without manual input. Take this example, if you want specific calculations or data checks to occur every time an Excel file is opened, you can use VBA event handlers like Workbook_Open. Here's what this looks like:

` ` `vba

Private Sub Workbook_Open()

RunPython ("import my_module; my_module.check_data_integrity()")

End Sub

` ` `

With this setup, every time the workbook opens, it will run the specified Python function to check data integrity automatically. This guarantees users are always greeted with verified information without requiring additional clicks or commands.

Excel also supports triggering scripts based on cell changes by employing Worksheet Change Events. This feature is particularly useful for dynamic applications where real-time analysis is needed based on user inputs:

` ` `vba

```
Private Sub Worksheet_Change(ByVal Target As Range)

If Not Intersect(Target, Me.Range("A1")) Is Nothing Then

RunPython            ("import            my_module;
my_module.update_analysis()")

End If

End Sub
```
` ` `

In this scenario, any change made in cell A1 will trigger an update analysis script written in Python—an efficient way to maintain current data insights based on user interactions.

To ensure reliability and performance when triggering scripts in response to events or user actions, it's essential to test each integration step thoroughly. Monitor execution times and handle potential errors gracefully by incorporating try-except blocks in your Python functions while logging any issues encountered during execution.

By combining these techniques, you can not only transform individual workflows but also enhance collaboration across teams relying on shared reports or dashboards integrated with live data processes. As colleagues utilize automated tools initiated by simple actions—like clicking a button—the focus shifts back toward insightful decision-making rather than routine data handling tasks.

Implementing these strategies fosters an environment where analysis thrives through automation while maintaining the essential human element of interpretation and insight generation—a true testament to marrying efficiency with creativity in our data-driven endeavors. Embrace these techniques as you refine how you leverage Python within your daily Excel routines; soon enough, you'll find yourself not only saving time but also elevating the overall quality of work produced within your team or organization.

Integration with Other Office Tools

Integrating Python with Microsoft Office tools can significantly boost your productivity and streamline your workflows. Each tool in the Office suite has its unique strengths, and when combined with Python, they can create a powerful synergy that simplifies complex tasks. For example, using Outlook for email automation alongside Excel for data analysis allows you to minimize manual effort while enhancing your reporting capabilities.

One effective application of this integration is automating email reports generated from Excel data. Picture this: sales figures are automatically compiled in an Excel sheet, and a Python script formats that information into a well-structured email. This not only saves time but also ensures consistency in communication. Let's explore how to set this up using the win32com library, which enables Python to interact with COM objects like Outlook.

First, ensure you have the pywin32 package installed:

```bash

pip install pywin32

```

Once you have the package, you can use the following Python script to send an email with data directly pulled from an Excel workbook:

```python

import win32com.client as win32


def send_email_with_report():

\#\# Initialize Outlook application
```

```
outlook = win32.Dispatch('outlook.application')

mail = outlook.CreateItem(0)  \# Create a new email item


\#\# Prepare the report from Excel

excel = win32.Dispatch('Excel.Application')

wb = excel.Workbooks.Open(r'C:.xlsx')

sheet = wb.Sheets('Sheet1')


report_data = sheet.Range('A1:B10').Value   \# Adjust the range as needed


\#\# Format the report content for the email body

body_content = "Sales Report:

for row in report_data:

body_content += f"row[0]: row[1]


\#\# Compose the email

mail.Subject = 'Automated Sales Report'

mail.Body = body_content

mail.To = 'recipient@example.com'


\#\# Send the email

mail.Send()


\#\# Cleanup
```

```
wb.Close(False)

excel.Quit()
```
` ` `

This script retrieves data from a specified range in your Excel workbook and formats it into an email body before sending it to a designated recipient. By running this script periodically or triggering it after completing tasks like month-end reports, you ensure timely communication without needing to compile and send emails manually.

Effective collaboration often requires sharing insights across multiple platforms, which leads us to integrating Microsoft Teams with Python applications. Take this example, when critical updates arise or data anomalies are detected in Excel, automated notifications can be sent directly to Teams channels using webhooks or direct API calls.

Here's how to set up such integration using the requests library to post messages to Teams:

` ` `python
```
import requests


def post_to_teams(message):

url              =              'https://outlook.office.com/webhook/
your_webhook_url_here'


payload =

text": message


requests.post(url, json=payload)
```

\#\# Example usage after a critical update in Excel

post_to_teams("Attention: Sales figures exceeded projections for Q3.")

` ` `

In this snippet, simply replace "your_webhook_url_here" with your actual Teams webhook URL. This integration facilitates real-time communication among team members, enhancing responsiveness without inundating anyone with unnecessary emails.

And, combining OneNote with Python opens up new avenues for organizing notes and tracking projects. You could automate note-taking from an Excel sheet directly into OneNote by creating structured summaries or progress reports based on spreadsheet data. By utilizing OneNote's API alongside Python, you can consolidate information while keeping it accessible and organized.

For example, if you're managing project milestones tracked in Excel, you might write a script that logs these milestones into OneNote as follows:

` ` `python

\#\# Example sketch; requires additional setup for OneNote API access.

import requests

def add_note_to_onenote(title, content):

url = "https://www.onenote.com/api/v1.0/pages

headers =

Authorization": "Bearer YOUR_ACCESS_TOKEN",

```
Content-Type": "application/json

data =
title": title,
content": content,


response = requests.post(url, headers=headers, json=data)
return response.status_code == 201   \# Returns True if
successful


\#\# Example usage after updating project status in Excel.
add_note_to_onenote("Project Update", "Milestones updated;
see attached Excel.")
` ` `
```

This example illustrates how you might structure interactions with OneNote through Python scripts aimed at enhancing collaboration within your projects.

The cumulative effect of these integrations is profound —creating an interconnected ecosystem where data flows freely between tools, reducing manual input errors while saving time. As you refine your approach to integrating Python with other Office applications, you'll discover that your ability to deliver impactful insights grows exponentially.

These advanced strategies not only improve workflow efficiency but also foster better communication among teams engaged in various aspects of business operations. The result is a cohesive environment where technology and human insight work together seamlessly to achieve organizational goals—an essential step toward mastering modern data-driven practices in any profession.

Workflow Automation Tools

Workflow automation tools are transforming the way professionals engage with data and manage their tasks, particularly when paired with Python and Excel. The true power of automation lies in its ability to reduce repetitive tasks, enabling you to dedicate more time to high-value work. Imagine a scenario where data entry, report generation, and even data analysis occur automatically. This not only minimizes the risk of human error but also frees you up for strategic thinking.

One standout tool in the automation landscape is Zapier. This platform allows users to connect various applications and automate workflows through simple triggers and actions. For example, you can create a Zap that automatically captures new entries from a Google Form, processes them in Excel, and sends out a confirmation email via Gmail—all without extensive coding. A practical application of this would be setting up a Zap that triggers a Python script whenever a new row is added to an Excel spreadsheet, enabling further analysis or updates to another system based on that data.

Consider this scenario: you're collecting survey responses through Google Forms and want to compile the results in Excel while notifying your team via Slack about new submissions. With Zapier, you can design a workflow where form submissions automatically populate an Excel sheet. Once the data is recorded, the workflow can trigger a custom Python script that generates insights or visualizations from the collected data before posting a summary message in your team's Slack channel.

Another powerful tool for automating workflows is

Microsoft Power Automate (formerly known as Microsoft Flow). This tool integrates seamlessly with Excel and other Microsoft services, allowing you to create flows that respond to various events within your Office suite. Take this example, if your team frequently shares updates on project status via Excel spreadsheets stored in OneDrive or SharePoint, Power Automate can monitor those files for changes. When an update is detected, it can automatically notify relevant stakeholders through email or Teams messages, ensuring everyone stays informed without the need for manual checks.

Power Automate also offers integration with external applications through its extensive connector ecosystem. If you regularly pull data from web applications or APIs into your Excel files, automated flows that keep this information updated can be invaluable. For example, if your sales data updates daily from an external CRM system, Power Automate can pull that information directly into your Excel workbook at specified intervals—eliminating the need for manual exports.

To maximize these tools alongside Python scripts, consider combining their capabilities for enhanced performance. Take this example, after Power Automate updates your Excel file with new data from an API, it could trigger a Python script to process this information and perform calculations or generate reports based on the latest figures.

Next is IFTTT (If This Then That)—another excellent option for workflow automation. IFTTT operates on similar principles as Zapier but often focuses more on personal productivity applications. It enables effortless connections between various online services; for instance, you might set it up so that whenever you add a new entry in an Excel spreadsheet (using the Google Sheets applet), it triggers actions such as creating a task in Todoist or posting an update on Twitter. IFTTT excels in scenarios where light-touch integrations enhance personal productivity without requiring complex coding.

The ultimate goal of utilizing these automation tools is not just to eliminate tedious tasks but also to foster a proactive work environment where insights flow freely and decisions are informed by real-time data. By implementing these workflows, organizations gain greater agility in responding to changes and challenges.

Integrating Python into these workflows further elevates their potential. Whether developing custom scripts tailored to specific business needs or optimizing existing processes through intelligent analysis, combining automation tools with Python creates an invaluable framework for boosting efficiency and effectiveness in any professional setting. This integration fosters a culture of continuous improvement— an essential mindset for anyone looking to thrive in today's fast-paced work environment.

Embracing these workflow automation strategies opens up new possibilities for productivity. As you begin incorporating these tools into your existing processes, you'll likely uncover innovative ways to streamline operations while enhancing overall performance across various projects and initiatives. The journey toward mastering this integration will not only simplify your work but also empower you to lead initiatives that effectively leverage data-driven insights across your organization.

Task Scheduling and Alerts

Task scheduling and alerts play a crucial role in enhancing workflow automation, especially when integrating Python with Excel. These features ensure that tasks are executed at optimal times, allowing users to concentrate on strategic activities while routine operations function smoothly in the background. Automating tasks such as data updates, report generation, or triggering alerts based on specific conditions in your Excel datasets streamlines processes and saves valuable time.

Python provides several libraries to facilitate task scheduling, with schedule and APScheduler being among the most popular options. The schedule library is particularly user-friendly, making it easy to create simple job schedulers. Take this example, if you need to run a Python script that processes your Excel data every day at 8 AM, you can set it up as follows:

```python
import schedule

import time


def job():

\#\# Code to process your Excel data

print("Processing Excel data...")


schedule.every().day.at("08:00").do(job)


while True:

schedule.run_pending()

time.sleep(1)

```

In this example, the job function will execute daily at 8 AM, handling the data as required. This method ensures consistent data management without the need for manual intervention, greatly enhancing operational efficiency.

For more complex scheduling requirements or when managing multiple tasks, APScheduler offers increased flexibility. It allows for job scheduling using cron-like expressions or intervals and can even handle jobs across different threads. Here's how you might set up a job that runs every Monday at noon:

```python
from         apscheduler.schedulers.blocking         import BlockingScheduler

def scheduled_job():
\#\# Your code here
print("Running weekly report...")

scheduler = BlockingScheduler()
scheduler.add_job(scheduled_job,                      'cron', day_of_week='mon', hour=12)

scheduler.start()
```

Integrating alerts into your workflows further elevates their effectiveness by notifying stakeholders of critical events or changes within your datasets. For example, you may want to send an alert when sales figures fall below a certain threshold. Python's compatibility with email services via libraries like smtplib simplifies the implementation of these notifications.

Here's an example of how you can set an alert if sales data dips below a specified limit:

```python
import smtplib
```

```python
def check_sales(sales_data):
threshold = 1000 \# Define your threshold here
if sales_data < threshold:
send_alert_email()

def send_alert_email():
server = smtplib.SMTP('smtp.gmail.com', 587)
server.starttls()

server.login('your_email@gmail.com', 'your_password')

subject = "Sales Alert
body = "Sales have dropped below the threshold!

message = f'Subject: subjectbody'

server.sendmail('your_email@gmail.com',
'recipient@example.com', message)

server.quit()
```
`` ` ``

This function checks sales data against a defined threshold and sends an email alert when necessary. By incorporating such checks within scheduled tasks, you can ensure timely responses to fluctuations in key metrics.

The combination of task scheduling and alerts not only boosts operational efficiency but also cultivates a proactive organizational culture where critical events are promptly addressed. Imagine running daily reports that automatically notify managers of performance metrics while simultaneously refreshing Excel datasets for real-time analysis. This integration facilitates better decision-making based on current data rather than outdated information.

As you implement these strategies, consider utilizing logging mechanisms to effectively track task executions and alert notifications. Libraries like logging can provide valuable insights into the success or failure of task runs—an essential aspect of maintaining robust workflows.

By mastering task scheduling and alerts within your Python-Excel integration projects, you gain enhanced control over your processes. This level of automation empowers teams to focus on high-impact activities while ensuring that foundational operations remain consistent and reliable—an invaluable advantage in today's fast-paced business environment, where responsiveness is key to success.

Monitoring and Optimization

Monitoring and optimization are vital elements of any automated workflow, particularly when integrating Python with Excel. These practices ensure that processes not only run smoothly but also adapt to evolving needs and enhance efficiency over time. By establishing robust monitoring systems, you can gain valuable insights into the performance of your automation, pinpoint potential bottlenecks, and make informed optimizations.

One of the primary tools for monitoring is logging. Python's built-in logging library allows you to track events within your scripts by capturing details such as execution times, errors, and user-defined messages. By logging key actions, you can analyze workflow performance over time. For example, if you're executing a series of data processing tasks on an hourly basis, you can configure logging to record the start and end times of each task alongside any encountered errors:

```python
import logging

import time


\#\# Configure logging

logging.basicConfig(filename='workflow.log',
level=logging.INFO)


def process_data():

start_time = time.time()

try:

\#\# Data processing logic here

logging.info("Data processing started.")

\#\# Simulate data processing

time.sleep(2) \# Placeholder for actual work

logging.info("Data processing completed successfully.")

except Exception as e:

logging.error(f"Error occurred: e")

finally:

end_time = time.time()

elapsed_time = end_time - start_time
```

logging.info(f"Process completed in elapsed_time:.2f seconds.")

process_data()

` ` `

This approach not only documents your workflow but also helps identify trends over time. If a particular task consistently takes longer than expected or frequently encounters errors, it signals a need for further investigation and optimization.

Following monitoring comes the optimization phase, where you leverage insights gained to enhance your workflows. Python offers a wealth of libraries to support this effort. Take this example, the cProfile module can help you profile your scripts to discover where most execution time is spent. By identifying slow functions or inefficient loops, you can target specific areas for improvement.

Take a script that aggregates large datasets in Excel using a loop; optimizing data handling can dramatically reduce execution time. Instead of manually iterating through each row, utilizing vectorized operations from libraries like Pandas can yield significant performance benefits:

` ` `python

import pandas as pd

\#\# Example data processing using Pandas

def aggregate_data(file_path):

df = pd.read_excel(file_path)

aggregated_data = df.groupby('Category').sum()   \# Vectorized operation

```python
aggregated_data.to_excel('aggregated_data.xlsx')


aggregate_data('sales_data.xlsx')
```
` ` `

In this example, leveraging Pandas' built-in grouping functionality provides a faster method for aggregating data compared to looping through individual rows.

Further optimization might involve reviewing your overall architecture. Are there redundant tasks? Can parallel processing be employed? Python's concurrent.futures module enables you to run multiple operations simultaneously, significantly reducing total processing time when dealing with independent tasks:

` ` `python

```python
from concurrent.futures import ThreadPoolExecutor


def task1():
\#\# Some workload here
print("Task 1 complete")


def task2():
\#\# Some workload here
print("Task 2 complete")


with ThreadPoolExecutor() as executor:
executor.submit(task1)
executor.submit(task2)
```

` ` `

By executing tasks concurrently, you maximize resource utilization and minimize waiting times.

In addition to these technical improvements, it's important to assess how your automated workflows align with broader business processes. Regular feedback from stakeholders regarding workflow effectiveness can provide qualitative insights that complement quantitative metrics. Such feedback loops encourage continuous improvement and foster a culture of innovation within teams.

Finally, while optimizing workflows is crucial, maintaining documentation of changes throughout this process is equally important. Clear records help teams understand the rationale behind specific decisions and serve as reference points for future adjustments.

the combination of monitoring and optimization creates a cycle of continuous improvement in Python-Excel integrations. By diligently tracking performance metrics and actively seeking enhancements based on those insights, organizations position themselves to adeptly respond to evolving demands—ensuring their workflows remain efficient and impactful in delivering results.

Building a Complete Automated Solution

Creating a fully automated solution using Python and Excel involves integrating various concepts covered throughout this book. By combining the strengths of both platforms, you can significantly enhance the efficiency and accuracy of your workflows. An effective automated solution can handle repetitive tasks, manage data processing, and generate reports with minimal human intervention.

Let's explore a practical example: generating a monthly sales report. This process typically entails collecting data from multiple sources, performing calculations, creating visualizations, and formatting the final document. Automating these steps can save you countless hours each month.

To begin constructing your automated solution, clearly define the workflow by mapping out each step—from data extraction to report generation. Utilize Python libraries such as Pandas for data manipulation and OpenPyXL or XlsxWriter for Excel operations, as these will serve as the backbone of your automation.

Imagine you have an Excel file containing sales data from various regions and products. The first step is to load this data into a Pandas DataFrame:

```python
import pandas as pd


\#\# Load the Excel file

sales_data            =            pd.read_excel('sales_data.xlsx', sheet_name='Sales')
```

Once the data is loaded, you can perform analyses or transformations on the DataFrame. For example, let's calculate the total sales for each product:

```python
\#\# Grouping by product to calculate total sales

total_sales            =            sales_data.groupby('Product')['Sales'].sum().reset_index()
```

After processing the data, it's crucial to visualize the results before finalizing the report. Using libraries like Matplotlib or Seaborn allows you to create charts directly within your

Python script:

```python
import matplotlib.pyplot as plt

\#\# Creating a bar chart for total sales per product
plt.bar(total_sales['Product'], total_sales['Sales'])
plt.xlabel('Product')
plt.ylabel('Total Sales')
plt.title('Total Sales per Product')
plt.xticks(rotation=45)
plt.tight_layout()
plt.savefig('total_sales_chart.png') \# Save chart image
```

With your data processed and visualized, it's time to automate the creation of your report in Excel. You can use OpenPyXL or XlsxWriter to create a new workbook or update an existing one:

```python
from openpyxl import Workbook

\#\# Create a new workbook and select the active worksheet
wb = Workbook()
ws = wb.active

\#\# Adding headers
ws.append(['Product', 'Total Sales'])
```

```
for row in total_sales.itertuples(index=False):

ws.append(row)


\#\# Insert chart image into the worksheet

from openpyxl.drawing.image import Image


img = Image('total_sales_chart.png')

ws.add_image(img, 'D1') \# Specify where to place the image


\#\# Save the workbook

wb.save('monthly_sales_report.xlsx')
```
` ` `

By implementing these steps in your Python script, you've established a solid foundation for an automated solution. The beauty of this approach lies in its repeatability; simply rerunning the script at the end of each month will regenerate the report with updated data.

To further enhance your solution, consider incorporating error handling routines. Take this example, using try-except blocks can help manage issues related to reading files or executing commands that may arise from unexpected inputs or formats.

Additionally, automating the scheduling of your script is crucial for practicality. Tools like Windows Task Scheduler or cron jobs (on Unix-based systems) can be employed to run your script at specified times without manual intervention. This guarantees that your reports remain current without requiring extra effort on your part.

Through this example of building an automated solution

for monthly sales reporting using Python and Excel, we've illustrated how each component interacts seamlessly. Whether you're managing financial reports, inventory systems, or any other repetitive tasks involving data manipulation and reporting in Excel, adopting this holistic approach empowers you to streamline those processes effectively.

The journey doesn't end here; ongoing refinement of your automated solutions will not only improve workflows but also yield valuable insights into how technology can enhance productivity within any organization.

CHAPTER 15:
CASE STUDIES
AND REAL-WORLD
APPLICATIONS

Overview of Real-World
Applications

T he integration of Python with Excel offers a wealth of real-world applications, reflecting the ever-evolving landscape of business and data analysis. Organizations across diverse sectors harness this powerful combination to boost productivity, enhance data accuracy, and streamline workflows. Whether in finance, marketing, operations, or education, incorporating Python into Excel can revolutionize data utilization and reporting practices.

In the finance sector, professionals often grapple with extensive datasets for budgeting, forecasting, and performance analysis. Python scripts can automate the retrieval and processing of financial data from various sources—such as databases or APIs—streamlining the analytical process. Take this example, a financial analyst might use the Pandas library to extract stock prices from an online source and calculate moving averages directly within Excel. This not only saves time but also minimizes human errors linked to manual data entry.

Marketing analytics similarly benefits from the synergy of Python and Excel through advanced data modeling techniques. Marketers frequently work with complex datasets to assess campaign performance, customer segmentation, and market trends. By leveraging Python libraries like Matplotlib or Seaborn alongside Excel, teams can create dynamic visualizations that effectively communicate insights—far surpassing traditional static reports. For example, a marketing team could automate the generation of weekly reports that highlight conversion rates for various campaigns, granting immediate access to critical insights that inform decision-making.

Operational efficiency is another area where this integration excels. Companies managing supply chain logistics often encounter challenges in inventory tracking and demand forecasting. Python's capabilities can enhance these processes by analyzing historical sales data and generating forecasts using machine learning algorithms. These results can then be fed back into Excel for reporting purposes. Picture an operations manager utilizing a Python script to predict stock levels based on seasonal trends—automatically updating inventory sheets in real time.

The education sector also reaps significant rewards from this integration. Educators can employ Python scripts within Excel to analyze student performance metrics across different assessments and demographics. By automating these analyses, they can identify trends in student achievement or pinpoint areas needing improvement without getting bogged down in tedious calculations. Take this example, a teacher might quickly assess class averages and visualize them through interactive charts embedded in their Excel workbooks.

Healthcare presents another compelling application of Python alongside Excel. Healthcare professionals often need comprehensive analyses for patient management systems or clinical trials. By tapping into Python's robust libraries, they can automate data extraction from electronic health records (EHRs), conduct statistical analyses on patient outcomes, and present findings within Excel dashboards. This enhances accuracy and allows practitioners to focus more on patient care rather than administrative tasks.

Finally, project management significantly benefits from this synergy as well. Project managers regularly track progress using spreadsheets that document timelines, resources, and budgets. With Python's assistance, they can automate status updates by pulling data from project management tools into Excel files for real-time reporting. For example, a project manager might set up a script that retrieves task completion rates from a tool like Jira and visualizes them in an Excel Gantt chart format—providing instant insights into project health.

In summary, the applications of Python in Excel are extensive and span numerous industries and functions. From automating financial analyses to enhancing marketing strategies and improving operational efficiencies, the benefits are both vast and varied. As organizations continue navigating an increasingly data-driven world, embracing this integration will not only foster productivity but also empower teams to make informed decisions based on real-time insights. The adaptability of these tools ensures that professionals equipped with Python skills will remain at the forefront of innovation in their respective fields.

Case Study: Financial Industry

In the financial industry, the integration of Python and Excel represents a significant shift in how analysts manage and analyze data. The enormous volume of data generated in finance demands robust tools that can efficiently handle vast datasets while providing flexibility for analysis and reporting. Python enhances Excel's capabilities, equipping financial professionals with a powerful toolkit for automating tasks, conducting complex analyses, and generating insights quickly.

For example, consider a financial analyst preparing quarterly reports. Traditionally, this process involves gathering data from multiple sources—such as databases or market feeds—entering that data into Excel, and performing calculations manually. This labor-intensive method is not only time-consuming but also susceptible to errors. However, with Python, analysts can streamline this workflow through automation. By utilizing libraries like Pandas, an analyst can write scripts to pull data directly from APIs or databases.

Here's a brief illustration of how this works:

```python
import pandas as pd

import requests


\#\# Fetching financial data from an API

response      =      requests.get('https://api.example.com/financials')

data = response.json()


\#\# Creating a DataFrame

df = pd.DataFrame(data)


\#\# Performing calculations
```

```
df['Net Income'] = df['Revenue'] - df['Expenses']
```
` ` `

This code demonstrates how analysts can access real-time financial data without manual input, ensuring both accuracy and efficiency. The resulting DataFrame can be exported back into Excel for further visualization or reporting.

Risk assessment in finance also greatly benefits from Python's analytical capabilities. Analysts often evaluate various risk factors that could impact investments or portfolios. By employing statistical models in Python, they can analyze historical data to forecast potential risks and returns more effectively than traditional methods allow. Take this example, Monte Carlo simulations can be used to project various outcomes based on historical volatility:

` ` `python

```
import numpy as np


\#\# Simulating stock price changes

np.random.seed(42)

price = 100 \# Initial stock price

returns = np.random.normal(loc=0.01, scale=0.02, size=1000) \# Simulated returns


\#\# Calculating future prices based on simulated returns

future_prices = price * (1 + returns).cumprod()
```
` ` `

The results from such simulations can be visualized directly in Excel using libraries like Matplotlib or Seaborn, facilitating clearer communication of potential outcomes to stakeholders.

Portfolio optimization is another vital area where Python proves invaluable. Financial analysts can apply optimization algorithms to determine the best asset allocation that maximizes returns while minimizing risk. Utilizing libraries such as SciPy allows them to implement techniques like Mean-Variance Optimization:

```python
from scipy.optimize import minimize


\#\# Example asset returns

returns = np.array([0.1, 0.15, 0.2])  \# Expected returns for three assets

cov_matrix = np.array([[0.1, 0.02, 0], [0.02, 0.08, 0], [0, 0, 0.05]])  \# Covariance matrix


def portfolio_variance(weights):

return weights.T @ cov_matrix @ weights


constraints = ('type': 'eq', 'fun': lambda x: np.sum(x) - 1)

bounds = tuple((0, 1) for asset in range(len(returns)))


result = minimize(portfolio_variance, num_assets * [1./ num_assets], bounds=bounds,

constraints=constraints)

optimal_weights = result.x
```

This optimization framework empowers analysts to dynamically adjust their portfolios based on evolving market conditions and client needs.

Finally, the automation of report generation tailored to specific client requirements or internal audits adds significant value as well. Instead of starting from scratch each time—a repetitive and time-consuming task—analysts can utilize Python scripts to automatically format and compile information into pre-designed templates within Excel.

Take this example:

```python
from openpyxl import Workbook


\#\# Creating an Excel workbook with report summaries

wb = Workbook()

ws = wb.active

ws.title = "Quarterly Report


\#\# Adding headings and content dynamically based on analysis results

ws.append(["Quarter", "Net Income", "Total Assets"])

for i in range(4):  \# Assuming four quarters of data are available

ws.append([f'Qi+1', df.loc[i]['Net Income'], df.loc[i]['Total Assets']])


wb.save("Quarterly_Report.xlsx")
```

` ` `

By leveraging automation alongside visual elements like charts generated through Python libraries directly within Excel workbooks, financial teams can produce insightful reports more efficiently than ever before.

In summary, integrating Python with Excel transforms workflows within the finance sector while enhancing analytical capabilities across all areas—from daily operations to long-term strategic planning. As technology evolves and organizations strive for greater efficiency amidst increasing data complexity, mastering these tools will be essential for success in any financial role.

Case Study: Inventory Management

Inventory management is a pivotal aspect of supply chain operations, where accurate data and timely insights can significantly influence profitability. In an environment characterized by fluctuating demand and intricate logistics, the combination of Python's analytical capabilities with Excel's user-friendly interface offers managers an effective solution for real-time decision-making and streamlined operations.

Consider the typical scenario of an inventory manager tasked with tracking stock levels across multiple warehouses. Traditionally, this would involve tedious manual updates to spreadsheets, a process prone to errors and delays. However, by integrating Python into this workflow, the approach shifts dramatically. Utilizing libraries like Pandas enables managers to dynamically source inventory data from databases or APIs, ensuring that records are consistently up-to-date without the burden of manual entries.

Take this example, an inventory manager can easily pull current stock levels into Excel for analysis with a few lines of code:

```python
import pandas as pd

import requests


\#\# Fetching inventory data from an API

response      =      requests.get('https://api.example.com/inventory')

data = response.json()


\#\# Creating a DataFrame from the fetched data

inventory_df = pd.DataFrame(data)


\#\# Filtering low stock items

low_stock_items = inventory_df[inventory_df['quantity'] < 10]
```

This script automates data retrieval and highlights low-stock items that need immediate attention. The results can then be exported back to Excel for further visualization or reporting.

Forecasting demand is another significant challenge in inventory management that benefits from automation. Accurate forecasts enable businesses to optimize stock levels and minimize costs associated with excess inventory or stockouts. With Python's statistical analysis capabilities, managers can employ models that assess historical sales data to predict future demand patterns.

For example, using linear regression with libraries like scikit-learn allows managers to forecast future sales based on past trends:

```python
from sklearn.linear_model import LinearRegression
import numpy as np

\#\# Historical sales data (e.g., past months)
months = np.array([[1], [2], [3], [4], [5]])
sales = np.array([100, 150, 200, 250, 300])

\#\# Training the regression model
model = LinearRegression()
model.fit(months, sales)

\#\# Predicting future sales for the next month
predicted_sales = model.predict(np.array([[6]]))
```

The output from this model provides valuable insights into expected sales for the upcoming month, enabling managers to adjust their inventory orders accordingly.

Supplier relationship management is yet another essential facet of inventory management that can be enhanced through automation. Ensuring timely deliveries while maintaining optimal stock levels requires effective communication and tracking of supplier performance. By utilizing Python scripts, managers can automate supplier evaluations based on criteria such as delivery times, quality metrics, and pricing trends.

Take this example:

```python
supplier_data =

'Supplier': ['Supplier A', 'Supplier B', 'Supplier C'],

'Delivery Time (days)': [2, 5, 1],

'Quality Score': [90, 80, 95]


suppliers_df = pd.DataFrame(supplier_data)

\#\# Evaluating suppliers based on delivery time and quality

best_supplier = suppliers_df.loc[suppliers_df['Delivery Time (days)'].idxmin()]
```

This code snippet demonstrates how automation simplifies supplier assessments by quickly identifying the best-performing partners based on specific metrics.

And, automating reorder processes presents another significant advantage of integrating Python into Excel workflows. By developing an automatic notification system that alerts managers when stock levels fall below predefined thresholds—such as sending emails or generating alerts through Excel's built-in features—businesses can ensure timely orders without relying on manual oversight.

Here's a simple example illustrating how to generate an email alert for low stock items:

```python
import smtplib
```

```
def send_email(low_stock_items):
server = smtplib.SMTP('smtp.example.com', 587)
server.starttls()

server.login('your_email@example.com', 'password')

subject = "Low Stock Alert!
body = f"The following items are low in stock:low_stock_items.to_string()

message = f'Subject: subjectbody'

server.sendmail('your_email@example.com',
'recipient@example.com', message)
server.quit()

if not low_stock_items.empty:
send_email(low_stock_items)
```

This integration not only saves time but also enhances responsiveness within the inventory management process.

By implementing these automated solutions, organizations foster better decision-making while minimizing the costly mistakes often associated with manual processes. The synergy between Python's robust data handling capabilities and Excel's familiar interface empowers inventory managers to concentrate on strategic initiatives rather than becoming mired in repetitive tasks.

In summary, leveraging Python in inventory management transforms traditional workflows into agile processes that adapt seamlessly to real-time market conditions. As businesses strive for efficiency amid increasing complexities in supply chain dynamics, this integration becomes crucial for maintaining a competitive edge in today's fast-paced marketplace.

Case Study: Marketing Analytics

Marketing analytics plays a crucial role for businesses looking to comprehend consumer behavior, optimize their campaigns, and improve overall performance. By combining Python's robust data processing capabilities with Excel's analytical tools, organizations can effectively analyze large datasets and extract actionable insights.

Consider the scenario of a marketing analyst tasked with evaluating the effectiveness of various advertising channels. Traditionally, this would involve wading through extensive spreadsheets filled with campaign data—a process that often leads to manual calculations, potential errors, and missed opportunities. By integrating Python into this workflow, analysts can automate data collection and streamline the analysis process. Libraries such as Pandas and Matplotlib empower them to conduct complex operations swiftly and visualize results clearly.

Take this example, if an analyst wishes to assess the return on investment (ROI) for different marketing channels—such as email campaigns, social media ads, and search engine marketing—Python can facilitate this process seamlessly. The following code retrieves campaign data from an Excel file and calculates the ROI for each channel:

```python
```

```
import pandas as pd

\#\# Load the campaign data from Excel
campaign_data = pd.read_excel('marketing_campaigns.xlsx')

\#\# Calculate ROI for each campaign
campaign_data['ROI']    =    (campaign_data['Revenue']    -
campaign_data['Cost']) / campaign_data['Cost'] * 100

\#\# Display the ROI for each channel
print(campaign_data[['Channel', 'ROI']])
```
```

Executing this code allows the analyst to quickly quantify the effectiveness of each marketing strategy, saving time and enabling immediate adjustments based on real-time data.

To enhance understanding among stakeholders further, visualizing these insights can be invaluable. The analyst might use Matplotlib to create a compelling bar chart that presents the ROI of different channels:

```python
import matplotlib.pyplot as plt

plt.figure(figsize=(10, 6))

plt.bar(campaign_data['Channel'],    campaign_data['ROI'],
color='skyblue')

plt.title('ROI by Marketing Channel')

plt.xlabel('Marketing Channel')
```
```

```
plt.ylabel('ROI (%)')

plt.xticks(rotation=45)

plt.tight_layout()

plt.show()
```
``` ` ` `

This straightforward visualization allows decision-makers to quickly grasp which channels are performing well. By presenting data visually, the analyst fosters informed discussions about resource allocation and strategic planning.

And, predictive analytics offers businesses the ability to anticipate customer needs and emerging trends. By leveraging machine learning algorithms in Python, analysts can develop models that predict customer behaviors based on historical data. For example, using scikit-learn for customer segmentation allows targeted marketing efforts that resonate more effectively with specific groups.

Here's how K-means clustering can segment customers based on their purchasing behavior:

```python
from sklearn.cluster import KMeans


\#\# Assuming customer_data is a DataFrame containing relevant features

X = customer_data[['Age', 'Annual_Spend']]


\#\# Applying K-means clustering

kmeans = KMeans(n_clusters=3)
```
```

```python
customer_data['Segment'] = kmeans.fit_predict(X)

\#\# Display segmented customer data
print(customer_data.head())
```
` ` `

This segmentation enables marketers to tailor campaigns specifically designed for each cluster's preferences and spending habits, ultimately boosting engagement rates and conversions.

In addition, email campaign analysis benefits significantly from A/B testing to refine messaging and strategies continuously. Analysts can automate the collection of engagement metrics—such as open rates and click-through rates—from multiple campaigns stored in Excel using Python. Quick statistical tests performed via libraries like SciPy or StatsModels ensure that decisions regarding which email versions resonate best with audiences are rooted in data rather than intuition.

For example:

` ` `python
```python
from scipy import stats

\#\# Open rates from two different email versions
open_rate_A = [0.2, 0.25, 0.3]
open_rate_B = [0.15, 0.18, 0.22]

\#\# Perform a t-test to compare open rates between two groups
t_statistic,    p_value    =    stats.ttest_ind(open_rate_A,
```

open_rate_B)

if p_value < 0.05:

print("Significant difference in open rates.")

else:

print("No significant difference in open rates.")

` ` `

This approach enhances an organization's agility in adjusting marketing strategies based on what truly works.

To wrap things up, incorporating Python into marketing analytics transforms how businesses operate by automating complex tasks while providing deeper insights than traditional methods allow. From calculating ROI to predicting future trends through machine learning models, this integration empowers organizations not only to analyze but also to act with precision in their marketing efforts. The ability to visualize these insights further strengthens cross-departmental communication, ensuring that every decision is informed by thorough data analysis rather than speculation or guesswork.

As companies navigate a landscape filled with competitive pressures and ever-evolving consumer expectations, leveraging these analytical tools becomes essential for sustained success in marketing strategies—demonstrating that when creativity meets technology, innovation thrives.

Case Study: Data Science and BI

Data Science and Business Intelligence (BI) have become essential in shaping strategic decision-making across various industries. The integration of Python with Excel empowers organizations to unlock advanced analytical capabilities, transforming raw data into actionable insights.

This combination allows professionals to leverage statistical methods, machine learning, and visualization tools, ultimately enhancing their data analysis.

Imagine a business intelligence analyst tasked with analyzing sales data to identify trends and patterns. Traditionally, this process would involve sifting through extensive Excel spreadsheets, manually filtering and sorting data—a time-consuming endeavor often prone to human error. However, by utilizing Python's robust data manipulation libraries like Pandas, analysts can streamline their workflows, making the analysis not only quicker but also more accurate.

For example, suppose the analyst wants to examine monthly sales trends across different regions. With Python, they can automate the loading and processing of sales data from an Excel file:

```python
import pandas as pd

\#\# Load sales data from Excel

sales_data = pd.read_excel('monthly_sales.xlsx')


\#\# Calculate total sales by region

total_sales            =            sales_data.groupby('Region')
['Sales'].sum().reset_index()


\#\# Display total sales by region

print(total_sales)
```

This concise snippet enables the analyst to swiftly generate a summary of total sales per region. By avoiding manual calculations or cumbersome pivot tables, which can lead to errors, the analyst gains a clear overview of regional performance at a glance.

Visualizing these results is crucial as well. A straightforward bar chart can effectively convey regional performance, helping stakeholders quickly grasp the implications of the data. Using Matplotlib, the analyst could create such a visualization:

```python
import matplotlib.pyplot as plt


plt.figure(figsize=(10, 6))

plt.bar(total_sales['Region'],                total_sales['Sales'],
color='orange')

plt.title('Total Sales by Region')

plt.xlabel('Region')

plt.ylabel('Sales Amount')

plt.xticks(rotation=45)

plt.tight_layout()

plt.show()
```

This visual representation fosters engagement with the data among team members, facilitating discussions about regional strategies and resource allocation.

Also, predictive analytics plays a vital role in BI today. Analysts can harness Python's machine learning libraries, such as scikit-learn, to build models that forecast future sales based on historical data. Take this example, applying a linear regression model can unveil insights into how various factors influence sales:

```python
from sklearn.model_selection import train_test_split
from sklearn.linear_model import LinearRegression

\#\# Prepare feature matrix and target variable
X = sales_data[['Marketing_Spend', 'Store_Count']]
y = sales_data['Sales']

\#\# Split the dataset into training and testing sets
X_train, X_test, y_train, y_test = train_test_split(X, y, test_size=0.2)

\#\# Create and train the model
model = LinearRegression()
model.fit(X_train, y_train)

\#\# Make predictions
predictions = model.predict(X_test)

\#\# Display predictions versus actual values
results = pd.DataFrame('Actual': y_test, 'Predicted': predictions)
print(results)
```

This method not only yields forecasts but also highlights key drivers of sales performance—empowering organizations to make informed decisions regarding marketing investments and operational adjustments.

Another significant advantage of incorporating Python in Data Science is its capability to handle unstructured data. For example, when analyzing customer feedback from surveys or social media interactions, natural language processing (NLP) techniques can be utilized. By employing libraries like NLTK or spaCy, analysts can efficiently extract sentiments from text data.

Here's a brief illustration using NLTK for sentiment analysis on customer feedback:

```python
import pandas as pd

from nltk.sentiment import SentimentIntensityAnalyzer


\#\# Load customer feedback data from Excel

feedback_data = pd.read_excel('customer_feedback.xlsx')


\#\# Initialize sentiment analyzer

sia = SentimentIntensityAnalyzer()


\#\# Analyze sentiments of feedback comments

feedback_data['Sentiment'] = feedback_data['Comments'].apply(lambda x: sia.polarity_scores(x)['compound'])


\#\# Display sentiment scores alongside comments
```

```
print(feedback_data[['Comments', 'Sentiment']])
```
` ` `

These insights into customer sentiment empower businesses to quickly adjust their strategies based on customer perceptions and experiences.

The interplay between Data Science and Business Intelligence demonstrates how integrating Python with Excel can revolutionize analytical capabilities within organizations. From automating complex analyses to delivering predictive insights and extracting valuable information from unstructured data—these elements significantly enhance informed decision-making processes.

In today's fast-paced market environment where agility is crucial, combining Python's versatility with Excel's familiarity equips analysts to effectively navigate challenges and seize growth opportunities. The outcome is not just improved analytical precision but also a strategic advantage that positions organizations for success in an increasingly data-driven world.

Case Study: Retail Operations

In the competitive landscape of retail operations, data-driven strategies can significantly enhance efficiency and profitability. Retailers are often inundated with vast amounts of data—sales figures, inventory levels, and customer preferences. By integrating Python with Excel, retailers can unlock powerful analytical capabilities that allow for a comprehensive examination of this data.

Consider a retail manager who seeks to optimize inventory levels across multiple stores. Traditionally, this task might involve tedious manual tracking in Excel spreadsheets. However, Python's automation capabilities enable the manager to analyze data quickly and accurately, facilitating informed decision-making.

To illustrate this, let's explore a practical scenario where a retail chain wants to monitor stock levels and forecast future inventory needs based on sales trends. Utilizing the Pandas library in Python, the retailer can efficiently load sales data from Excel:

```python
import pandas as pd

\#\# Load sales data from Excel

sales_data = pd.read_excel('retail_sales_data.xlsx')

\#\# Preview the first few rows of the dataset

print(sales_data.head())
```

Once the data is loaded, the manager can group it by product to calculate total units sold. This analysis helps identify which items are selling quickly and which are stagnating on shelves:

```python
\#\# Calculate total sales by product

total_sales = sales_data.groupby('Product')['Units Sold'].sum().reset_index()

\#\# Sort products by units sold in descending order

total_sales = total_sales.sort_values(by='Units Sold', ascending=False)

print(total_sales)
```

With a clearer picture of product performance, the next step is to forecast future demand using time series analysis. The statsmodels library in Python offers robust tools for this purpose. Assuming we have historical monthly sales data available, we can proceed as follows:

```python
from statsmodels.tsa.holtwinters import ExponentialSmoothing

\#\# Prepare data for time series analysis

monthly_sales = sales_data.groupby(['Month'])['Units Sold'].sum()

\#\# Fit an exponential smoothing model to forecast future sales

model = ExponentialSmoothing(monthly_sales, trend='add', seasonal='add', seasonal_periods=12)

model_fit = model.fit()

\#\# Make predictions for the next 12 months

forecast = model_fit.forecast(steps=12)

print(forecast)
```

These forecasts empower retailers to anticipate stock needs ahead of time, effectively reducing both overstock and stockouts—two critical challenges in retail management.

To convey these insights more intuitively, visualizing the data is crucial. A simple line chart can effectively showcase historical sales alongside forecasts using Matplotlib:

```python
import matplotlib.pyplot as plt

plt.figure(figsize=(12, 6))
plt.plot(monthly_sales.index, monthly_sales.values, label='Historical Sales')
plt.plot(forecast.index, forecast.values, label='Forecasted Sales', linestyle='--')
plt.title('Monthly Sales Forecast')
plt.xlabel('Month')
plt.ylabel('Units Sold')
plt.legend()
plt.show()
```

Armed with accurate forecasts and compelling visualizations, retail managers can make strategic decisions regarding ordering cycles and promotional campaigns tailored to peak selling periods.

Another vital aspect of retail operations is analyzing customer purchase behavior. Understanding what drives consumer purchases allows retailers to tailor their marketing efforts effectively. By employing clustering techniques such as K-means through Python's scikit-learn library, retailers can segment their customer base into distinct groups based on purchasing patterns:

```python
from sklearn.cluster import KMeans
```

```
\#\# Select relevant features for clustering (e.g., purchase
frequency and average spend)

customer_features = sales_data[['CustomerID', 'Frequency',
'AverageSpend']]


\#\# Implement K-means clustering

kmeans = KMeans(n_clusters=3) \# Assuming we want three
clusters

customer_features['Cluster']                              =
kmeans.fit_predict(customer_features[['Frequency',
'AverageSpend']])


\#\# Display clustered customers alongside their segments

print(customer_features.head())
` ` `
```

This segmentation provides actionable insights into which marketing strategies may resonate most effectively with each customer group.

Lastly, we should consider operational efficiency within the supply chain itself. Python's capabilities extend beyond analytics; they can also streamline logistical processes. By integrating APIs that provide real-time data about shipments or supplier lead times directly into Excel through Python scripts, retailers gain immediate visibility into their supply chains.

For example:

```python
` ` `python
import requests
```

```
\#\# Fetch real-time shipment data from an API
(hypothetical endpoint)

response = requests.get('https://api.example.com/
shipment_status')

shipment_data = response.json()


\#\# Load shipment status into a DataFrame for further
analysis or reporting

shipment_df = pd.DataFrame(shipment_data)

print(shipment_df.head())
` ` `
```

By automating these integrations and analyses within Excel using Python scripts, retailers not only improve their operational efficiency but also empower teams to make quicker decisions based on real-time insights.

This exploration illustrates how integrating Python with Excel can transform retail operations—enhancing inventory management, personalizing marketing strategies, and streamlining supply chain logistics. Retailers equipped with these advanced tools are not merely surviving; they are thriving in an increasingly data-driven marketplace.

Learning from Case Studies

The insights derived from real-world applications of Python in Excel are incredibly valuable, showcasing not only the potential of this powerful combination but also its transformative impact across various industries. By examining case studies, we can learn best practices, recognize common pitfalls, and ignite new ideas for our own projects.

For example, in the financial sector, analysts routinely deal with extensive datasets. A leading investment firm adopted Python to automate the compilation of daily market data into Excel reports. Previously, analysts spent hours extracting data manually from different sources. However, after implementing Python scripts to gather and process this information automatically, they significantly reduced report generation time. This streamlined workflow allowed analysts to concentrate on analysis rather than data collection, ultimately enhancing productivity.

A particularly striking instance involves a firm that utilized Pandas to clean and structure messy stock data sourced from multiple APIs. Each morning before the market opened, the team ran a script that fetched the latest prices and corrected discrepancies in real-time:

```python
import pandas as pd

import requests


\#\# Fetch stock data

response = requests.get('https://api.stockdata.com/v1/stocks')

stock_data = response.json()


\#\# Convert to DataFrame

df = pd.DataFrame(stock_data)


\#\# Clean data: remove duplicates and fill missing values

df.drop_duplicates(inplace=True)
```

```python
df.fillna(method='ffill', inplace=True)
```

\#\# Save cleaned data to Excel

```python
df.to_excel('cleaned_stock_data.xlsx', index=False)
```
` ` `

With just a few lines of code, this firm improved accuracy and significantly shortened reporting timelines, allowing analysts to generate insights in a fraction of the time previously required.

Another compelling application can be seen in retail operations. Retailers have successfully leveraged customer segmentation through clustering models to drive targeted marketing efforts. By analyzing customer purchasing behaviors using K-means clustering, businesses can tailor promotions that resonate more effectively with distinct groups. A leading retail chain, for instance, increased sales by 20% after implementing personalized marketing strategies based on these insights.

In the healthcare sector, organizations have also tapped into Python's capabilities to boost operational efficiency. One hospital network integrated Python scripts with Excel to manage patient appointment scheduling more effectively. By analyzing historical appointment data alongside patient flow patterns, they developed predictive models that optimized scheduling processes:

` ` `python

```python
from sklearn.linear_model import LinearRegression
```

\#\# Sample dataset: number of appointments vs patients seen

```
data = pd.read_excel('appointment_data.xlsx')

X = data[['Appointments']]

y = data['Patients Seen']


\#\# Create a linear regression model

model = LinearRegression()

model.fit(X, y)


\#\# Predict future patient flow based on scheduled appointments

predicted_flow = model.predict(X)

print(predicted_flow)
```
` ` `

This predictive capability enabled healthcare managers to proactively adjust staffing levels based on expected patient volume—a crucial improvement in an industry where timing is often critical.

Logistics companies managing large fleets also illustrate the benefits of using Python with Excel. By automating data uploads from GPS tracking systems into Excel for analysis, these companies could assess route efficiency and fuel consumption effectively, leading to significant cost reductions.

Reflecting on these diverse examples—from finance and retail to healthcare and logistics—reveals a common thread: organizations are reaping substantial benefits by integrating Python into their Excel workflows. They are not merely adopting new tools; they are redefining their operational capabilities through enhanced efficiency and smarter decision-making processes.

Learning from these case studies extends beyond understanding what worked; it provides invaluable lessons about strategically implementing technology in business operations. Each scenario serves as a template for innovation that others can adapt or refine according to their unique challenges.

these stories inspire us by demonstrating tangible outcomes driven by creativity and technical expertise. They remind us that effective integration of Python with Excel not only boosts productivity but can also lead organizations toward greater success in their respective fields.

Applying Lessons to Your Work

Integrating insights from case studies into your workflows can lead to significant improvements in both efficiency and effectiveness. Each example serves as a reminder of the potential at the intersection of Python and Excel, illustrating not only the "how" but also the "why" behind these tools.

One key takeaway is identifying areas where manual processes can be automated. Reflect on your daily tasks —whether they involve data entry, report generation, or data analysis. For example, if you find yourself spending hours collating information from various spreadsheets, implementing a Python script to automate this process could free up valuable time for strategic analysis. A practical application involves using libraries like Pandas to manage repetitive data manipulation tasks. You might start with something as straightforward as merging multiple data sources into a single Excel sheet:

```python
import pandas as pd
```

```python
\#\# Load multiple Excel files into DataFrames
df1 = pd.read_excel('sales_data_jan.xlsx')
df2 = pd.read_excel('sales_data_feb.xlsx')

\#\# Combine DataFrames
combined_df = pd.concat([df1, df2])

\#\# Save to a new Excel file
combined_df.to_excel('combined_sales_data.xlsx', index=False)
```

This simple code snippet can significantly reduce the manual effort involved in combining datasets, streamlining your workflow from the outset.

Equally important is the value of data cleaning and preprocessing. Many organizations highlighted in case studies have reaped benefits from effectively preparing their data before analysis. If you frequently handle datasets that are prone to inaccuracies or missing values, integrating error-checking scripts into your workflow can greatly enhance data quality. Take this example:

```python
\#\# Checking for null values
missing_values = combined_df.isnull().sum()

print(missing_values)


\#\# Filling missing values with zeros
```

```
combined_df.fillna(0, inplace=True)
```
` ` `

Incorporating such checks into your data preparation process ensures that you work with reliable datasets, leading to more accurate analyses and conclusions.

To apply these insights practically, consider adopting a project-based approach. Identify specific projects within your role where integration could boost productivity. Take this example, if your team regularly prepares monthly reports, creating a Python script that automatically pulls necessary metrics and formats them for Excel can save time and reduce errors associated with manual entry.

Collaboration within teams is another critical aspect that can benefit from these lessons. Sharing knowledge about Python's capabilities can foster innovation across departments. Organizing a lunch-and-learn session to demonstrate how you've automated tasks could inspire colleagues to explore their own workflows and discover opportunities for automation.

As you enhance your workflows through Python and Excel, continuous learning should remain a priority. Engaging with communities or platforms dedicated to Python users exposes you to diverse problem-solving approaches and innovative ideas implemented by others. Participating in forums or attending webinars can keep your skills sharp and current.

Adopt an experimental mindset as you integrate these practices into your work. Take inspiration from those case studies; experiment with different scripts or libraries that suit your specific needs. Begin small—automate one aspect of a task before expanding to more complex workflows. This iterative process will not only enhance your technical skills but also boost your confidence in leveraging Python for various tasks.

applying these lessons means committing to an ongoing journey of improvement and exploration within your work environment. By incorporating automation techniques and promoting collaboration, you're fostering not just personal growth but also organizational advancement—creating a culture of innovation that embraces efficiency and productivity at every level. The fusion of Python with Excel isn't merely about mastering tools; it's about reshaping our approach to work, challenging norms, and striving for excellence across all domains.

CHAPTER 16: FUTURE TRENDS AND OPPORTUNITIES

*Emerging Technologies
in Excel and Python*

T he landscape of data analysis is constantly evolving, shaped by innovations that redefine our interaction with tools like Excel and Python. These emerging technologies do more than enhance existing functionalities; they fundamentally transform workflows, allowing users to extract insights more effectively than ever before.

A notable advancement in this arena is the integration of artificial intelligence (AI) within Excel, which streamlines data processing and analysis. AI can automatically identify patterns in datasets, suggest relevant formulas, or generate visualizations based on user inquiries. Take this example, Excel's built-in Ideas feature utilizes machine learning algorithms to help users uncover trends and insights without requiring extensive technical expertise.

Python complements these advancements seamlessly, offering extensive libraries for AI and machine learning, such as Scikit-learn and TensorFlow. By leveraging Python's capabilities alongside Excel's intuitive interface, users can develop sophisticated models to predict outcomes based on historical data. Imagine creating a predictive model for sales forecasting in Python and then visualizing the results in Excel. This synergy fosters a hands-on approach to data analysis, empowering professionals not only to obtain results but also to grasp the underlying mechanics driving those outcomes.

Cloud computing represents another significant shift in how we engage with data. The move toward cloud-based solutions enhances collaboration and provides on-demand access to substantial computational power. Platforms like Microsoft Azure allow users to execute complex Python scripts directly on cloud-hosted datasets, enabling the analysis of large volumes of data without the constraints of local machine specifications.

For example, using Azure Notebooks with Python allows for real-time analytics across distributed datasets while utilizing Excel as the primary reporting tool. A simple connection through APIs or ODBC enables seamless integration of live data into your Excel reports. This capability to merge real-time insights from cloud databases with the familiarity of Excel can significantly enhance decision-making processes within organizations.

Another important trend is the rise of automation in data workflows. Robotic Process Automation (RPA) tools integrate effectively with both Python scripts and Excel macros, simplifying repetitive tasks that often consume valuable time and resources. Take this example, combining RPA with a Python script can automate the retrieval of reports from various sources, execute calculations, and update an Excel dashboard—all without human intervention.

This automation allows teams to focus on higher-value tasks rather than being bogged down by routine operations. A practical application might involve scheduling tasks that trigger Python scripts at set intervals to pull weekly sales reports from different databases into a centralized Excel file, providing stakeholders with timely metrics at their fingertips.

And, advancements in Natural Language Processing (NLP) are making it easier for non-technical users to interact with data analytics tools using natural language queries instead of complex SQL commands or Python scripts. Imagine asking an AI assistant integrated within your Excel environment questions like "What were our top three sales regions last quarter?" and receiving immediate answers generated by backend Python analysis—without needing direct coding or manual data manipulation.

As we explore these advancements, it's essential to consider their implications for skill development in the workforce. Professionals must not only master new technical skills but also adopt a mindset geared toward continuous learning and innovation. Engaging with communities focused on these emerging technologies offers invaluable networking and knowledge-sharing opportunities that can propel careers forward.

Staying ahead in this dynamic field requires experimenting with new tools as they emerge—perhaps dedicating time each week to explore new libraries available in Python or testing newly released features in Excel designed specifically for AI integration. The journey doesn't conclude once you've mastered existing processes; it continues as new technologies redefine what's possible within this ecosystem.

At its core, the interplay between emerging technologies in Excel and Python ushers professionals into an exciting era where intuition meets innovation—a landscape ripe for exploration where data-driven decisions evolve into transformative actions within any organization's strategy.

Integrating AI and Machine Learning

The integration of artificial intelligence (AI) and machine learning (ML) into tools like Excel and Python signifies a fundamental shift in how we analyze and interpret data. These technologies empower users to extract deeper insights, transforming standard spreadsheets into dynamic analytical platforms.

One practical application of machine learning is predictive analytics. In Python, libraries such as Scikit-learn simplify the process of building these models. Take this example, if you aim to predict future sales based on historical data, you can structure your dataset in Excel and then leverage Python to develop a linear regression model that identifies trends and generates forecasts. Here's how the process unfolds:

1. Prepare Your Data: Begin by organizing your historical sales data in Excel, ensuring you have clearly defined columns for time periods, sales figures, and other relevant variables.

2. Load Data into Python: Utilize the Pandas library to import this data into a DataFrame for analysis.

``` python
import pandas as pd


\#\# Load the Excel file

df = pd.read_excel('sales_data.xlsx')
```

1. Train Your Model: Use Scikit-learn to create and fit a linear regression model.

```python
from sklearn.model_selection import train_test_split
from sklearn.linear_model import LinearRegression

\#\# Define features and target variable
X = df[['Time']] \# Independent variable
y = df['Sales'] \# Dependent variable

\#\# Split the dataset into training and testing sets
X_train, X_test, y_train, y_test = train_test_split(X, y, test_size=0.2)

\#\# Create and fit the model
model = LinearRegression()
model.fit(X_train, y_train)
```

1. Make Predictions: After training the model, you can generate predictions using new input.

```python
predictions = model.predict(X_test)
```

1. Visualize Results in Excel: Finally, return the predictions to Excel for visualization or further analysis with charts or dashboards.

This synergy between Python's robust modeling capabilities and Excel's powerful visualization tools allows professionals to communicate insights effectively. It transforms raw data into actionable strategies that inform business decisions.

Beyond simple forecasting, integrating AI with Excel opens up advanced functionalities like anomaly detection in datasets. For example, when analyzing financial transactions, machine learning algorithms can be trained to flag unusual patterns that may indicate fraud or data entry errors. By applying unsupervised learning techniques such as clustering in Python with libraries like KMeans or DBSCAN, you can effortlessly identify these anomalies.

And, incorporating natural language processing (NLP) into your workflow enhances user interaction with data analytics tools. Imagine an AI-driven feature in Excel that allows you to type inquiries like "Show me last month's top-selling products," instantly generating visualizations powered by underlying Python scripts. This capability effectively bridges the gap between technical complexity and user-friendly interfaces.

Also, these integrations pave the way for real-time analytics, where your data updates continuously based on external inputs or shifting market conditions. By utilizing APIs that connect Python scripts directly with real-time databases, your analytical models can automatically adjust as new data streams in. Take this example, a script that pulls daily sales figures from an online database ensures that your forecasts remain current without requiring manual updates.

As organizations increasingly recognize the value of combining AI and ML with traditional tools like Excel, there's a growing demand for professionals skilled in navigating this blended landscape. Continuous learning becomes essential; engaging in online courses or community discussions will equip you with the foundational knowledge and cutting-edge skills necessary to leverage these technologies effectively.

integrating AI and machine learning into your workflows

not only boosts productivity but also fosters a culture of innovation within teams. By incorporating these techniques into your projects, you'll transition from merely reacting to data to proactively shaping outcomes based on insights derived from intelligent analysis—an approach that distinguishes leading professionals in today's data-driven world.

Cloud-Based Excel Solutions

Cloud-based Excel solutions mark a significant advancement in the management, sharing, and analysis of data. By harnessing the power of cloud computing, organizations can store large volumes of data, access it from anywhere, and collaborate in real time. This not only boosts productivity but also cultivates a more agile work environment. The integration of Python with these cloud solutions further enhances their capabilities, enabling advanced analytics and automation that were previously difficult to achieve.

Take Microsoft Excel Online as a prime example of a cloud-based solution. This version allows users to create and edit spreadsheets directly within a web browser, eliminating the need for installation and making it accessible across various devices—whether desktop, tablet, or smartphone. One of its standout features is its collaborative functionality; multiple users can work on the same document simultaneously, with changes appearing in real time for everyone involved. Imagine a finance team analyzing quarterly performance data together from different locations—this seamless collaboration reduces the need for endless email exchanges and version control issues.

Integrating Python with Excel Online opens up exciting possibilities for data manipulation and analysis. With tools like PyXLL or xlwings, you can run Python scripts that interact with your Excel Online files hosted on OneDrive or SharePoint. This integration facilitates complex calculations, generates visualizations using libraries such as Matplotlib or Seaborn, and automates repetitive tasks— all while preserving the collaborative advantages of cloud storage.

Take this example, consider an organization that uses cloud storage to manage sales data across various regions. By employing Python, you could create a script that extracts this data from Excel Online and performs automated analysis to identify trends over time. Here's how you might set this up:

1. Accessing Cloud Files: Utilize the openpyxl library alongside pandas to read Excel files stored on OneDrive.

``` python

import pandas as pd

import openpyxl


\#\# Load your Excel file from OneDrive

df = pd.read_excel("https://your_onedrive_url/path/to/your_file.xlsx")
```

1. Data Manipulation: Once loaded into a DataFrame, filtering and analyzing your sales data becomes straightforward.

``` python
\#\# Filter for sales greater than 1000

high_sales = df[df['Sales'] > 1000]
```

1. Generating Insights: You can then leverage this

filtered data to produce reports or visualizations.

```python
import matplotlib.pyplot as plt

\#\# Plotting high sales regions
high_sales.groupby('Region')['Sales'].sum().plot(kind='bar')
plt.title('Total High Sales by Region')
plt.show()
```

Automating such reports not only saves time but also minimizes errors by ensuring consistent calculations every time new data is entered into the Excel file.

Security is another crucial aspect of cloud-based solutions. When handling sensitive information like financial records or customer data, robust security measures are essential. Most cloud platforms provide built-in encryption for data at rest and in transit, safeguarding your information against unauthorized access. Additionally, using secure APIs when integrating Python scripts ensures that your connections remain protected.

And, adopting cloud-based Excel solutions facilitates seamless updates and maintenance without the hassle of manual installations or upgrades. Users benefit from automatic access to the latest features and security patches deployed by service providers, allowing teams to focus more on analysis rather than technical logistics.

As organizations increasingly embrace remote work models and digital transformation initiatives, the role of cloud-based solutions will continue to grow. The ability to access and manipulate data flexibly will become an essential skill set for professionals across various industries. Integrating

Python not only enriches these capabilities but also equips users for a future where data-driven decision-making is paramount.

In summary, the rise of cloud-based Excel solutions has transformed traditional spreadsheet applications into dynamic platforms capable of real-time collaboration and advanced analytics through Python integration. By effectively leveraging these tools, we can unlock new levels of insight and efficiency that will propel our projects forward in an ever-competitive landscape.

Advancements in Data Science

Advancements in data science have significantly transformed the analytics landscape, fundamentally altering how organizations gather, process, and extract insights from their data. As we explore the complexities of this field, it's important to recognize the evolving synergy between Python and Excel. This relationship enhances analytical capabilities in ways previously unimaginable, making it a powerful combination for professionals.

The rise of big data has prompted the need for more sophisticated analytical tools. With enormous volumes of data streaming into systems every second, traditional methods are often inadequate. Enter Python, which has established itself as a key player in data science. Its robust libraries—such as NumPy for numerical computations, Pandas for data manipulation, and Scikit-learn for machine learning—enable analysts to navigate complex datasets efficiently and derive actionable insights quickly.

The integration of Python with Excel further amplifies these capabilities. For example, consider a company that receives daily sales transactions from various regions. By employing Python scripts within Excel spreadsheets, analysts can automate the aggregation of this data into insightful dashboards. This marriage of Excel's user-friendly interface with Python's computational strength streamlines processes that would otherwise demand considerable time and resources.

A practical illustration of this integration is performing exploratory data analysis (EDA) directly within Excel using Python. EDA is essential for gaining an understanding of datasets before moving on to modeling or hypothesis testing. Analysts can write scripts that summarize key statistics or visualize distributions without needing to export data to separate software tools. Take this example, if we want to analyze sales distribution across product categories, we could follow these steps:

1. Load Data into a Pandas DataFrame: Start by importing the sales data from an Excel file.

```python
import pandas as pd

df = pd.read_excel("sales_data.xlsx")
```

1. Generate Summary Statistics: Quickly analyze basic statistics like the mean and standard deviation.

```python
summary_stats = df['Sales'].describe()

print(summary_stats)
```

1. Visualize Sales Distribution: Use Matplotlib or Seaborn for effective visualization.

```python
import matplotlib.pyplot as plt

plt.hist(df['Sales'], bins=30)
```

```python
plt.title('Sales Distribution')

plt.xlabel('Sales Amount')

plt.ylabel('Frequency')

plt.show()
```
```

Such analyses empower businesses to make informed decisions based on real-time insights derived from their operational datasets.

Machine learning has also seen remarkable advancements, allowing businesses not only to understand historical trends but also to predict future outcomes based on current patterns. By integrating libraries like Scikit-learn and TensorFlow into Python scripts executed through Excel, organizations can utilize predictive analytics models without leaving their familiar spreadsheet environment.

For example, if a company aims to predict customer churn based on historical purchasing behavior, the process might look like this:

1. Preparing the Dataset: Load historical customer behavior data.

```python
df = pd.read_excel("customer_data.xlsx")
```
```

1. Feature Engineering: Create relevant features that may influence churn.

```python
df['AveragePurchaseValue']    =    df['TotalSpent']    /
df['TotalPurchases']
```
```
```

1. Model Training: Use Scikit-learn's logistic regression model.

```python
from sklearn.model_selection import train_test_split

from sklearn.linear_model import LogisticRegression


X = df[['AveragePurchaseValue', 'VisitFrequency']]

y = df['Churn']


X_train, X_test, y_train, y_test = train_test_split(X, y, test_size=0.2)


model = LogisticRegression()

model.fit(X_train, y_train)


predictions = model.predict(X_test)
```

This predictive capability transforms how businesses approach customer retention strategies by providing solid analyses rooted in statistical methods.

Additionally, advancements in natural language processing (NLP) allow organizations to glean insights from unstructured data sources such as customer feedback or social media comments. The integration of Python libraries like NLTK or SpaCy with Excel enables analysts to extract sentiments or keywords seamlessly within their spreadsheets.

Take this example, when analyzing survey feedback stored in

an Excel workbook:

1. **Sentiment Analysis Preparation:

```python
import pandas as pd
from textblob import TextBlob

df = pd.read_excel("customer_feedback.xlsx")
```

1. **Analyzing Sentiment:

```python
df['Sentiment']        =        df['Feedback'].apply(lambda        x:
TextBlob(x).sentiment.polarity)
```

1. **Visualizing Sentiment Scores:

```python
import matplotlib.pyplot as plt

plt.hist(df['Sentiment'], bins=20)
plt.title('Customer Feedback Sentiment')
plt.xlabel('Sentiment Score')
plt.ylabel('Frequency')
plt.show()
```

This combination of textual analysis and numerical evaluation provides deeper insights into customer attitudes toward products or services.

The convergence of these advancements creates a powerful toolkit for professionals eager to harness the full potential of their data with enhanced analytical rigor and precision in decision-making processes. As technology continues to advance—especially with emerging trends like AI integration—the collaboration between Python and Excel becomes increasingly vital for maintaining competitiveness in today's fast-paced business environment.

understanding these advancements not only helps you keep pace with industry changes but also empowers you to lead initiatives that effectively leverage innovative analytical techniques within your organization—making you an invaluable asset on any team striving for excellence in data-driven decision-making.

The Role of Python in Future Excel Versions

The integration of Python into future versions of Excel is set to transform how users engage with data in this widely-used spreadsheet application. As organizations increasingly depend on data-driven insights, the synergy between Excel and Python provides a powerful solution that addresses evolving analytical needs. This combination enhances productivity and analytical capabilities, making it an attractive option for users seeking to maximize their efficiency.

Excel is renowned for its accessibility and user-friendliness. However, as datasets expand and grow more complex, traditional spreadsheet functionalities can become unwieldy. This is where Python emerges as a game-changer. Upcoming versions of Excel are expected to deepen their integration with Python, enabling users to perform advanced data manipulation and analysis tasks more smoothly. Take this example, analysts could write Python scripts directly within Excel to automate repetitive tasks, extract valuable insights from large datasets, and carry out complex calculations—all while utilizing the familiar Excel interface.

One notable advantage of this integration is the potential for improved data visualization. Users will be able to leverage libraries such as Matplotlib and Seaborn within Excel to create sophisticated visual representations of their data that surpass the basic charting options currently available. Imagine generating advanced heatmaps or interactive visualizations without having to switch tools or contexts. This capability not only enhances the aesthetic quality of presentations but also aids in storytelling with data, making insights clearer for stakeholders.

Take, for example, a financial analyst tasked with visualizing cash flow projections over several years. By embedding a Python script in Excel, they can create a dynamic line chart that automatically updates as new data is entered or modified. Here's how such a script might look:

```python
import pandas as pd

import matplotlib.pyplot as plt


\#\# Load cash flow data from an Excel sheet

cash_flow_df = pd.read_excel("cash_flow_data.xlsx")


\#\# Generate a line chart

plt.plot(cash_flow_df['Year'], cash_flow_df['CashFlow'])

plt.title('Projected Cash Flow Over Time')

plt.xlabel('Year')

plt.ylabel('Cash Flow')
```

plt.show()

` ` `

This functionality enhances the user experience by facilitating quicker decision-making through real-time visual feedback.

In addition to improving visualizations, the collaboration between Python and Excel is expected to revolutionize how users manage and manipulate data using machine learning algorithms right within their spreadsheets. Users no longer need extensive programming knowledge or separate software tools to develop predictive models; everything can be accomplished directly in Excel. With libraries like Scikit-learn accessible through the Excel interface, even those with limited technical expertise can apply machine learning techniques effectively.

Take this example, if an organization aims to predict sales based on historical performance, analysts can utilize Python's capabilities without leaving Excel:

` ` `python

from sklearn.model_selection import train_test_split

from sklearn.linear_model import LinearRegression

\#\# Load historical sales data

sales_data = pd.read_excel("historical_sales.xlsx")

\#\# Prepare features and labels

X = sales_data[['AdvertisingBudget', 'MarketTrends']]

y = sales_data['Sales']

```
\#\# Split into training and testing sets
X_train, X_test, y_train, y_test = train_test_split(X, y,
test_size=0.2)

\#\# Train the model
model = LinearRegression()
model.fit(X_train, y_train)

\#\# Predict future sales
predictions = model.predict(X_test)
` ` `
```

By embedding such scripts directly into their workflows, professionals can enhance their analytical outputs and empower teams across departments to make swift, data-informed decisions.

And, the collaborative features arising from this integration will promote teamwork. For example, when various departments require tailored analytical functions, the ability to share custom Python scripts within an organization's Excel framework encourages knowledge sharing and consistency in reporting methodologies. Teams can build libraries of reusable code snippets accessible for everyone to use or adapt for their specific projects.

As we anticipate these developments, it's essential for users to embrace continuous learning and adaptability. The capabilities that Python will introduce into future versions of Excel are substantial but necessitate a proactive approach to exploring new functionalities. Familiarizing oneself with Python not only positions users as forward-thinking professionals but also enhances their value within their organizations.

In summary, the integration of Python into future iterations of Excel represents a significant shift toward more powerful and efficient analytics workflows that blur the lines between programming and spreadsheet management. By harnessing these tools together, analysts can streamline repetitive tasks while pushing the boundaries of data exploration and insight generation—an essential evolution for anyone committed to excelling in the field of data analytics.

Continuous Learning Pathways

Mastering Python for Excel is not a destination but a continuous journey that requires dedication to ongoing learning. In our fast-paced technological landscape, staying updated on new developments can significantly enhance your data analysis skills and effectiveness. This proactive mindset not only equips you to tackle current challenges but also positions you favorably for future opportunities.

One effective way to expand your knowledge is by engaging with online resources. Platforms like Coursera, Udacity, and edX offer specialized courses tailored to all skill levels, from beginners to advanced practitioners. Many of these courses include real-world projects that allow you to apply your learning directly in Excel and Python contexts. For example, a course focused on data analysis with Pandas can deepen your understanding of data manipulation while providing hands-on experience that complements your Excel skills.

Additionally, participating in community forums and discussion groups can greatly enhance your learning experience. Websites like Stack Overflow, Reddit's r/learnpython, and dedicated Excel forums are rich with practitioners who share their challenges and solutions. Engaging in these communities not only provides answers to your questions but also exposes you to a variety of problem-solving techniques. You may find yourself helping others, which reinforces your understanding through teaching—a powerful method of consolidating knowledge.

To further strengthen your theoretical foundation, consider reading books that explore both Excel and Python applications. Titles focusing on data science or machine learning with Python can provide valuable insights applicable to real-world scenarios. These resources often include case studies that illustrate how experts tackle complex problems using Python within Excel environments. By applying concepts from these books to your own projects, you'll gain perspective on advanced methods that can elevate your work.

Seeking out workshops or webinars can also enrich your learning experience. Many organizations host sessions led by industry experts who share best practices and innovative solutions involving Excel and Python integration. Attending these events not only sharpens your skills but also expands your professional network—an invaluable asset in an era where collaboration drives success.

Practice is crucial when mastering any skill, especially programming languages like Python. Undertaking small projects or automations within Excel based on real business needs will enhance both your coding abilities and your familiarity with common libraries like Pandas or Matplotlib. Start by identifying repetitive tasks at work that could be streamlined through automation; this practical approach encourages experimentation and often leads to unexpected discoveries.

As technology continues to advance, keeping an eye on emerging trends will help you stay ahead of the curve. Following blogs or subscribing to newsletters focused on Excel enhancements or Python developments ensures you're aware of new tools and techniques as they emerge. The introduction of features such as artificial intelligence and machine learning integration signifies an exciting future for professionals willing to embrace change.

Additionally, pursuing certifications can provide a structured way to validate your skills formally. Certifications in data analysis or specific Python frameworks demonstrate both commitment and proficiency, making them valuable additions to your resume. They can help distinguish you in a competitive job market while instilling confidence when facing complex analytical tasks.

Finally, cultivating an innovative mindset will prove invaluable as new opportunities arise. Embrace challenges as avenues for growth rather than obstacles; every problem solved adds another tool to your skillset arsenal. As you navigate the evolving technologies and methodologies in both Excel and Python integration, maintaining a sense of curiosity will keep the process engaging—and ultimately rewarding.

In summary, committing yourself to continuous learning fosters an environment ripe for professional growth and innovation within the context of integrating Python with Excel. The more knowledge you accumulate and apply— whether through courses, community engagement, practice projects, or staying updated—the greater impact you'll have within your organization and beyond.

Exploring New Frontiers

Navigating the rapidly evolving intersection of Python and Excel unveils a wealth of possibilities that can transform our approach to data analysis, reporting, and automation. Many professionals stand on the brink of this transformation, eager to adopt not only existing tools but also the innovative frontiers that lie ahead. This journey goes beyond merely utilizing new features; it's about fundamentally reshaping workflows, boosting productivity, and nurturing a culture of continuous improvement.

One of the most promising areas emerging on the horizon is the integration of artificial intelligence (AI) with Excel and Python. As companies increasingly rely on predictive analytics to guide their decision-making processes, tools like TensorFlow and PyTorch have become essential for developing machine learning models that can be seamlessly applied within Excel environments. For example, consider the possibility of creating a model that predicts sales trends based on historical data from Excel spreadsheets. By leveraging libraries such as Scikit-learn or Keras, you can train models to analyze patterns and extract insights that were previously out of reach with traditional methods.

Take, for instance, a retail analyst tasked with forecasting inventory needs for the upcoming quarter. They can gather data on past sales, seasonal trends, and market conditions using Excel. With Python's robust libraries for machine learning, they can construct a model that accurately predicts future demand. This approach not only streamlines inventory management but also minimizes costs associated with overproduction or stockouts.

Another exciting development is the emergence of cloud-based solutions that blend Python's versatility with Excel's user-friendly interface. Platforms like Microsoft Azure and Google Cloud facilitate the deployment of scalable applications capable of processing large datasets in real time. These services support integration with APIs that deliver live data feeds—such as financial market information or social media trends—automatically updating relevant Excel dashboards.

Imagine a scenario where financial analysts receive daily reports populated with real-time market data without any manual effort. By utilizing Python scripts executed on cloud platforms, routine updates are streamlined, allowing teams to concentrate on strategic analysis rather than tedious data collection.

And, collaborative tools like Jupyter Notebooks are enhancing data storytelling capabilities. The ability to share insights visually alongside code snippets enables stakeholders to grasp not just raw numbers but also their contextual implications. When analysts merge Python's technical prowess with narrative clarity in Excel reports, businesses can drive better outcomes.

The potential applications of augmented reality (AR) and virtual reality (VR) in conjunction with Python and Excel are also emerging as compelling avenues for exploration. Imagine visualizing complex datasets in three-dimensional space, allowing users to interactively manipulate variables through AR tools while drawing from live Excel data sources. These technological advancements could revolutionize how businesses interpret large datasets and engage stakeholders during presentations.

In addition to these technological innovations, cultivating soft skills such as data storytelling remains crucial as these tools evolve. For analysts, effectively communicating insights is just as important as gathering them. Mastering the art of narrating data-driven stories can significantly influence decision-making within an organization. By explaining findings in accessible language and utilizing visuals, you ensure your analyses resonate with diverse audiences.

To wrap things up, venturing into these new frontiers requires an adaptable mindset willing to embrace change and innovation. The integration of AI, cloud solutions, collaborative tools like Jupyter Notebooks, and even AR/VR signifies a shift in how we interact with data daily. Keeping pace with these developments not only positions you as an informed practitioner but also as a leader capable of guiding your organization through transformative changes.

As you step into these exciting frontiers, remember that continuous learning is not just beneficial; it's essential for thriving in this dynamic landscape where Python meets Excel in groundbreaking ways. Maintaining curiosity and an open mind will empower you to effectively harness these advancements—transforming challenges into opportunities for innovation.

Final Thoughts and Encouragement

The journey of integrating Python with Excel is one of transformation and innovation, opening up a world of possibilities. As we've explored various tools, techniques, and real-world applications, it's important to recognize the significant impact this knowledge can have on your professional landscape. The ability to automate tedious tasks, analyze complex datasets, and generate insightful reports positions you at the forefront of modern data analysis. This experience goes beyond mere technical skills; it embodies a mindset that embraces change and leverages technology to enhance efficiency.

Incorporating Python into your Excel workflow not only sharpens your technical abilities but also encourages a more strategic approach to problem-solving. Each script you write or function you create adds to a narrative of efficiency and insight. Imagine transforming mundane tasks into automated workflows, freeing up your time for critical thinking and creative analysis. This shift from manual processes to automated solutions signifies a fundamental change in how we approach our work—making data analysis less about the tools and more about the insights they help us uncover.

Throughout this guide, we have emphasized practicality, focusing on actionable steps that yield tangible improvements in your daily operations. As you apply what you've learned, consider the specific challenges you encounter in your role. Whether it's streamlining reporting processes or enhancing data visualization techniques, apply these skills with intention. True mastery emerges in this application. Reflect on the scripts or methods that resonated with you and envision how they can seamlessly integrate into your existing workflows.

It's also vital to cultivate a culture of continuous learning within your team or organization. Share your experiences and newfound skills with colleagues, encouraging them to explore Python tools alongside Excel. This collaborative spirit not only enhances collective knowledge but also positions you as a leader who values growth and innovation. Foster discussions around data storytelling and automation strategies, reinforcing that mastery is not solely an individual pursuit but a shared journey.

As you progress in this field, anticipate challenges—whether in debugging code or integrating new libraries. Each obstacle presents an opportunity for growth and deeper understanding. Approach these moments with curiosity rather than frustration; they are stepping stones toward resilience in navigating complex data environments.

Consider the broader implications of your work as well. The insights derived from integrating Python with Excel extend beyond individual projects, contributing to informed decision-making across your organization. The ripple effect of accurate forecasting or streamlined reporting influences strategic directions and business outcomes.

your engagement with this material signifies more than just acquiring technical skills; it reflects a commitment to becoming an innovative problem-solver in a data-driven world. Embrace this identity as you continue to explore new tools and techniques, creatively adapting them to address your unique challenges.

As you reflect on your accomplishments, take pride in the powerful toolkit you've developed—one that marries the analytical strengths of Python with the accessibility of Excel. With each project you undertake, let this toolkit evolve by experimenting with advanced functionalities or exploring emerging trends like AI integration or cloud-based solutions.

Your journey is just beginning; it marks the start of an exciting exploration into new frontiers of data analysis and automation. Stay curious, remain engaged, and continue pushing boundaries as you navigate this dynamic landscape where technology meets human ingenuity. Let this guide serve as both a reference and an inspiration as you carve out your path forward—a path filled with opportunities for innovation and impact.

CONCLUSION

The integration of Python with Excel has transformed how data professionals approach their work, providing a versatile toolkit that elevates traditional spreadsheet tasks. This journey through Python's diverse functionalities has equipped you not only with technical skills but also with a mindset focused on innovation and efficiency. Mastering this integration goes beyond grasping syntax or formulas; it involves a fundamental shift in how you analyze and interpret data.

As you reflect on the techniques covered in this guide, consider the range of skills you've developed—from basic data manipulation to advanced automation. Each tool is designed to streamline your workflow and enhance your analytical capabilities. You've likely automated repetitive tasks, freeing up time for deeper analysis and strategic thinking. This transition allows you to leverage your expertise not just in executing tasks but in deriving meaningful insights from data and communicating them effectively.

Looking ahead, keep in mind that the true strength of Python lies in its adaptability. The libraries and tools we've discussed are foundational elements that empower you to create tailored solutions for the unique challenges within your professional environment. Whether you're generating reports, visualizing complex datasets, or conducting sophisticated financial analyses, your ability to integrate these tools will distinguish you in the data landscape.

The importance of continuous learning cannot be overstated. As technology evolves, so should your skills. Engaging with emerging trends—whether they involve advancements in machine learning or new Python libraries —will help you remain at the forefront of data analysis. Participating in communities or forums can further enhance your growth; collaboration often ignites innovative ideas and provides support when facing challenges during implementation.

Embrace the obstacles that arise as you apply these concepts in real-world scenarios. Debugging code or troubleshooting automation scripts may initially seem daunting, but these experiences are crucial for developing your expertise. Each challenge you overcome builds your confidence and reinforces the idea that mastery requires perseverance and a willingness to learn from setbacks.

Additionally, don't underestimate the value of sharing knowledge with others. Educating colleagues about Python's capabilities within Excel fosters a culture of innovation and collaboration that benefits everyone. By leading discussions on data practices or new tools, you position yourself as a catalyst for change within your organization.

The insights gained from integrating Python into Excel workflows extend beyond personal development; they significantly contribute to informed decision-making processes within your team or business unit. The analyses and predictions generated through this integrated approach can have far-reaching implications, influencing strategic directions and enhancing overall productivity.

what you've cultivated throughout this guide is more than just a collection of techniques; it's a comprehensive framework for tackling data challenges with confidence and creativity. With every project you undertake using these skills, you're not merely executing tasks; you're crafting narratives supported by data that drive meaningful outcomes.

As you embark on this new chapter in your professional journey, let this experience inspire ongoing exploration and experimentation. Each step taken with Python in Excel opens up new possibilities for innovation and efficiency. Your commitment to mastering these tools positions you as an influential figure ready to drive positive change for yourself and those around you.

Take pride in your achievements thus far while remaining open to the future opportunities that await. The landscape of data analysis is ever-evolving, filled with potential for those willing to explore it fully. Carry this momentum forward; let curiosity guide your path as you navigate the intersection of technology and insight-driven decision-making.

- **Reflecting on Your Learning Journey**

Reflecting on your learning journey is just as important as the knowledge and skills you've gained. Each interaction with Python and Excel has added depth to your understanding, transforming you into a more skilled data professional. In the beginning, you may have approached these tools with hesitation, viewing them as complex challenges. However, over time, this uncertainty evolved into confidence as you faced obstacles and celebrated small victories.

Recall your initial experiences using Python within Excel. Maybe it started with a straightforward task—automating data extraction from multiple sheets or generating a simple report. Each successful execution not only reinforced your grasp of the syntax but also ignited ideas for more ambitious projects. That early success laid the foundation for more complex automations and integrations, eventually allowing you to create scripts that significantly changed how you manage data.

Throughout this journey, you've built a robust toolkit that goes well beyond basic functionality. Your experiences with libraries like Pandas and OpenPyXL have revealed how streamlined processes can drastically enhance efficiency. This evolution wasn't just about improving technical skills; it also shifted your perspective on data—helping you see it not merely as rows and columns but as a powerful resource that can drive decision-making.

As you reflect on the various projects you've undertaken, consider the moments that demanded problem-solving or creative thinking. Whether troubleshooting unexpected errors or optimizing scripts for better performance, these experiences have shaped your analytical mindset. Overcoming each hurdle deepened your understanding of both Python's nuances and Excel's limitations, imparting valuable lessons in resilience and adaptability.

You may have discovered that collaboration amplifies your learning experience. Sharing knowledge with peers or seeking help from community forums cultivates an environment where ideas can thrive. Engaging in discussions about best practices or new tools fosters collective growth, pushing boundaries further than any individual effort could achieve alone. Learning is inherently social; sharing experiences not only reinforces your understanding but also inspires others on similar paths.

Let's also acknowledge the value of continuous experimentation in your learning process. Your willingness to try new methods or explore different libraries has greatly enriched your skill set. For example, experimenting with visualization libraries like Matplotlib or Seaborn can open new avenues for presenting data in engaging ways, offering insights that static tables might miss. These explorations often lead to those "aha!" moments—discoveries that shift how you approach data challenges going forward.

As you continue this journey, it's vital to keep questioning and exploring new methodologies within Python and Excel. The rapidly evolving landscape of technology requires a mindset geared toward lifelong learning. Stay informed about emerging trends—whether they involve advancements in machine learning integrations or updates in Python libraries—that could add new dimensions to your analytical repertoire.

Consider documenting your progress along the way. Keeping a journal of what has worked—and what hasn't—can be an invaluable resource for future projects. Reflective practice allows you to track growth over time while providing insights into areas for further improvement.

mastering Python in Excel is about more than simply acquiring skills; it's about developing an innovative approach to problem-solving driven by curiosity. By reflecting on both successes and challenges encountered along the way, you position yourself to embrace future opportunities with enthusiasm rather than apprehension.

Your growth as a skilled practitioner isn't solely defined by technical expertise; it's also about the creative application of these tools in real-world situations. With every task you automate or analysis you perform using Python within Excel, you're not just executing functions—you're crafting narratives shaped by data that inform strategic decisions and foster growth within your organization.

So take pride in where you've been and where you're headed; each step enriches not only your personal development but also positively impacts those around you. Embrace this pivotal moment in your career with an open heart and mind as new challenges await on the horizon—each promising another opportunity for growth and exploration.

- **Building a Community of Practice**

Building a community of practice is a powerful way to enrich your learning journey with Python and Excel. Engaging with others who share your interests not only reinforces your skills but also cultivates an environment filled with collaboration and innovation. When like-minded individuals come together, they create opportunities to share insights, tackle challenges, and celebrate successes, fostering a collaborative spirit that can accelerate your mastery of these tools.

One of the most rewarding aspects of being part of such a community is the diverse range of perspectives it offers. You'll encounter individuals at various stages of their learning paths—some may be beginners, while others are seasoned professionals. Each member brings unique experiences and knowledge, creating a rich resource for problem-solving and inspiration. Take this example, a beginner may ask fresh questions that prompt more experienced users to rethink their approaches, resulting in an environment where everyone learns from one another.

Consider forming study groups or joining local meetups focused on data analysis and automation with Python and Excel. Online platforms like GitHub or specialized forums can also serve as excellent venues for connecting with peers. In these spaces, you can share code snippets, seek advice on troubleshooting issues, or discuss the latest libraries and techniques that enhance productivity. The mutual support found in these communities can be invigorating; knowing that others face similar challenges can help sustain your motivation, especially when projects become daunting.

Participation in online courses or webinars can further enrich your community experience. Often led by experts in the field, these sessions offer opportunities to learn new skills while engaging with fellow participants in real time. Sharing insights gained from these sessions back within your community amplifies the benefits for everyone involved, encouraging deeper exploration of discussed topics and allowing members to collaboratively apply what they've learned.

In addition to structured gatherings, consider leveraging social media platforms like LinkedIn or Twitter to connect with professionals worldwide who are passionate about integrating Python with Excel. Engaging in discussions around trending topics or challenges fosters continuous learning while expanding your network. Following industry leaders or joining relevant groups exposes you to fresh ideas and innovative applications of Python in Excel that you might not have encountered otherwise.

Creating a space for knowledge-sharing is just as important as participating in existing ones. You might start a blog or contribute articles reflecting on your experiences automating tasks with Python in Excel. Documenting your projects not only solidifies your understanding but also gives back to the community by offering guidance to others on similar paths. Writing down your thoughts—whether troubleshooting tips or new techniques—strengthens your own knowledge base while inspiring those around you.

Mentorship also plays a crucial role within communities of practice. As you gain experience, consider offering guidance to newcomers eager to learn. Mentorship fosters a supportive ecosystem where knowledge circulates freely and nurtures growth for both mentors and mentees alike. This relationship often leads to surprising insights; teaching someone else reinforces your understanding while encouraging you to explore concepts from different angles.

Lastly, remain open-minded about evolving practices within both Python and Excel environments as technology advances rapidly. A thriving community adapts alongside these changes, fostering innovation through shared learning experiences. Regular discussions about new developments keep everyone informed about cutting-edge tools that can enhance efficiency or solve persistent problems more effectively.

Building a robust community of practice extends beyond mere skill enhancement; it's about creating lasting connections throughout your career journey. By investing time in nurturing relationships with peers and actively engaging on various platforms, you're not just improving yourself—you're contributing to a collective knowledge base that uplifts everyone involved. Embrace this aspect wholeheartedly; as you share both triumphs and setbacks, you'll find greater fulfillment in mastering Python in Excel alongside an inspiring network of dedicated practitioners committed to excellence.

· Resources for Continued Development

To maintain momentum in your journey toward mastering Python for Excel, exploring diverse resources for continued development is essential. As technology and data analysis continuously evolve, leveraging various tools and materials can significantly enhance your knowledge and keep you at the forefront of the field.

Online platforms such as Coursera, Udacity, and edX offer structured courses that focus specifically on integrating Python with Excel. These courses often include practical exercises, enabling you to apply your newfound skills immediately. For example, you may find modules that teach you how to automate report generation or manipulate data frames using Pandas. Engaging with these platforms not only provides theoretical knowledge but also offers hands-on experience, solidifying your understanding of key concepts.

In addition to formal courses, video tutorials on platforms

like YouTube can be invaluable. Many channels dedicated to programming provide detailed walkthroughs on specific libraries and techniques used in Python and Excel integration. Watching experts tackle real-world problems can give you insights into best practices and shortcuts that written guides might overlook. This visual learning approach caters to different styles, making it a useful complement to your study regimen.

Books also serve as an essential resource for deepening your understanding of Python in Excel. Look for titles that specifically address automation or data analysis with these tools; they can act as comprehensive references as you navigate complex projects. Authors with industry experience often share real-world insights, helping you bridge the gap between theory and practice. Reading case studies within these texts allows you to see how others have approached similar challenges, providing inspiration for your work.

Community forums present another rich source of information. Websites like Stack Overflow and Reddit's r/learnpython create spaces where users can ask questions and share solutions related to Python programming and its applications in Excel. Actively participating in these communities not only helps you find answers but also exposes you to diverse perspectives on common issues faced by learners at all levels. Also, sharing your insights reinforces your own understanding while aiding others on their learning journeys.

Documentation is often underestimated but should never be overlooked. Each library used for integrating Python with Excel comes with extensive documentation detailing its functionalities and capabilities. Take this example, exploring the Pandas documentation reveals numerous methods tailored for data manipulation—insights that may not be readily available elsewhere. Learning how to navigate these documents effectively can save time when debugging or implementing new features.

Podcasts have gained popularity among professionals seeking continuous learning opportunities while on the go. Many shows focusing on data science, analytics, or programming feature discussions about the latest trends in technology and best practices for using Python with Excel. Listening to experts share their experiences can inspire innovative applications of your skills.

Networking within professional organizations related to data science or analytics can also significantly enhance your growth trajectory. Many organizations host events, webinars, or conferences where members showcase their projects or share recent findings involving Python applications across various industries. Engaging with these communities opens doors for collaboration and keeps you informed about industry standards and emerging technologies.

Finally, don't underestimate the value of personal projects for continued development. Applying what you've learned through self-initiated tasks reinforces concepts while allowing room for experimentation without external pressure. Whether building a financial model using historical market data or automating daily reporting tasks at work, hands-on practice ensures that your knowledge is retained more effectively than through passive learning alone.

By utilizing a diverse array of resources—from online courses and video tutorials to community forums and personal projects—you build a robust foundation for ongoing development in mastering Python alongside Excel. Each resource complements the others, creating a well-rounded approach that not only enhances your technical skills but also fosters confidence as you tackle increasingly complex challenges head-on.

- **Final Words of Inspiration**

Mastering the integration of Python with Excel is more than just a technical skill; it represents a transformative journey. Consider the countless hours you've spent grappling with data, striving to extract meaningful insights from spreadsheets overflowing with numbers and text. Each moment of frustration, each yearning for a more efficient method of data manipulation, has been part of your quest for increased productivity and creativity. Now, equipped with the knowledge and skills gained from this guide, you stand on the brink of that transformation.

As you move forward, view the challenges that lie ahead as opportunities for growth. The landscape of data analysis is constantly changing, and your journey is far from over. With Python at your fingertips, you've opened the door to a vast universe of possibilities. Envision automating repetitive tasks that once drained your energy, or crafting dynamic reports that convey stories with elegance and clarity. Consider how you can harness these capabilities not only to streamline your own workflow but also to inspire your colleagues. By innovating within your processes, you can become a catalyst for change, encouraging others to explore new ways of thinking and working.

Remember that mastery is a continuous journey. As you dive deeper into advanced topics or tackle more complex projects, setbacks are inevitable. Each challenge you encounter serves as a stepping stone toward greater understanding. Embrace these hurdles; they are integral to your growth narrative. Seek out resources that ignite your curiosity—be it articles, forums, or community groups where fellow practitioners share their experiences and insights. Engaging with others enriches your learning and exposes you to diverse problem-solving perspectives.

As you apply what you've learned, let curiosity be your compass. Experimentation is crucial in both Python and Excel; don't shy away from trying new libraries or techniques as they emerge in the field. You'll discover that some solutions may resonate better than others depending on the specific context of your projects. Your ability to adapt and refine your approaches in light of new information will distinguish you as a leader in data analysis.

Additionally, consider documenting your journey— celebrating both your successes and learning from failures. Keeping track of what works and what doesn't not only benefits you but also provides invaluable insights for those who follow in your footsteps. Sharing these insights nurtures a culture of collaboration within your team or organization, where collective knowledge enhances individual capabilities.

Reflect on how far you've come since embarking on this journey into Python and Excel integration. Each line of code you've written and every formula you've mastered has armed you with tools to significantly boost your workflow efficiency. Your newfound skills empower you not just as an analyst but as an innovator—someone who views data not merely as numbers but as narratives waiting to be discovered.

As we conclude this guide, carry forward the spirit of exploration and innovation that defines the world of data analytics. The skills you've developed here are just the beginning; they form a foundation upon which to build even greater expertise. With every project undertaken and every challenge faced, remember that you're not merely solving problems; you're influencing how data is understood and utilized.

Embrace this knowledge with confidence and enthusiasm as you embark on new projects or refine existing ones. Your ability to merge Python's powerful capabilities with Excel's familiarity positions you at the forefront of modern data analysis—an exciting realm brimming with opportunities for creativity and success. Keep pushing boundaries, seeking knowledge, and inspiring those around you. The world of data eagerly awaits your contributions; step boldly into this new frontier.

www.ingramcontent.com/pod-product-compliance
Lightning Source LLC
LaVergne TN
LVHW051219050326
832903LV00028B/2159